Jeremy Thorpe: a Secre

Lewis Chester is the co-author of ten books including *Hoax*, an account of the Irving/Hughes affair, which won the Crime Fact Book award in 1972. He was formerly editor of the *Sunday Times* Insight team.

Magnus Linklater is an assistant editor of the *Sunday Times*, for which he has also been editor of the colour magazine and news editor. He previously worked for the *Daily Express* and for the London *Evening Standard* where he edited the Londoner's Diary column. He is co-author of *Hoax*.

David May joined the staff of the *Sunday Times* in 1977. He was formerly co-editor of the London magazine, *Time Out*.

Jeremy Thorpe: a Secret Life

Lewis Chester
Magnus Linklater
David May

Fontana Paperbacks
in association with
Andre Deutsch

Contents

Preface

The trial of Jeremy Thorpe, former leader of the Liberal Party, on charges of conspiracy and incitement to murder, ended on 22 June 1979 with his acquittal on both counts. Three other men charged with him were also found not guilty of conspiring to murder Norman Scott, with whom Thorpe had once been friendly. This book does not challenge those verdicts, nor seek to lead the reader to any different conclusion. What it does aim to do is to offer a full account of the extraordinary events and characters which led to Thorpe's appearance in the dock at the Old Bailey, and to the final destruction of his political career. It goes on to chart the crucial episodes in what was to become an absorbing and controversial trial.

In piecing the story together, we have been helped by many people – politicians, lawyers and other journalists – to whom we express our gratitude. Many of them gave us their time and helped to clarify events by providing us with invaluable documentation. Of the journalists we are most indebted to John Shirley who worked directly with us on aspects of our inquiries. In addition we thank the following: the BBC and producer Gordon Carr, David Blundy, Peter Chippindale, Susan Clarke, Susan Crosland, Roy East, Paddy French, Derek Humphry, Parin Janmohamed, Michael Jones, Keith Kyle, David Leigh, Graeme McLagan, the late James Margach, Andrew Medlicott, the Press Association, Barrie Stephens, the editorial staff of the *Western Morning News* and Hugo Young.

The book could never have been produced with such speed without the informed tenacity of our editor, Alison

Wade, and the patience and skill of our typesetters, Unwin Brothers Ltd of Woking.

We owe much to Harold Evans, editor of the *Sunday Times*, who first proposed the idea of the book, and make special mention of the investigative work done by Barrie Penrose and Roger Courtiour.

Lewis Chester
Magnus Linklater
David May

London, August 1979

1. An Extraordinary Performer

In early February 1951, an audience of undergraduates sat spellbound in the debating chamber of the Cambridge Union, listening to a speech from the newly elected president of their rival union at Oxford. The young man who held their attention was as striking in dress as in his style of delivery. He had arrived wearing a top hat and opera cloak, and carrying a silver-topped cane. Now he stood elegantly by the dispatch-box, immaculate in tail-coat and white tie.

Slightly built and almost unnaturally pale, he spoke nevertheless with such force and vigour, his words accompanied by such dramatic and extravagant gestures, that at least one of those present became suddenly convinced that he was listening to an old-fashioned theatrical monologue rather than a speech attacking government policies. A torrent of anecdotes, each accompanied by imitations of some of the best-known voices in the land, had his audience convulsed with laughter, at the same time leaving them with the distinct impression that the speaker was already on intimate terms with the rich and the famous. When, finally, the familiar growl of Winston Churchill echoed across the room there was a burst of spontaneous applause.

But not everyone listening was completely seduced by this performance. Rising to respond, Mr Roland Brown, then a promising lawyer, later Attorney-General in Tanzania, injected a note of acid into the proceedings.

'Mr President,' he said, 'we have heard, this evening, from Winston Churchill, from Lloyd George, from many other distinguished people. But the one person from whom we have not heard a word is Mr Jeremy Thorpe himself. Mr President, he must indeed have something *terrible* to hide.'

Leaning back in his seat, twenty-one-year-old John Jeremy Thorpe laughed as heartily as the rest, applauding a shrewd piece of political repartee. But Brown, unconsciously perhaps, had put his finger on the one aspect of Thorpe's character which was most to trouble his friends and alarm his colleagues in the course of a glittering but controversial career.

For behind the dazzling showmanship of a man whose wit, charm and energy were to make him at one point the most popular political figure in the country, outstripping two Prime Ministers in the opinion polls, there lay a deep and complex personality whose secrets were guarded from the outside world, and even from close acquaintances, with uncompromising determination.

'There are things that one passionately wants to keep private,' he was to say some twenty years later. 'Things that are no one's business. What isn't realised is how professionally I don't expose what I don't want to.'

To his contemporaries at Oxford there was nothing particularly secret about what made the young Jeremy Thorpe run. His ambitions were public, unashamed, and pursued with a single-mindedness which was notable even for Oxford, where political ambition was not exactly unknown. For some it was just a little too naked. In the immediate post-war years, many undergraduates were in their late twenties or early thirties, a generation which had returned to university after fighting a war that had convinced them of the need to find a new kind of idealism to replace the old political conflicts. In this atmosphere it was generally felt that the pursuit of political office for its own sake should not rank high on the list of priorities, or at least should be conducted with some decorum. Thorpe, only nineteen when he first went up to Oxford, was quite unabashed. He set out to achieve the highest goal of all – presidency of the union, the post which has always been seen as a springboard to political greatness – and along the way he determined to pick up a clutch of lesser trophies. He won them all, and although his methods shocked some of his fellows, and left one or two with a distinct feeling of uneasiness, he conducted his campaigns with such exuberance that it was hard to take offence. From his very first day at university he seemed to command gifts of easy persuasion which other politicians spend a lifetime seeking to acquire.

'Jeremy sprang, as it were, fully armed from the womb,' said one contemporary. 'His political qualities seem to have been formed at an incredibly early age.'

He was also a convinced, though not always a convincing Liberal.

By every normal index, however, he should have been a staunch Conservative. His family, highly political on both sides, was Conservative. His father, John Thorpe, was a distinguished KC and Tory MP for Rusholme in Manchester. His mother was a pillar of her local Conservative constituency in Surrey. Jeremy himself liked to trace the political line back to Mr Speaker Thorpe who was beheaded by a mob in 1371. But it was his maternal grandfather who was, perhaps, the most striking and singular figure in the family tree. Sir John Norton-Griffiths MP was the last man to be decorated by Tsar Nicholas II before the Revolution. Known as 'Empire Jack' for his passionate devotion to British imperialism, he distinguished himself by blowing up Rumanian oil-wells during the First World War so that the Germans could not capture them. The story is told that before he actually blew up the wells he went to the King of Rumania to ask for permission. 'But what about compensation?' asked the King. 'I am a British officer,' replied Sir John haughtily, 'and I will sign you a letter.'

Somewhere along the line, the young Jeremy began to rebel gently against this formidable tradition. Perhaps it was the fact that as the youngest of three children he was allowed an independence which the others never had. His two sisters, born before their mother was eighteen, were separated from Jeremy by seven years. His younger sister, Camilla, who was tragically to commit suicide in 1974, said that she and her sister Lavinia were kept in the background while young Jeremy got the attention and the limelight.

11

But only later was there much resentment. 'Warm, emotional, neurotic, close' was how Thorpe once described his family.

They grew up in a comfortable red-brick house in Kensington. Recalling his earliest political experience, Thorpe said he remembered, at the age of five or six, watching his mother ringing the bell to summon the parlour-maid with more coal for the fire. He asked his mother why she didn't do it herself, and was unconvinced by her reply, which was that she simply wasn't very good at it.

At about this time Jeremy was taken seriously ill. Tubercular glands were diagnosed in his abdomen, and for seven months he was forced to lie on his back in a spinal carriage, tended mainly by a housekeeper and his nanny. The illness left its physical, if not emotional, legacy, since it ensured that the sporting life, so useful to success in the career of any privately educated British schoolboy, was never his strongest point. Ever since those days he has been forced to take exercises for a painful back which can, at any moment, 'seize up'.

British prep schools between the wars tended to be institutions of stifling tradition, run on strict disciplinarian lines and a precarious budget. But in 1940, when Jeremy was eleven, he was rescued. The advent of the war persuaded many middle-class families, especially those living in the south of England, that their children would be safer in America. Jeremy, with his younger sister, was dispatched to Connecticut where he stayed with his aunt, and attended the Rectory School. Modelled on distinctly British lines, and containing a fair number of English exiles, the Rectory was nevertheless a relaxed and easy-going contrast to its prototypes. Its headmaster, John Bigelow, described it as 'more like an overgrown family than a school', and amongst the forty or so pupils Jeremy made an immediate impression. He was already a self-confident and precocious boy, clever, witty, more popular perhaps with teachers than with fellow-pupils, good at French, more than proficient at the violin, a good actor and a budding public speaker. His gift for mimicry was already developing, and he was able to pick up a deep southern American accent which is by far the hardest to imitate well. He was also prepared to stick his neck out. John Bigelow recalls that one day Jeremy discovered that a neighbouring farmer was feeding the leftovers of some scarce and rationed food to his pigs. He accosted the man and delivered a stern lecture on the iniquities of selfishness in the course of a war. The farmer, more taken aback than anything, appears to have accepted the reproof.

Thorpe himself claims to have picked up his first radical inclinations as a reaction to the Republicans with whom he found himself in contact at his aunt's house. 'Perhaps it was the sheer cussedness of a child,' he said later, 'or because I couldn't stand Republicans. But I went round sticking Roosevelt pins on them all.' It was certainly true that by the time he returned to England – in 1943, aboard a destroyer – he was sufficiently changed to resent the discipline of Eton, the school to which he was now sent.

Within months of coming back, Jeremy's father, John Thorpe, had a severe stroke which left him deprived of speech.

The effect on Jeremy was deep. He had always felt particularly close to his father, a romantic Irishman with a rich sense of humour. Born in Cork but brought up in England, John Thorpe had lavished warmth and affection on Jeremy, making up perhaps for the unhappy childhood he had experienced as a boy – his own father had been a cold and narrow-minded churchman.

For some time, desperately unhappy, Jeremy tried everything, including the services of a faith healer, to help his father. Although unable to speak, John Thorpe could still take in all that went on around him, and his inability to contribute to family life caused him growing distress. When finally he died, Jeremy was distraught.

He and his mother now became far closer. Ursula Thorpe was, and is, a striking, even formidable lady, with a distinct penchant for the eccentric. Friends recall her wearing an 'Eton crop' haircut, a Tyrolean hat with a feather in it, and

13

sporting a monocle. The monocle continued for a long time, only finally to be abandoned as a concession to Thorpe's political image. Thorpe himself recalls a typically uncompromising incident from his childhood when Mrs Thorpe was throwing a children's party. One of the nannies who was there with her infant charge was rude to her, so Mrs Thorpe dismissed her on the spot. Later she rang the child's mother and announced: 'It's been so nice having your son here. But I've given his nanny notice.'

For a period she dominated all her children by the sheer force of her personality. 'We were all frightened of her,' admitted Thorpe. But after his father's death, the two were thrown together. She became not only his most ardent political admirer, but a confidante as well, and their close relationship was to continue through both his marriages.

One other effect of John Thorpe's death was that the family began to find itself in severe financial difficulties, and it was only because Mrs Thorpe's brother-in-law came to their assistance with a timely covenant that Jeremy was able to stay on at Eton.

This unhappy period hardened his antipathy towards school. Eton had not immediately taken to this precocious youngster with his embryo radicalism. Though perfectly used to nurturing rebel vipers, Eton was, and is, an institution where observing the rules of the game is part of the business of survival. It is just possible that Jeremy committed the unpardonable error of not taking the place seriously enough. He boasted about his middle-class background, complained about the powers of 'the library' – the group of senior boys which runs each house – and was beaten for smoking in bed. He was tiresome about the merits of American democracy. True, he won prizes for his violin-playing, but Eton has never regarded that as one of the pinnacles of achievement. He was not sorry to leave.

At home during the holidays he was more pleasantly occupied. Following his father's death he began to see more of that great Liberal family, the Lloyd Georges. Jeremy had always been impressed by David Lloyd George. He had been introduced as a child to the old man who had shown him round his orchard. But it was Lloyd George's daughter, Megan, who was to be his real mentor. Megan and Jeremy's mother had been girlhood friends, bridesmaids at each other's weddings, and Megan was Jeremy's godmother. It was she who now began introducing him to the romantic appeal of Lloyd George Liberalism.

The name Lloyd George inspires differing reactions amongst British politicians today. For some he is 'the people's champion', synonymous with the great Liberal government which took office in 1906, led by one of the strongest cabinets Britain has ever seen, and which went on to introduce a range of social reforms so far-reaching that no single government has ever managed subsequently to equal them. For others he is the man whose high-handed conduct of the First World War split the Liberal Party and effectively destroyed it as a major political force – there are still Liberals today who can scarcely bring themselves to utter his name. For others still he is a man whose private life and sexual conduct was a running scandal, a man whose reputation was kept intact in his lifetime only by the manipulation of power.

But for Jeremy, learning his Liberalism at the feet of the great man's daughter, his appeal was probably more as a man of action, whose personal magnetism and powers of rhetoric scattered the opposition where lesser mortals would have held back. He was a link with an age where political leaders were larger than life. Of course the Liberal Party of the late 1940s, with only twelve members of parliament, was only a poor shadow of its former self. But it was still a national platform. And what a challenge to try and lead it back one day towards its former glory!

There was, for Jeremy Thorpe, on leaving Eton, only one chore to face before he could get to grips with politics at Oxford. National Service was compulsory, and two years of it essential. In the event he served only six weeks. Quite why the Rifle Brigade and Private Thorpe parted company is something which remains a secret between them. Medical records are not open to public scrutiny, and Thorpe himself has always been reticent on the subject. The most he will say is that he was judged 'psychologically unsuitable', the army's description of a man who cannot adjust to the rigours of military discipline. One close friend says merely: 'He managed to convince the army that they wouldn't survive if he stayed.'

So Thorpe moved smoothly on to Trinity College, Oxford. He chose his father's subject, law, and gave it a minimum of his time. Instead he concentrated on taking Oxford by storm, and, on the whole, Oxford reacted favourably. There was room for flamboyance, and Thorpe supplied it. He took rooms in The High, the university's main street, at number 69, and set about creating a distinctly Edwardian style of living which he was to favour for most of his career. His dress was the most obvious reflection of that age of elegance. Frock coats, stove-pipe trousers, brocade waistcoats, buckled shoes, even spats and a 'frog' (a decorative fastening for the front of a military coat, much favoured by nineteenth-century bloods) were all part of the Thorpe wardrobe. The clothes and the style suggested wealth, but, as was so often to prove the case, Thorpe never had quite as much as the image suggested.

One Oxford contemporary, Michael Ogle, who shared rooms with Thorpe, pointed out that most of Thorpe's Edwardian clothes had been left to him by his father, and were worn for reasons of expediency as much as anything. 'It was all part of creating a lifestyle more spacious than his circumstances would permit,' says Ogle.

The shortage of money was, of course, relative. There was just enough to indulge his taste for Chinese objets d'art, with special reference to the T'ang and Han dynasties, and to acquire a reputation as an expert on ceramics. But the violin-playing began to suffer. As Thorpe himself said later: 'I think I was good enough to become a professional second violin in a third-rate orchestra.' And that was not quite what he had in mind.

Instead he cultivated entertaining friends and useful allies. A regular weekly lunch took place in the Shamrock Restaurant near the Bodleian Library, where friends of Thorpe would meet to discuss Oxford gossip, talk about politics and music, or dwell lightly on the meaning of life. Thorpe would sometimes fling wide the bay window and address the 'multitude' below. The multitude, on these occasions would, by and large, pass onwards unconcerned, being well accustomed to such undergraduate eccentricities.

His circle of acquaintants stretched wide and included several who would later make their own mark on public life. In politics there were people like William Rees-Mogg who was to become editor of *The Times*; Robin Day who, as one of the sharpest television interviewers of his day, would frequently cross swords with Jeremy Thorpe MP; Keith Kyle, a political journalist; Dick Taverne, a Labour MP who would rebel against his own party and resign the whip, but would refuse the alternative of joining the Liberals; Timothy (later Lord) Beaumont, a fellow-Liberal who would later become president of the party, only to fall out with his leader; John Gilbert, who shared Thorpe's taste for elegance and went on to become a Labour minister; Stanley Brodie, a QC whom Thorpe would call on to help run the Liberals' shaky finances; Christopher Bourke, another lawyer, who was to serve in the office of Director of Public Prosecutions; Ann Chesney (later Ann Dummett), active in civil rights and a great champion of Thorpe in later years; Patrick Hutber, an influential City editor who would use his column to castigate Thorpe's financial judgement.

At the same time Thorpe fostered relations with the 'grown-up' world outside university. Unlike most of his contemporaries, he relished the company of his mother's generation. Ursula Thorpe was a frequent visitor to his digs in The High, so was Lady Megan Lloyd George, and even Lady Norton-Griffiths, his grandmother. They enjoyed his company as much as he did theirs. One fellow-undergraduate, Jeremy Maas, who occupied rooms opposite his, remembers an occasion when he was expecting his own mother to arrive. Confused by the two 'Jeremies' marked on the entrance, she walked into Jeremy Thorpe's rooms instead, and stayed on to talk for more than an hour, so greatly enjoying the company of 'that charming young man' that she was loth to leave.

But perhaps his most important 'contact' with the outside world, and with the Liberal Party, was Dingle Foot, a senior and influential Liberal whose career in politics and the law was to bring him ministerial rank, wide experience of the constitutional affairs of emergent nations in Africa and the Far East, and a knighthood. He was one of the four remarkable sons of Isaac Foot, an elder statesman of the party, and a towering figure amongst West Country Liberals. Three of Isaac's sons had been presidents of the Oxford Union, while the fourth, Hugh Foot (later Lord Caradon), became president of the Cambridge Union instead. All went on to political careers of distinction.

Thorpe took strongly to Dingle Foot and cultivated him, inviting him to speak in Oxford and helping him to campaign in North Cornwall. He acquired the gift of imitating the different voices of all four Feet, but his speciality was Dingle's. 'One of the sights of Oxford', recalled Keith Kyle, 'was seeing Jeremy Thorpe and Dingle Foot walking down The High, talking to each other in Dingle Foot's voice.'

This was the public face of Jeremy Thorpe, 'a personality whose vivacity, wit and easy manner stand in sparkling relief to the drab stage of Oxford life,' as the university magazine *Isis* described him. But his circle was wide, and there were other friends who would also surface later in Thorpe's life, having preserved a remarkable and consistent loyalty – the one quality which Thorpe was to value above all others. They included Philip Watkins, who worked his way up through the Liberal Party organization to emerge, under Thorpe's aegis, as treasurer of the party at a critical point in its development; and David Holmes, later best man at Thorpe's first wedding, later still co-defendant in the dock at the Old Bailey, accused with him of conspiracy to murder

And George Carman, the QC who would defend Thorpe in that court.

There was no doubt, however, which of these worlds received most of Thorpe's time. 'His energies have not only been poured into the whirl of union affairs', noted the same *Isis* article, 'but they have also been hurled with concentrated fury upon the Liberal Club, the Law Society, and the Russell and Palmerston Club.' He became president of them all in his race for the union, and he achieved office amidst clouds of controversy which have never entirely dispersed.

There are two schools of thought about how he got to the top. One claims that he did nothing worse than 'playing at politics'; that if he did break any conventions they were essentially trivial and deserved to be broken; that everybody else was doing it too; and that anyway he was a poor Machiavellian because he was always getting caught. The other school, drawn mostly from the older generation, professed itself shocked at the insensitivity with which he ran his campaigns for office.

The Liberal Club was his first and most obvious goal. He became social secretary, then secretary, and finally president. There was no doubting his qualifications for the job – impeccable Liberal principles, a fine gift for oratory, and an enthusiasm which built up the club's membership towards the level of its two rivals. In fact so smooth was his rise that he wanted to cut out the secretary stage altogether but he was persuaded against this by Keith Kyle, and he accepted the delay gracefully enough.

Next, and most unpromising, was his bid for the presidency of the small but influential Law Society. Here his claim was thin, since not only was there a strong and obvious contender – a woman – but Thorpe's attention to his legal studies had not been thorough. He still decided to run, seeking at the outset to convince his opponent that she should stand down. She refused. Thorpe nonetheless achieved a landslide victory though his vote comprised a remarkably high proportion of normally inactive Society members – including some who were now practising in London.

But these were merely skirmishes along the road. The real battle was for the union presidency itself. He began by quietly eliminating a serious rival. Under Robin Day's term as president the union's rules had been amended to allow those whose university career had been interrupted by the war to stand for election. Thorpe, as a member of the committee, voted for the change, but then realised that it let in a serious contender for office in the shape of Keith Kyle. He therefore secretly launched, and encouraged from the sidelines, a campaign of protest against his own committee's decision. Such dissension followed that Kyle withdrew his candidacy rather than cause any further trouble.

Thus, by the Michaelmas term of 1950, when Godfrey Smith (now a senior editorial executive on the *Sunday Times*) was president, the field had been narrowed to three candidates: William Rees-Mogg who was Conservative, Dick Taverne, Labour, and Jeremy Thorpe, Liberal. Their performance during that term's debates would be crucial to their success, and the first test was the important opening debate of the season.

The motion attacked the Labour government's record in office, and Smith began casting around for speakers from outside the university to support it. Conservative politicians were reluctant to take part on the eve of a General Election, so Thorpe took it upon himself to bypass his president and find a Liberal speaker instead. This was considered an outrageous interference with the presidential choice, and Smith promptly cancelled the invitation Thorpe had issued. Smith then set off for the Liberal Party conference in Scarborough to find someone for himself. Once there, however, he began encountering a distinct *froideur*. Those Liberals he approached turned him down flat. His requests for help were ignored. Dingle Foot, amongst others, rejected his polite invitation with uncharacteristic brusqueness.

'I gradually became aware that they had been nobbled,' recalls Smith. 'It seemed to me that Thorpe had been deliberately discouraging them from coming to speak. It was only many years later that it dawned on me how thoroughly he must have "put the boot in". I'll never forget that bleak reception in Scarborough.'

The result was a desperate, last-minute search for stand-in speakers, and honour was only just saved in time. The retribution exacted on Thorpe was his omission from the list of main speakers, and a committee of inquiry was set up, with Keith Kyle in the chair, to investigate his conduct. After much solemn deliberation Thorpe was censured, though no one could agree on a suitable punishment. Thorpe referred to the whole thing gleefully as 'the Balliol plot', since most of his critics were Balliol men. In the union he was branded openly as 'a fiddler', to which he promptly retorted: 'I will fiddle till Balliol burns!'

Despite this debacle, Thorpe was still very much in the race. In the presidential debate at the end of that term, he faced Dick Taverne across the floor. Taverne delivered what most people considered to be the finest speech of his under-graduate career, but Thorpe responded with a speech of such brilliance that he stole the show. His subsequent election was assured, and next term – Hilary, 1951 – he took his seat as president.

It is easy, in retrospect, to read more into these student escapades than they deserve. Michael Ogle, for instance, who knew Thorpe perhaps better than most, claims that the political side of his character was artificial, an outer layer put on for display only, concealing a better, more generous nature underneath. 'I never liked his political persona – it didn't do him justice,' he says. 'He would don a carapace of insensitivity which more and more concealed the private side of him.'

Others, who knew him less intimately, were left with a distinct feeling of uneasiness about his judgement which never quite left them as they watched his later career. Rees-Mogg recalls a conversation with Taverne in which they agreed that it would be hard to forget the way in which Thorpe had behaved at university, and it was not until many years later that they began to be convinced that he had acquired the seriousness of a major political figure. Keith Kyle, while admiring him as a politician, felt that he might well come to grief if he continued to 'cut corners' as he had at Oxford; and another contemporary, the late Ivan Yates, was convinced that there was a distinct unbalance somewhere in his character. *Isis*, concluding a profile of him in 1951, wrote: 'His likes and dislikes are often too violently expressed, and some feel that as a future politician he would be wiser to be more discreet. An interesting and stimulating career lies ahead of him, provided he does not let his enthusiasm over-reach his wisdom.'

It was, perhaps, inevitable that someone who attracted so much attention should be subjected to more searching analysis than most. More than one of his friends noted a streak of ruthlessness beneath the light-hearted veneer, and some detected more – a kind of brooding introspection. One of them referred to 'the dark side' of his character, and Godfrey Smith recalls a disquieting remark made by William Rees-Mogg. Discussing Thorpe in his room one day, Rees-Mogg suddenly remarked: 'We must watch Jeremy. One day he will be driven to the brink of suicide.' This may have been an instinctive reaction to what Thorpe calls the Irish side of his character. 'My Irish relations have periods of acute melancholy', he told the journalist Susan Barnes, 'and for days on end collapse in an Irish heap. I do have moments like this.'

For the time being, however, they were few and far between. Thorpe still had one more prize to win at Oxford – and one minor setback to overcome. The prize was his fourth presidency – that of the Russell and Palmerston Club, which had only just been revived by Timothy Beaumont. It was a club founded in memory of two great Whig politicians, and there was indeed something convincingly whiggish about Thorpe's manner at this time. In the course of an argument he would often strike a pose, his back to the fireplace, and exclaim: 'God, how I *hate* the Tories!'

The setback concerned the small matter of his degree. He

had not devoted much time to lectures or tutorials, and the approach of his finals induced a considerable panic. In the end he only just managed to scrape a third. 'Jeremy carried all before him except his degree,' remarked his mother philosophically.

It was enough, however, for him to proceed to the Inner Temple where he was called to the Bar on the same night as his friend Stanley Brodie. But while Brodie went on to become a QC, Jeremy's path lay in a different direction. His political feelers had been put out long before, and by the end of his first year at Oxford the executive of the Liberal Party was well aware of his existence. At first he felt that his best chance of securing a seat in parliament would be to launch an assault on Lloyd George country in Wales, and he had even begun to learn Welsh in preparation. But when, in 1949, he was asked to take a team of fellow-Liberals down from Oxford to the West Country to help another of the Foot brothers, John Foot, to campaign in the Cornwall constituency of Bodmin, he began to realise that this might be a more promising area. Thorpe's 'university commandoes', as they were known, would descend *en bloc* on an unsuspecting town or village and subject it to a barrage of doorstep interviews, loudhailer slogans and marketplace meetings. Led by Thorpe himself, already wearing an extraordinary brown bowler, which was to be the subject of much agonised debate later in his career, the young Liberals stormed through Bodmin for a week. 'It was ballyhoo', recalls Foot, 'but perfectly legitimate. And even in those days Jeremy had this astonishing instinct for politicking. You knew from the beginning that this was a very remarkable chap, he was an extraordinary performer.'

The West Country, with its strong methodist tradition, which had long gone hand in hand with an equally strong inclination to Liberalism, was therefore obvious territory. There was, however, nothing particularly obvious about the constituency of North Devon, though the Thorpe family had taken occasional holidays in the local resort of Woolacombe. The Tories enjoyed a seemingly invincible majority of over 12,000 votes, and the Liberals had slumped by 4000 since the war. But then there was no such thing any longer as a safe Liberal seat, and even if there had been there was a waiting list of distinguished senior Liberals who would have had first claim. So Thorpe applied for North Devon and was accepted. In 1952 he was adopted as candidate, and began the long task of nursing the Liberal vote in North Devon back to strength.

His speeches in this early period tended to revolve round foreign policy, which was always his speciality and on which he articulated sound Liberal views. He attacked apartheid in South Africa and neo-colonialism in South-East Asia. They sound safe enough subjects today, but in the early 1950s, with the Cold War dominating Western attitudes, it took some political confidence to advance such openly combative opinions. There was, perhaps, less emphasis in his speeches on economic strategy. The subject was never to be one of his strong cards and would expose him in the future to attacks from his political opponents. But to compensate, there were plenty of spirited assaults on the two main parties as the end of Winston Churchill's post-war term of office approached.

It was, however, on the political stump in North Devon itself that Thorpe's genius lay. No one has ever disputed his formidable talent for vote-winning which enabled him to build up such popularity in his constituency that it was to carry him through the deepest slumps in Liberal fortunes. His success was based, first, on a phenomenal memory for people and faces which allowed him to recall not only the Christian names of local people but the names of their friends, their relations and even their pets, leaving everyone to whom he spoke with a vague sense that they occupied a special place in the heart of their prospective MP. As well as this, however, there was the sheer hard work he put in, and which he expected his (unpaid) party helpers to assist with. He visited every house in every remote village in his constituency at some stage during the run-up to his first election, and established which local issues concerned them. 'Show me a village with no electricity and I'll show you a village which is going to vote Liberal next time,' he used to say.

He began building up a system by which every time a new voter came of age he would receive a leaflet welcoming him into the fold and suggesting where he might place his first cross when it came to an election. To help Thorpe commit local details to memory he would use a small notebook containing useful information, such as: 'Mrs J.'s garden newly planted, door needs lick of paint, dog poorly.' Next time he visited Mrs J. he would dash up the garden path, clasp her by the hand and beam: 'Glad to see the garden coming on so well since you planted it this spring. Tut tut, still haven't got round to that door yet? How's poor Snuffles then? Got over his cold has he?' Five minutes later Mrs Jones would be talking excitedly to her neighbour about 'Our Jeremy' and what he had been saying. Meanwhile Our Jeremy was six doors down, telling Mrs S. in broad dialect about the goings-on up at the 'Big House', and how the squire was causing an awful fuss by fencing off the local footpath, and wasn't it time something was done to change the way things were going on around here? Then he would catch up with the local milkman down at the end of the street and insist on taking over the wheel of his truck and delivering bottles at every door, seizing the opportunity to point out how there was nothing to distinguish between Labour and Tory candidates except the colour of their rosettes. By the time he left the village the place would be a-buzz with gossip, rumour – and excitement.

'Which do you want to vote for – the free man or the party stooge?' he would cry from some vantage point on which he would perch with deliberate casualness. 'A vote for the Liberals is a vote for freedom.'

North Devon was open to the Thorpe appeal. And with the backing of the Foot brothers who came down to speak on his behalf, the Liberals went into the 1955 election with all the panache of an American congressional campaign, which it strongly resembled. The Tories, with their candidate, the Honourable James Lindsay, were accused of using 'smear and fear' tactics in an effort to reverse the trend. 'The Tories may be surprised to hear this,' snapped Thorpe, 'but politicians do not all go into politics to seek the rewards of office . . .'

The eve-of-election rally was addressed by another party stalwart, Frank Byers, former MP for North Dorset, and was attended by more than 1000 singing, cheering supporters. Extra police were called in as Thorpe himself appeared at the window of the Queen's Hall in Barnstaple, and a chant which was to become familiar in North Devon went up: 'JE-RE-MEEE . . . JE-RE-MEEE . . . .' Next day, in a steady downpour of rain, 82 per cent of the electorate turned out and slashed the Tory majority in half. Mr Lindsay was returned, but with only a 5226 majority. Two months later Thorpe was unanimously re-adopted as candidate, and, with two other Liberals on the platform – Jo Grimond, a future leader, and Peter Bessell, a neighbouring candidate – announced to a cheering, sweltering crowd in his now perfected Devon accent: 'Us be gwain do it again!'

Of that there was little doubt, but it had been an expensive campaign, and if they were to make the final breakthrough it would be even more expensive. A full-time agent with a car was essential. Then there must be separate divisions within the constituency – forty in all, Thorpe thought – and they should aim for a starting minimum of 5000 paid-up members. Speaking from the same re-adoption platform, he challenged the crowd to raise £300 and bet them his wing collar and tie that they would not do it. When the hat came back £475 had been collected in thirty minutes, and Thorpe flamboyantly paid up. It was impressive testimony to another of his gifts: the ability to raise money was to become one of his most telling contributions to the party, and a source of bitter controversy in the future.

In the meantime he was ensuring that his presence was felt in London as well as in the West Country. He was already on the Liberal Party executive, to which he had been elected at the age of twenty three, and he rapidly made himself known to the party hierarchy. Amongst other things, he dutifully sat on an agricultural sub-committee set up to thrash out party policy. One of those who belonged to it recalls that Thorpe seemed less interested in the finer points of farming subsidies than in hearing the latest party gossip, which increasingly revolved around the leadership of Clement Davies, a much-loved Liberal of the old school, friend of Winston Churchill, and a steadying hand at the tiller. Thorpe had joined a group within the party called the Radical Reform Group, whose aim was to move the party gently leftwards. They were not hostile to Davies personally, but as time went on some of the younger and more restless members, Thorpe amongst them, became convinced that a change was necessary.

At the Liberals' annual conference in 1956, Clement Davies, amidst scenes of great emotion, announced his decision to 'step down from the bridge and go below', handing over command to Jo Grimond. Amidst the cheering and the weeping, Thorpe was seen to turn and comment: 'Isn't Clem marvellous?' as he joined in the applause. Immediately a cynical colleague shot back: 'Crocodile tears, Jeremy?'

Outside politics his career was taking two directions. He was by now a practising barrister on the Western Circuit with a modest reputation, perhaps better known as an 'advocate' than an academic lawyer; that is, his defence of civil and minor criminal cases relied more on the style of presentation in court than on a meticulous analysis of legal precedent. He was a genial and popular companion at the various assizes he attended, and those watching his progress were reasonably certain that were he ever to take his attention off politics and concentrate on a legal career he would go to the top.

But more appealing to Thorpe, and extremely useful to his political ambitions, was his second career – television. He had landed a job with Independent Television in the

27

days when current affairs programmes were beginning to take shape, and he began almost immediately to establish himself as an interviewer of rare talent. All his sharpness of observation, his barbed wit and his quick-thinking responses seemed made for television, and later, as an MP, he was to make great capital out of it. In the meantime, he not only became a face familiar to the public on various current affairs programmes, including the influential 'This Week', but began establishing useful contacts with statesmen in various quarters of the globe: Hussein of Jordan, Kaunda of the African National Congress, Banda of Nyasaland with whom he secured a 'scoop' interview shortly after Banda's release from prison under the British. It was here that Thorpe's friendship with Dingle Foot was helpful since Foot was on close terms with many of the emerging African leaders because of his legal work in the Third World. Thorpe's links with Africa and the Middle East were further established when, in 1958, he became a partner in a political consultancy, External Development Services, set up by an undergraduate friend and fellow-Liberal, Grenville Jones. The services they offered included advice on trade and economic matters, and took Thorpe to places as far apart as Nigeria, Tunisia, Uganda and Dubai. It was also to cause him, and Jones, some embarrassment later when he found his pro-Israeli views clashing with his business interests in the Arab states. He made several trips to India, too, where he was handsomely rewarded for giving legal advice to a friend coping with a complex trust fund.

But now Thorpe faced a crucial General Election. It was 1959, and, at the age of thirty, he was about to discover whether the seven long years he had spent nursing North Devon would finally pay off. There was some reason for confidence. In March of the previous year, Mark Bonham-Carter, grandson of the former Liberal Prime Minister, H.H. Asquith, had won a spectacular by-election victory in the neighbouring constituency of Torrington, thanks partly to the indefatigable help given him by Thorpe.

A few days before the election in October, Thorpe sat

with his former Oxford colleague, Keith Kyle, discussing his prospects. He began calculating the slim majorities he might expect from various divisions in the constituency, and then added 500 votes on top for the 'personality vote' he thought he would get. 'I think that'll just about give me a majority of 300,' he announced.

On 10 October, amidst scenes of incredible tension in the Queen's Hall, the votes were counted. When the results were read out to a delirious crowd, they revealed that John Jeremy Thorpe, Liberal, had succeeded in obliterating the Conservative majority and had captured the seat by just 362 votes. His prophecy had been uncannily accurate.

For the first time since 1935 North Devon was Liberal again. As the news spread through the countryside, excited Liberals poured out of their doors, while outside the hall itself a crowd of several thousand cheered itself hoarse for half an hour. Next day, Thorpe, accompanied by his mother, gave his victory speech from the balcony of the local party headquarters. 'This is not my victory, but our victory,' he said, his voice trembling with emotion. 'I think you know how much I love North Devon and the people who live within its borders.' That evening a crowd of 6000 surged through the streets in a torchlight procession, their new MP leading them beneath a yellow banner which had last proclaimed victory twenty four years before.

That night, as Thorpe retired, exhausted, to bed in a local hotel, there were two disturbances. The first was the arrival of an excited Peter Bessell, the neighbouring Liberal candidate for Bodmin, who had just failed to capture his seat but had cut the Conservative majority from more than 7000 to 2000. The two were congratulating each other when there was a knock at the door and three embarrassed sailors walked in. They had been sent by the commanding officer of their ship to secure the autograph of the newly elected MP, as an initiative test. Amidst much merriment Thorpe duly signed, thus fulfilling the first of many thousands of similar duties which are part of the lot of a duly elected member of parliament.

2. Quest for Shangri-La

On his first visit to the House of Commons as a fully fledged member of parliament Jeremy Thorpe was shown his personal coat-hook just inside the members' entrance. The first thing he noticed was a scarlet loop hanging from it. 'What on earth is that?' he asked the attendant. 'That, sir, is where you hang your sword,' was the murmured reply. 'How absurd,' said Thorpe, delighted and astonished. 'An MP has a place to hang his sword, but no desk to work at!'

New arrivals at the House of Commons – 'the finest club in Europe' – react in different ways to their surroundings. Some are appalled by its antiquated conventions, its cramped office-space and its public-schoolboy atmosphere. Others take to it instinctively. Thorpe, from his very first day, was in his element, able to relish the traditions while mocking them at the same time. He rapidly mastered the intricacies of parliamentary procedure but was not afraid to point out some of the drawbacks.

He was amongst the first group of new MPs to be sworn in, and lost no time in making a maiden speech. He was soon acquiring a reputation as a wit and a master of back-bench repartee, while amusing the gossip writers with tricks like 'borrowing' dirty British Railways linen from his train and presenting it to the Minister of Transport in the Commons to demonstrate how badly cleaned the carriages were.

On the more important issues of the day he established a position on the left of his party. His early activities centred round civil liberties in various foreign states – he campaigned actively by collecting petitions for the release of political prisoners, attending rallies, and taking part in demonstrations. He was even banned from entering Spain after urging a political amnesty there. He attacked the absence of democracy in Ghana, and urged the boycott of South African goods. When the Conservative Prime Minister, Harold Macmillan, axed seven of his cabinet in 1962, Thorpe's parliamentary observation was accounted the sharpest. 'Greater love', he said, 'hath no man than this, that he lay down his friends for his life.'

Like most bachelor MPs Thorpe was the object of some speculation. On the campaign trail and other public occasions, the functions normally discharged by an MP's wife were undertaken by his mother. The newspapers, naturally eager to marry off any unattached public figure, wrote up the new MP for North Devon as 'eligible'.

In March 1960, two months before the wedding of Princess Margaret and Anthony Armstrong-Jones, the security services asked for an investigation to be carried out into Thorpe's background. It was prompted by the rumour that Armstrong-Jones might well ask Thorpe to be best man at his forthcoming wedding, and it was carried out by the then Chief Constable of Devon, Lieutenant Colonel R.R.M. (now Sir Ranulph 'Streaky') Bacon. Thorpe and Armstrong-Jones had been at Eton together and Thorpe was fond of saying – it was one of his jocular party pieces – that his greatest ambition was to marry Princess Margaret. The investigation was a discreet affair. Few people knew about it, indeed it appears that Bacon made most of the inquiries personally. He spoke to a local constable in the Barnstaple area and discussed the matter with 'known associates' of Thorpe in Devon. Thorpe was not interviewed personally, but he was kept under surveillance for a time. In submitting the results of his investigation to Whitehall, Bacon reported that many people believed that Thorpe had homosexual tendencies. Bacon's report was noted on the security file which is opened on every MP as soon as he is elected.

Homosexual activity at that time was a criminal offence, though since the mid-1950s it had been an area of the law under increasing attack. Up until that time public attitudes to homosexuality had scarcely been tested since the trials of the playwright Oscar Wilde in 1895. The outrage and offended sensibilities then paraded in court by the prosecution had reinforced the late Victorian view of homosexuality as an offence against nature. The Solicitor-General, Sir Frank Lockwood, who prosecuted Wilde, judged it as 'vice in its most hideous and detestable form' and those who indulged as 'somewhat lower than the beasts'. Wilde himself, writing later from Reading Gaol, described Lockwood's passion on the subject as being 'like one of Savanarola's indictments of the Popes of Rome', but it was dutifully echoed by the newspapers of the day. Thereafter it had been quietly swept under the carpet as a subject not fit for public discussion.

In 1954 a sensational trial involving three men, Lord Montagu of Beaulieu, Michael Pitt-Rivers and Peter Wildeblood – accused of belonging to an upper-class homosexual circle – had reopened the debate. While serving his sentence, Peter Wildeblood prepared a moving book, *Against the Law*, putting the case for toleration. Three years later a further change in social and moral attitudes was signalled by Sir John Wolfenden's report on prostitution and homosexuality which recommended far-reaching changes in the law. In particular it recommended that homosexual activity between consenting adults aged over twenty-one should cease to be against the law. At that time the maximum sentence for buggery, the most serious homosexual offence, was life imprisonment.

Wolfenden went a long way to dispelling outdated ideas about homosexuality, including the suggestion that it was a disease and a perversion, and recommended a more tolerant and understanding response to it. Members of the Liberal Party, amongst many other progressive groups, welcomed his report and urged that its recommendations should be written into a parliamentary bill. It was, nonetheless, still an emotive issue and the law remained unreformed under the Tory administration despite the growing weight of liberal opinion.

One reason for this inflexibility was that homosexuality had come to be regarded as in some way prejudicial to the security of the state. The defection to Soviet Russia of Guy Burgess and Donald Maclean, both Foreign Office men with homosexual proclivities, had shocked the security services. The 1956 report of the Conference of Privy Councillors into their defection agreed that in addition to communist sympathies, character 'defects' should also be grounds for exclusion from state posts. The 'defects' encompassed 'drunkenness, addiction to drugs, homosexuality, or any loose living'. The report was firm in its conclusion: 'It is right to continue the practice of tilting the balance in favour of offering greater protection to the security of the state rather than in the direction of safeguarding the rights of the individual.' In 1962 a young homosexual civil servant called John Vassall, employed by the Ministry of Defence, was convicted of spying and sentenced to ten years in prison. The vulnerability to blackmail of homosexuals in positions of power was widely discussed, and attitudes began to harden once more.

Jeremy Thorpe was on uncertain ground in this aspect of the national debate because of the doubts about his own sexuality. At Oxford he had, by general account, led a life of almost total 'asexuality'. Not that there was anything particularly surprising about this, since undergraduates in those days led a far more restricted life than is the case today. Thorpe's occasional advances towards the opposite sex were made, it seemed, almost more as a matter of form than anything else.

In the years following, his closest relations, outside the circle of his mother's friends, had been with men, and he derived most pleasure and stimulation from their company. His homosexual tendencies were acknowledged among a small group of friends. He was, thus, doubly vulnerable as an MP. An indiscreet association might not only land him in trouble with the law but also permanently damage any chance of his holding government office. In the autumn of 1961 a young man came into his life who was to precipitate both disasters. His name was Norman Josiffe though he was to achieve ultimate notoriety under the name Norman Scott.

Norman Josiffe was an intriguing young man. Tall and slim with strong features, he would have been formally handsome but for the troubled expression about his eyes and the pouting set of his mouth which suggested sensuality and petulance, though not necessarily in that order.

He was to complain of a lack of love and affection in his childhood but it had not·been totally without joy. He was born in Sidcup, Kent, in February 1940, the fifth of Mrs Ena Josiffe's six children. Shortly after his birth, the family moved to Bexleyheath where Norman spent most of his youth. Although robust in appearance, the family contained hidden complexities.

Norman's three older brothers and his sister were the offspring of his mother's first marriage to Albert Merritt, an executive with the Shaw Saville shipping line. Mr Merritt had died, leaving Ena, still not long out of her twenties, with four children to support. The young widow had turned to a local accountant and family friend, Albert Josiffe. Her marriage to Josiffe was not a huge success and after the birth of her sixth child, another son, they separated. Albert Josiffe moved to Orpington leaving his wife with the children in Bexleyheath. As was thought proper in such situations at the time, Norman's parents operated on the 'clean break' principle, though modern psychological findings show that this is rarely the best policy for the child. Norman, like his younger brother, had no memories of his father as a child, a fact that was to assume great significance in later years.

Ena Josiffe was a woman of strong, self-reliant character. She worked as a switchboard operator and eventually achieved supervisory rank on the London staff of Pan American Airways. In bringing up the children she was helped by the presence in the near neighbourhood of her mother, Mrs Lynch. Grandma Lynch, an Irishwoman and a strong Roman Catholic, led the family procession to Mass each Sunday. As the children grew up Ena Josiffe was even able to indulge an interest in Conservative Party politics in the area. The local MP was a promising young Tory politician called Edward Heath.

The children's evolving view of the world was necessarily disciplined and sometimes brusque – so large a family needed a timetable – but it was not emotionally deprived. Norman remembered being a happy child at Bexleyheath's Upton Road County Primary School, where he was good at English, poor at maths, and invariably top in religious instruction. He loved the rich ritual of Mass on Sundays.

His real problems started at secondary school. At St Stephen's, a local Roman Catholic school, his performance rapidly declined. The harsher discipline of the authorities and the more rumbustious play of the children both inhibited his sensitive nature.

Norman was more at ease when the family moved and he was transferred to the local secondary modern school where the discipline was less stringent and academic pretensions more modest. But school was never a pleasure. His older brothers held their own through their ability at sports such as football and cricket. Norman could only admire and envy their prowess; he was not good at games. Aged fourteen, Norman secured an effective escape from the conventional world of his peers by persuading his mother to let him have a pony.

The pony, 'Listowel', became the emotional centre of his existence; its genuine needs provided a ready excuse for stolen absences from school. While his brothers assembled the necessary qualifications and attitudes to equip them for solid, middle-class citizenship, Norman sought release from such concerns in solitary rides around the Kent countryside. Within the family Norman came to be regarded as someone bound to go his own way, a sweet boy but a dreamer. 'Norman', said his mother, 'was always looking for some Shangri-La.'

But for the adolescent Norman the sweet, dream-like nature had come to conceal some dangerously blocked psychological energies. He began to deal with the absence of his father by denying the reality of his existence. The next stage in the development of a fantasy paternity could not be long delayed. As for his mother, her strength and ability to cope only seemed to put the development of his own manhood in question. He dealt with these feelings of inadequacy by turning on her, if only in his head. Mrs Josiffe's political activities inevitably widened her circle of male acquaintance in the neighbourhood. Norman came to see such acquaintance as predators on his mother's affections, denying him the substance of his own needs. In his case the brute possessiveness of a child had been dangerously prolonged into adolescence.

The situation worsened dramatically shortly after Norman left school, aged fifteen. On 23 April 1956, he was found guilty on two charges of larceny at Bromley Juvenile Court, Kent, and put on probation. His offences had been to steal a saddle and some feed for his pony. Norman viewed the episode as a form of revenge for his mother's inattention to his problems; though a deeper diagnosis would more probably point to the absence of a father. Norman was already beginning to perceive himself as a victim.

The probationary period did, however, enable him to obtain a better idea of what to do with his life. A short spell working as a clerk in a solicitor's office had already convinced him of his unsuitability for office work. The Home Counties' countryside afforded opportunities for working in the open air with animals and Norman, encouraged by his probation officer, sensibly decided to take one by becoming a pupil at the Westerham Riding School near Oxted, Surrey. By the age of seventeen he had left the orbit of his family and was working as a riding instructor at a stables in Altrincham, Cheshire.

While Norman developed a genuine skill in handling horses there was no similar progress in his dealings with people. In an attempt to master his own inner conflicts, Norman put on airs. He called himself Lianche-Josiffe (the Lianche being a Frenchified version of his grandmother's Irish surname) and when asked about his social background would hint at some darkly tragic circumstance that had left him virtually alone in the world. By the age of nineteen when he moved back south to learn dressage and to work in the Kingham Stables at Chipping Norton, Oxfordshire, he was well on the way to becoming a frightful prig. His redeeming, and ultimately saving, feature was an alert sense of fun that would often break through the false mask of his own devising.

The owner of the Kingham Stables, a Mr Brecht de Vater, had a wide circle of social acquaintances, though his high sense of style was accounted by some as a veil for what he perhaps regarded as rudimentary origins. The Kingham owner's original name was simply Vater, the same as his Welsh coalmining father. Among those Vater counted as friends was the new Liberal MP for North Devon. Sometime in 1960, in the course of a visit to the stables, Jeremy Thorpe was introduced to Norman Josiffe. They had a brief conversation during which Thorpe told Norman that if he ever found himself in difficulty he should feel free to look him up at the House of Commons.

As Norman approached his twenty-first birthday he found his difficulties multiplying. Although he had found a girl-friend in the area, he was losing faith in his ability to sustain friendships of any kind. The blocked energies in his make-up meant that he tended to overreact to simple gestures of friendship and frighten away well-wishers with his inten-sity. Norman often felt that people were looking at him in crowds. He began to suffer from sleeplessness, irritability and apparently inexplicable crying fits. He experienced doubts about his sexuality though he would react strongly against any suggestion that the effeminacy in his nature might have a homosexual significance. His relations with his employer, an aggressively confident man, deteriorated.

The distressing habit of inventing stories to make his situation appear even more piteous than it was in reality was now deeply ingrained. The 'father' that Norman had invented for himself and others had died tragically. He had been an architect working on the design of a new city in

Brazil. The plane carrying VIPs to visit the new city had crashed and his 'father' had been among those who lost their lives.

Early in 1961, Norman consulted a local GP and was prescribed a course of the tranquillizer Largactil. The doctor also encouraged him to attend the Ashurst Clinic, a special unit attached to the Littlemore Hospital in Oxford, where he might get a chance to tackle the problems that underlay his symptoms. In those days the Ashurst treatment-formula for disturbed patients was a mixture of Librium, psychotherapy and contact with people.

On 12 May 1961 Norman attended the out-patients clinic and appeared ready to entertain the idea that his case might be most suitably treated by admission as a full-time patient. On 23 May he failed to keep an appointment to discuss the matter further. On 24 May he was admitted to the casualty department at the Radcliffe Infirmary, Oxford, suffering from an overdose of Largactil.

It was essentially a cry for help, rather than a serious suicide attempt. Like many people on the verge of breakdown, Norman was dramatising his desperation but trying to avoid a simple acknowledgement of his need for assistance. In June he became a voluntary in-patient at the Ashurst where he had some opportunity to explore his own griefs with others who were similarly disturbed. He still, however, maintained the fiction of a dead father. The other patients thought that Norman was very young for his age. 'A little boy,' said one. Despite the violence in his nature exhibited by the suicide attempt, his condition excited pity rather than fear. They also thought he was almost certainly a virgin.

In July Norman discharged himself from the Ashurst with two other patients, an older bisexual man and a married woman in her forties. Together they set up a bizarre *ménage-à-trois* in a flat in Polstead Road, Oxford. It turned out an exceptionally volatile establishment and rapidly split up. The two older members returned to the Ashurst before the end of the month. Norman stayed in touch with the clinic but moved on to lodgings in the village of Church Enstone where he was for a while sustained by the friendship of a young man of his own age. But his basic problems still remained unresolved and broke out again in severe form when the young man rejected his company for that of a girlfriend. Norman made another 'suicide' attempt with his drugs.

A local doctor became so concerned about Norman's hysterical behaviour that he thought there were grounds for a 'section' – an order under section 29 of the Mental Health Act, 1959, for compulsory detention in a mental institution for three days. On 28 October Norman was returned to the Ashurst.

Three days later he left the Ashurst for good. In theory, the clinic could have detained him, but Norman's psychological problem was not the kind that could be best treated under a compulsory regime. He was therefore free to seek his own solutions. Norman had already decided what he was going to do. His parting words to a member of the staff were: 'I've had Oxfordshire and I'm off.' He would take up the offer of help so lightly made by Jeremy Thorpe a year earlier.

On the afternoon of 8 November 1961 Norman Josiffe came to Westminster with his Jack Russell terrier, 'Mrs Tish'. Finding that dogs were not allowed in the House of Commons, Norman took the terrier round to the Whitehall office of the Anti-Vivisection League for temporary safe-keeping. Once inside the high, domed visitors' lobby of the Commons he filled out the regulation 'green card' with a request to see Mr Jeremy Thorpe, MP.

He did not have long to wait. Thorpe apparently remembered him from his visit to the Kingham Stables and readily granted an interview. Norman tumbled out a sketch of his story. He explained how he had eventually left Mr de Vater on what could only be described as poor terms and how an accumulation of problems had forced him to become a patient in an Oxford clinic. His general situation was desperate. He was without money and had nowhere to stay. He had no immediate prospects of a job and, as a consequence of his awkward departure from the ranks of the employed, he had no valid national insurance card. Thorpe was immediately sympathetic and ready to promise moral and practical support. He told Norman to pick up his dog and arranged to meet him later in the day.

That evening Norman and 'Mrs Tish' accompanied Thorpe as he drove from the House of Commons. They went first to Dulwich where Norman was introduced to two male friends of the MP and then on to Oxted in Surrey where Thorpe's mother lived in a house called 'Stonewalls'. On the drive there Thorpe suggested it would make things easier if he could introduce Norman to his mother as a member of the camera crew that was to accompany him on a visit abroad the next day.

Norman's version of events, given later in a statement to the police, and repeatedly denied by Thorpe, is that a homosexual affair began that night. His detailed description of what he claims happened in his bedroom at Stonewalls was to form an important part of the prosecution case against Jeremy Thorpe at the Old Bailey seventeen years later.

3. Bunnies Can and Will

That first night in Mrs Thorpe's house was, by Norman Josiffe's account, the beginning of a long and troubled affair. Thorpe has always denied that there was any homosexual element in their relationship. There is, however, no dispute about the fact that it was – for a while at least – intimate and affectionate.

Thorpe initially helped Josiffe with accommodation, clothing and work. The young man moved into a small service flat in Draycott Place, near the House of Commons, and was attached to the staff of Len Smith, a Liberal Party official who was then organizing the British Honduras appeal for victims of a hurricane disaster. It rapidly emerged that there were problems involved in helping Josiffe. When the job with the appeal fund came to an end Josiffe inadvertently walked off with Len Smith's briefcase. A more serious incident arose when a Mrs Ann Gray, whom Josiffe had known at the Ashurst Clinic, told police that he had stolen her suede coat.

When a policeman sought to question Josiffe about the alleged theft, Thorpe insisted on the interview taking place in his own office near the House of Commons. At the interview on 8 February 1962, Thorpe explained that he was 'more or less a guardian' to Josiffe as he had apparently lost both parents, the father having been killed in an air crash and the mother's whereabouts being unknown. The policeman formed the impression that Norman Josiffe was a weak personality, under severe mental strain and completely dominated by the MP.

The extent of Thorpe's involvement with the young man was underlined by a letter he wrote to Josiffe five days later.

At that time Josiffe had just, with Thorpe's assistance, found a position with a farming family in Withypool, Somerset, helping with the horses. The content of Thorpe's letter, which was to be used in evidence against him seventeen years later, was as follows:

My dear Norman,

Since my letters normally go to the House, yours arrived all by itself at my breakfast table at the Reform, and gave me tremendous pleasure.

I cannot tell you just how happy I am to feel that you are really settling down, and feeling that life has something to offer.

This is really wonderful and you can always feel that whatever happens Jimmy and Mary and I are right behind you. The next thing is to solve your financial problems and this James Walters and I are on to. The really important point is that you are now a member of a *family* doing a useful job of work – with Tish – which you enjoy. Hooray!! Faced with all that no more bloody clinics.

I think you can now take the Ann Gray incident as over and done with.

Enclosed another letter!! I suggest you keep them all – just in case – but will you send back the photo? Thank the guy but say you are fixed up.

Bunnies *can* (and *will*) go to France. In haste.

Yours affectionately
Jeremy

I miss you.

Jimmy and Mary were James Collier and his wife who had taken Josiffe into their home in Culmstock, Devon, over Christmas. Collier was a friend of Thorpe's and the prospective Liberal candidate for Tiverton. James Walters was a London solicitor who had been consulted by Thorpe to see whether Josiffe had any expectation from the estate of his allegedly deceased father. The reference to a letter enclosed related to another response to an advertisement in *Country Life* which Thorpe had placed to help Josiffe find employment. 'Bunny' was Thorpe's pet name for him. The reference to going to France was an allusion to Josiffe's ambition to study dressage in that country.

Josiffe was not, however, as happily settled as the letter appeared to indicate. The family he was with found him highly strung and emotional and it became clear that the living-in arrangement was not working out. Thorpe meanwhile had begun investigating Josiffe's lie about his parentage with the assistance of a solicitor friend, James Walters, who soon became apprehensive about the nature of his assignment.

He told Thorpe in February 1962 that he felt some apprehension about the case, 'since if we press too far and destroy the story with which we have been presented we may well find that this has disastrous consequences so far as Josiffe himself is concerned ...'. He was afraid that if Josiffe had thought himself up a world of fantasy with which he had come to terms, then in showing that the fantasy was without foundation they might find themselves in even greater difficulties.

In his letter of reply Thorpe agreed that they must be careful 'not to open a Pandora's box'. In April Walters naturally discovered what had long been the case: Mrs Josiffe resided at her old address in Bexleyheath; Mr Josiffe senior was still alive and well and living in Orpington.

In May, Walters wrote to Thorpe reporting a telephone conversation he had just had with Mrs Josiffe: 'She is vicious about you ... as being largely responsible for the rift between her son and herself.'

Josiffe, meanwhile, was still on the move in the West Country. By May of 1962 he was living at Porlock Weir in Somerset with the family of a Dr Keith Lister. In response to a letter from the Listers inquiring about the young man's background Thorpe sent a brusque note giving the addresses of Josiffe's parents. Its tone suggested an abrupt cooling of relations between the two men. Other correspondence by Thorpe at the time indicates that he had sorted out Josiffe's problems over his national insurance card which had been a hang-over from his earlier employment with Thorpe's Chipping Norton friend, Brecht de Vater. The Ministry of Pensions and National Insurance had sent Josiffe a new card in April. Josiffe was to claim that this card was later retained by Thorpe who assumed the role of his employer and responsibility for paying his contributions. This claim was not accepted by Thorpe.

By the summer of 1962 it is apparent that Thorpe was of the view that any obligations he had to Norman Josiffe were at an end, except in the most peripheral sense. This did not conform with Josiffe's view of the situation. Despite acute pangs of guilt over the content of their relationship, Josiffe now felt he was in love with Jeremy Thorpe. The feeling had become the most important thing in his unhappy life.

In September, Josiffe wrote to Thorpe to tell him that his dog, 'Mrs Tish', had been put down after killing Dr Lister's ducks and to ask him if he would return a photograph of the dog. Thorpe's reply, which was later produced in evidence against him, was on House of Commons notepaper, dated 30 September 1962. It was friendly enough but distinctly cooler in tone than the earlier surviving letter:

My dear Norman,
   This is indeed terribly sad news about poor little Miss Tish, and I know what a blow this must have been to you. You have all my sympathy.
   I am afraid that I shall not be home for a little while and cannot therefore send you the photo (at the moment I'm in N. Devon). I have a horrible feeling I may have pasted it into an album which will make it difficult for me to dislodge. However....
   I hope otherwise things go well.

                              Yours
                              Jeremy

The episode with the ducks marked the end of Josiffe's stay with the Listers. He was to be charitable about the ending of the arrangement – 'The Listers already had four children, they didn't need me as a fifth.' He returned to London and, by his account, immediately resumed a relationship with Thorpe though of a more perfunctory kind. Thorpe himself was later to say that he only met Josiffe on two further occasions.

According to Josiffe, he began to realise that his real needs were parental, and his faith in Thorpe declined. Josiffe's mother pleaded with him to break off his association with Thorpe. He sought the consolation of religion but after confessing to a Roman Catholic priest was refused absolution until he broke free from the association. His feelings were transmuted into bitterness. Josiffe talked wildly to a young lady acquaintance in Draycott Place about killing Thorpe and committing suicide. The talk was reported to the police.

On 19 December 1962, when Josiffe was staying at the Easton Hotel near Victoria Station, two policemen came to interview him. They took him to Chelsea police station where Josiffe volunteered a statement which began: 'I have come to police to tell you about my homosexual relations with Jeremy Thorpe, who is a Liberal MP, because these relations have caused me so much purgatory and I am afraid it might happen to someone else.' He was examined by a police doctor who confirmed that he was a practising homosexual. The policemen also took possession of the two 'My dear Norman' letters from Thorpe. The statement indicated that Josiffe had been a minor when he first met Thorpe but this may not have been a deliberate deception on his part. One of Thorpe's letters was mis-dated — February 1961 instead of 1962 — and the police themselves may have placed events a year too early.

Although the statement alleged explicit instances of homosexuality it was never followed up by an interview with Thorpe, seemingly on the grounds that the allegation would have been strenuously denied. It did, however, remain on the police files and eventually found a home in the confidential safe of Assistant Commissioner (Crime) Richard Jackson; the file was to be of considerable consequence at a later date.

Josiffe claims that he continued to see Thorpe after giving the statement; but if that were so it cannot have been on very friendly terms. In February 1963 Thorpe received a bill from the Bond Street outfitters, Gieves Ltd, with a request for payment for a pair of silk pyjamas. They had been ordered on his account by Norman Josiffe two months earlier. Thorpe promptly wrote back to say that he refused to accept liability as Josiffe had no authority for such a purchase. 'Unfortunately,' Thorpe concluded, 'I have no idea of Mr Josiffe's present whereabouts, although I believe he has gone abroad.'

Josiffe had, in fact, gone to County Down in Northern Ireland to resume his erratic equestrian career. There is no record of any further direct correspondence between the two men. Although Josiffe claims there were further personal letters from Thorpe, these have never materialised.

Politically, 1963 was a good year for Thorpe. He had emerged from the ruck of young backbenchers as a parliamentarian of great promise. As the Conservative administration of Harold Macmillan began to lose its touch, the parties of the left exercised a greater hold on the public imagination. There was a sense of the country being ready for a new phase of radical politics. For Thorpe, well to the left of his party on most issues, this was an exhilarating trend.

For much of the year politics was dominated by the Profumo Affair, of which the central event was the resignation of Macmillan's War Minister, John Profumo, as a result of his association with the call-girl Christine Keeler who had also been a girlfriend of the Russian naval attache, Eugene Ivanov. As the ramifications of the scandal were explored by the press, intoxicated by the mixture of high politics, sex and spying, suspicion fastened on other members of the cabinet. Thorpe contributed to the general paranoia by suggesting in a speech that two other ministers would almost certainly be forced to resign for 'personal reasons'.

When Lord Denning's official report on the scandal was published later in the year, Thorpe's presumption was found to have no basis on the available evidence. Thorpe gracefully ate his words in a personal statement which was received in silence by the House of Commons: 'I accept Lord Denning's findings and I would wish to apologise for any pain which this publicity might have caused. This in itself indicates that standards of our public life stand higher than many at times thought possible.'

Thorpe's mistake came to be pardoned as the natural excess of a spirited young man, but it did provide early evidence of a recklessness that was to be an element in his political life. The Denning inquiry had an additional relevance for Thorpe, as it did for all MPs and public officials with homosexual tendencies. In his report, Denning carefully reviewed the specifics of Profumo's involvement with Christine Keeler, of the letters that he wrote her (some on War Office notepaper) and of the blackmail risk attendant upon their falling into unscrupulous hands. He then posed the wider question that the specifics inevitably led to: What is a Security Risk?

All the rumours reported to me were to the effect that a minister or person prominent in public life had been guilty of immorality or discreditable conduct of some kind or other. But it is not every piece of immorality or discreditable conduct which can be said to be a 'security risk'.

In my opinion immorality or discreditable conduct is only a security risk if it is committed in such circumstances that it might expose the person concerned to blackmail or to undue pressures which might lead him to give away secret information.

For instance, I would normally regard homosexual behaviour, or perverted practices with a prostitute as creating a security risk, at any rate if it was of recent

date. Again, I would not ordinarily regard adultery as a
security risk, at any rate when committed clandestinely
with a person who was not likely to resort to blackmail.
   Much must depend, however, on the circumstances.
The Vassall Case showed how photographs may be taken
of persons in compromising situations. The existence of
such photographs heightens the security risk: so also do
compromising letters. They would be a most potent
weapon in the hands of a blackmailer, even after several
years.

Thorpe's other contributions to the national debate were
more studied though usually spiced with some wit. His
speech on parliamentary re-organization – advocating Amer-
ican-style committees in the Commons to curb executive
secrecy and power – was reckoned to be the high point of
the 1963 Liberal assembly. In it he demonstrated a bur-
geoning gift for Tory-bashing. Noting that loyalty to the
Conservative whip, rather than parliamentary oratory, was
the best guarantee of honours for MPs in the government
party, Thorpe delighted delegates with his image: 'How
justly we can refer to the Tories as the party of dreadful
knights.'
   In 1964 Thorpe won wide public attention through a
campaign against the Egg Marketing Board on behalf of egg-
packaging interests in his constituency. With considerable
flair he managed to upgrade a localised argument – over the
right to process second-quality eggs – into an issue dramatising the problems of insensitivity and waste in the bureau-
cracy. When the country went to the polls in October 1964,
Thorpe had a national as well as a local reputation. On the
national level he was a lively exponent of libertarian policies
and an enemy of government inefficiency. In Devon he was
regarded as the very best kind of constituency MP. Thorpe
was returned with an increased majority and although the
Liberal representation in the Commons remained small –
nine seats – its prospect of influence on the government was
greatly enhanced. Labour, under the leadership of Harold

Wilson, had finally ended thirteen years of Conservative rule but its overall majority of three seats was too slight for comfort. The Liberal vote was now close to controlling the balance of power between the two major parties and Thorpe's influence on that vote was increasing rapidly. He was already being spoken of as a future leader of the party.

Norman Josiffe, meanwhile, was floundering. He had taken to calling himself the Honourable Lianche-Josiffe and upgraded the status of his 'deceased' father to a peer of the realm. To the portfolio of sad stories about himself he had added another about his young wife who had died in a car accident. Jeremy Thorpe remained his 'guardian'.

In reality, he drifted through a succession of riding jobs in Northern Ireland and the Midlands. He was a good instructor but his fitful personality and uncertain concentration rendered him less well equipped for routine stable work. He had hoped to become engaged to a girl he met at Fred Hartill's training stables near Wolverhampton, but nothing came of it. When asked to leave the house of other friends in Wolverhampton, Mr and Mrs Weight, he had taken another overdose of sleeping pills.

Shortly after the 1964 election Josiffe got in touch with Thorpe again to ask whether he could help get him a job on the continent. In December 1964 Thorpe advanced him the money to go to Porrentruy in Switzerland where he was to work as a groom for a Dr Francois Choquard. Josiffe arrived before his luggage, took a strong dislike to what he saw of his new position and promptly returned to London without his luggage. Thorpe agreed to do what he could to retrieve his belongings.

In January 1965 Josiffe left England again to try and find work in the Republic of Ireland. His luggage still had not been recovered from the Swiss venture and he soon found himself in difficulties again. In Dublin, Josiffe was befriended by a Jesuit priest, Father Michael Sweetman, who tried to calm him and sort out his affairs. While Father Sweetman was working on his behalf, Josiffe took an opportunity to work on a stud farm forty miles outside Dublin at Redcross in County Wicklow. The owners of the farm, Mr and Mrs Quirke, found him in a very agitated state.

When Josiffe left after three hectic weeks, Mrs Marie Quirke wrote a long and kindly letter to Jeremy Thorpe. The letter, dated 6 March 1965, was a painfully clear indication of the fact that Josiffe was still a very long way from resolving his problems of identity. It read as follows:

Dear Mr Thorpe,

Three weeks ago Norman Josiffe came here to learn Stud work. I met him in Dublin and drove him down. The first morning, within half an hour, he came in and told me he was going and would I take him to Dublin. Captain [——] (a friend staying with us) drove him into Wicklow where he could catch a bus. Even though he insisted he could take a taxi – Dublin is 38 miles from us! That afternoon he telephoned from Dublin to apologize and said he would like to come back. A friend drove him down the next day but wouldn't come in.

My husband offered him pocket money whilst he was learning the job £3 a week and he would live with us as one of the family. Norman said he would not dream of accepting anything and it was very good of us to have him. We just put it down to foolish pride.

We did everything we could to make him feel at home, especially as he then told us he was an orphan. He then went on to say his mother was French and his father a well-known English Peer. He travelled on a French passport and his name Josiffe was his mother's name also, his mother was dead.

Three times in as many weeks he said he was going and the last time, two evenings ago when he was talking about a certain horse with my husband and they disagreed as to ownership I told him to look it up in *Horses in Training*. He did so and was proved wrong. He turned on my husband and said 'I'm not spending all night arguing with you. I will be leaving here tomorrow morning.'

Frankly we were shocked. The next morning (yesterday) we drove him into Dublin parting on good terms. . . .

I am writing to you as he told us you were his Guardian and we feel there is something wrong with the boy. We have made all efforts. Especially, as he was widowed at such an early age and his past history seems to play on his mind.

A stud farm is very exacting work and we run it seriously. It is not a holiday camp. It is quite impossible to teach Norman anything as he will not be told but at the same time asks plenty of questions. Then walks away whilst one is trying to tell him.

He will certainly have to pull up his socks if he intends to settle down to anything, and as his Guardian I feel you have a right to know what has happened here. My husband gave Norman £10 yesterday and had given him a couple of pounds before. We wouldn't like to see him stranded. It's such a pity as he can be such a charming boy and just as quickly he can be very nasty.

Please let us know if he turns up alright. If you are ever over in Ireland we would be delighted if you would give us a call.

Yours sincerely

On 11 March, Thorpe wrote back:

Dear Mrs Quirke,

Thank you so much for your letter of March 6th. I am very sorry you have had so many unfortunate experiences with Norman Josiffe.

In fact I am not his Guardian, but merely tried to help him on occasions which have proved at times rather hairraising. I think honestly that he has a split personality and does seem incapable of standing on his own feet for long.

51

I fear I have no responsibility for his actions. I believe that his mother is alive and lives in Kent.

Yours sincerely

Back in Dublin with Father Sweetman, Josiffe's most pressing immediate concerns were the fate of the luggage he had sent to Switzerland and the non-payment of a hotel bill. He decided on the desperate strategy of writing to Jeremy Thorpe's mother. For Mrs Thorpe, the arrival of this letter, which set out in bleak detail Josiffe's claim to have had a homosexual affair with her son, must have been a sickening experience. The letter – which was to be read out in full at the trial of Jeremy Thorpe – made a series of accusations against him, all of them suggesting that Josiffe had been shamefully mistreated. It ended:

'You are probably shattered by all this. I am so sorry, but what can I do. Will you ask Jeremy to please lend me at least the money for the luggage. I hate asking because I know it may cause friction, and I know how close you both are. This is really why I'm writing to you. Jeremy owes me nothing. Possibly I owe him a lot, though I feel we balance out. Now instead of helping a cast off "friend" I appeal to his finer feelings as a "man" to help me who is in real need. I promise I shall repay every penny as soon as I am on my feet. Believe me I mean this.'

The last line of a postscript to the letter read: 'Can you understand any of this, Mrs Thorpe? I'm so sorry. Please believe me I'm desperate for help.'

On receiving the letter, Mrs Thorpe passed it directly to her son.

4. Enter Joe Disaster

For Jeremy Thorpe, who no longer wanted to have anything to do with Norman Josiffe, the letter presented a stark choice: he could either treat it with contemptuous silence or he could brusquely dismiss the appeal for help and challenge Josiffe to do his worst. Both courses risked provoking more desperate action so Thorpe turned for advice to his friend and fellow MP from the West Country, Peter Bessell.

It was a fateful step which was to dominate future events; but Bessell was not a surprising choice as confidant. Not only was he Thorpe's closest friend in the House of Commons, but a few weeks earlier the two men had had a long conversation over lunch in the members' dining-room which had turned to a discussion of their own sexuality. According to Bessell, he had adopted the role of elder brother, confiding that he himself had had homosexual tendencies as a youth. Thorpe had responded with his own admission. Thorpe later claimed that the conversation was a light-hearted one, not to be taken seriously. However, their friendship made it natural that he should contact Bessell, his confidant, to discuss the implications of Josiffe's letter.

He invited Bessell to join him for lunch at the Ritz Hotel where they could speak with more privacy than at the Commons, and after ordering their food he handed him the letter and asked him to read it.

The conversation which followed did not dwell on the relationship itself but centred round the question of whether Josiffe posed a real threat to Thorpe's career and if so what might be done about it. Finally Bessell volunteered to 'assess the situation' by flying to Dublin to see Josiffe himself and the Irish priest he had mentioned. Thorpe's relief, according to Bessell, was visible, and he proceeded to eat the steak tartare which he had ordered with a ravenous appetite.

By taking Bessell into his confidence, however, Thorpe had entrusted him with his reputation. It was a disastrous decision. Rarely can the House of Commons, let alone the Liberal Party, have harboured an MP whose career was so chequered; any examination of Bessell's life and times suggests that in most of his dealings, financial and otherwise, he combined plausibility with an almost congenital incapability of keeping his side of a bargain. Charming, imaginative, witty and elegant, he lacked one element which he considered essential to public life – money. From the late 1950s when he first dipped his toes into the choppy waters of the London and New York finance markets until January 1974 when he was forced, ignominiously, to flee from his creditors to Mexico, Bessell searched for the elusive 'big deal' which would give him the wealth and security he so desperately wanted. There were periods of apparent success, but they were inevitably followed by new crises when he would turn to others to bail him out. The fact that he so adroitly avoided bankruptcy for so long and was still capable of persuading people to finance him, is a remarkable testament to his personality.

One New York real estate broker, Eliot Steuer, who was a close friend and business associate for over fourteen years summed up Bessell's curious appeal thus: 'Let's put it this way. You go into a clip joint and you know you're going to be clipped. The same thing with Peter. I knew that I was being taken, but I really got a bang out of it. I liked him. I knew he was a faker but I liked him.' Between them Bessell and Steuer were involved in countless proposed deals involving millions of dollars of which *not one* came through. 'Do you know what I called him in the end?' says Steuer. 'Joe Disaster. Everything he touched was a disaster.'

Peter Bessell's long climb to parliament, and the prospect of real wealth, started with his demob as a Ministry of Information lecturer in 1945, after a war-time career which he had begun as a conscientious objector. As a young married man of twenty four he returned to his native town of Bath and his family's tailoring and dry-cleaning business. A small investment brokerage service that his father, J. Edgar Bessell, owned, had slumped before his death in 1940. In later years Bessell would ascribe a more colourful career to his father, claiming that he had been a test driver at Brooklands and involved in intelligence work, dying 'on active service for his country'.

In Bath Bessell joined the Young Liberals, and campaigned for them in the 1945 General Election. He began to combine a growing interest in politics with a taste for amateur dramatics, but both were overshadowed by the death of his wife from leukaemia in 1947. He remarried the next year and in 1949 moved with his family to Paignton in Devon where he took over another tailoring and cleaning business. A further setback occurred when his business premises were gutted by fire, but, undaunted, he moved on to Torquay where he became the manager of the Jaycell Same Day Cleaners, serving the customers and pressing the clothes himself when necessary. At the same time he threw himself into local activities, joining the local Liberal association, and acting enthusiastically in amateur dramatic productions (his proudest moment was playing the role of Rochester in *Jane Eyre*). In 1953 he produced a spectacular coronation pageant which won loud acclaim throughout the area and brought him valuable publicity. In 1955 he became prospective Liberal candidate for the division and fought a useful election, halting the decline in Liberal votes.

His success in this first contest evoked an enthusiastic response from party headquarters when a by-election was declared for December 1955. A spectacular list of speakers was promised, including Lady Violet Bonham-Carter and Jo Grimond, as well as every Liberal candidate in Devon and Cornwall. One speaker not mentioned on the list was Jeremy Thorpe. Driving through the town in a battered old van,

55

loudspeakers precariously balanced on the roof, Thorpe 'blitzed' the area in support of Bessell. It was the start of a political, business and personal friendship which was to last for twenty years.

Bessell increased his share of the vote by 25 per cent in that election, but it took a move to another traditional Liberal stronghold, the neighbouring constituency of Bodmin, for his political hopes to be transformed. In Bodmin, where he was officially adopted as candidate in 1957, he inherited the 'Isaac Foot chapel vote', an indigenous blend of non-conformism, methodism and Liberalism that guaranteed the Liberal candidate 10,000 votes come election day. He also won the approval of Isaac Foot himself and borrowed money from him. Foot was an old man by now but still a force to be reckoned with in the West Country (he had fought every election at Bodmin from 1910 to 1938).

Bessell had got some idea of the Isaac Foot approach when the old man asked him after one meeting: 'Well, Mr Bessell, what arrangements have you made to get the Bible Christians to vote?' Bessell promised to look into it. Clearly West Country Liberalism was more of a religious crusade than a matter of party politics. He was already a congregationalist lay preacher, and he would hurry from chapel to church and back again to take the Sunday lesson. In the afternoons he would shed his black gown and take part in meetings of the all-male Brotherhood Movement, or 'pleasant Sunday afternoons' as they were sometimes known. Founded on vague notions of Liberal international brotherhood at the end of the nineteenth century, the movement had enjoyed its heyday between the wars. Nevertheless in parts of Cornwall up to a hundred men, sometimes more, would still gather together to sing hymns and listen to music or speakers. 'Where else', remarked one local Liberal, 'can you guarantee to find a captive audience on a Sunday afternoon?'

Bessell was not, however, cowed by the weight of this tradition. He may have looked completely out of place at times in this largely rural area – he had developed a taste for lightweight suits in irridescent bronze or blue – but he would not conform. 'If you think I'm going to dress up as a fisherman every time I go to Looe, or as a farmer every time I go to Liskeard, then you've got another think coming,' he used to say. 'I am what I am, and people had better accept it.'

His politics were idiosyncratic. Liberal on most things, he was, however, in favour of the death penalty, and later would support Ian Smith's rebellion in Rhodesia and the American presence in Vietnam. Lord Foot – Isaac's third son – put it charitably:

'He managed to combine this appeal to the old Liberalism with being something of a heretic on the basic issues. I'm not suggesting he didn't have perfectly genuine interests but I found it rather difficult to see how a person could combine rather curious views about Rhodesia and hanging and so on with this Liberal non-conformist appeal. However, he managed to bring them all off. He was desperately anxious of course to succeed in politics, and when people are as eager as all that some things, sometimes, go by the board.'

But in politics, nobody, especially not in the Liberal Party, complains about a winner. In 1959 Bessell slashed the Tory majority by two-thirds, and went on to lay down the tactics for a stunning victory next time. His technique owed nothing whatsoever to Isaac Foot or the chapel vote.

He toured the constituency with a huge cavalcade of cars consisting of himself in a large black Cadillac, his name emblazoned along each side, followed by the 'Bessell Belle', a Land Rover to which was fitted a platform with floodlights and loudspeakers so powerful that they could be heard up to a mile away. Following the Land Rover would be a convoy of cars, sometimes a hundred or more, which would block every main street it came to. On a typical campaign evening the cavalcade would sweep through the constituency – progress only occasionally halted by the Cadillac failing to negotiate a particularly narrow lane – taking in up to a dozen villages. The whole division had been carefully plastered with posters bearing the legend BESSELL X in lurid colours, and as the convoy came to a halt spotlights would pick out The Candidate, invariably dressed in a white trenchcoat, etched into the darkness. Then The Voice would roll over the crowd, and far into the moorland beyond. It was a splendid voice, rich and reassuring. And if some people were bewildered by this razzamatazz there was one thing they could recognize. On his coat Bessell would wear a blue and gold rosette in the traditional colours of the Liberal division which were also the racing colours of its president, Viscount Clifden.

For Bessell was accepted at the top as well as further down the scale of the local hierarchy – an important asset financially as well as politically. He was offered for a low rent, and accepted, a fine Georgian house near Looe, Cornwall, and he was a favoured visitor at Lanhydrock House, the rambling Victorian gothic mansion of Lord Clifden where everything, including the occupants, seemed to have been stopped in time. Lord Clifden's sister, the Honourable Everilda Agar-Robartes, was particularly fond of the new candidate and keen to help him. One day at Lanhydrock, as lunch was being served, she told Bessell that she understood he was driving a large American car in the district, and she did not approve. She ordered her chauffeur to find something more suitable. A few weeks later Bessell was the proud owner of a Bentley.

In his financial career Bessell needed all the help he could get. He had left behind him in Torquay a pending court case in which an early business partner was suing him. Undeterred, he embarked on an ambitious scheme to build a chain of eight motels across the country, close to tourist centres such as Oxford. A company, Travellers Inns Ltd, was formed, and trips made to America to raise finance, estimated at £1,600,000. It was big enough for *Fortune* magazine, bible of the business world, to run a profile of him, noting that he was engaged in a major deal. 'In his spare time he is a Liberal politician,' added the magazine. This would scarcely have delighted the Liberals of Bodmin, but Bessell was always careful to combine both his careers to their mutual advantage. He took time out to speak at various United Nations meetings, and met Eleanor Roosevelt, later taking tea with her. He would often refer to his 'friendship' with her when impressing others with his American connections.

The rapid demise of the motel project through lack of funds was succeeded by an alternative proposal – to build a hotel at Heathrow Airport. Another company, Twentieth Century Securities, was formed, and a wealthy local Liberal persuaded to put £2000 into it. A furniture company was formed to supply the furnishings, and a local Liberal, Gerald Whitmarsh, who was to be an important supporter of Bessell in future years, took on his accounting work. Whitmarsh would later become secretary of a number of Bessell's companies and in turn offer Bessell directorships in some of his own. He also became Bessell's private banker and from 1959 until 1974 advanced him around £50,000 and provided a mortgage for Bessell to buy his house. Whitmarsh allowed Bessell to register his companies at his accountancy practice in Plymouth, an address which Bessell found convenient to list as one of his own offices. The Heathrow deal foundered, however, when the giant Sheraton hotel chain, with whom Bessell had been negotiating, pulled out, and he lost his option on the proposed site.

The next schemes were eventually to succeed, though despite rather than because of Bessell's contribution. This time Jeremy Thorpe, who admired Bessell's ostensible business flair, became involved. The idea was suggested by a local doctor, Mervyn Cooper, who proposed that he and Bessell should set up a company to bring light industry to the area. Manhattan Equipment Ltd was to manufacture and market felt-tip pens – the British end of an American agency. It had five directors, Bessell, Dr Cooper, Thorpe and Whitmarsh, as well as an American businessman who put up half the capital. The company enjoyed a modest success, and later a subsidiary, Drinkmaster Ltd, which manufactured drink-vending equipment, was formed. Both Bessell and Thorpe could now point to the way in which their businesses were bringing employment to the south west, but the American partners were unhappy about the low returns and eventually sold up.

Although the collapse of the Heathrow deal had left the investors in financial difficulties, Bessell himself landed on his feet. He was recommended as a suitable executive to the Canadian Oshawa group which wanted to start a leasing operation for coin-operated washing machines in the United Kingdom. Bessell impressed the Canadian director, Ray Wolf, by producing his *Fortune* magazine clippings, mentioning his friendship with Eleanor Roosevelt, and dropping the name of several cabinet ministers he knew. Oshawa brought him on to the board of two companies, Coinwash and Coin-a-Matic, formed in Britain, and appointed him managing director of the second, in which he was also a shareholder. Oshawa paid for new offices in Mayfair, to which Bessell transferred his own business, and paid him a good salary.

To find outlets for his machines Bessell turned once again to Liberal connections, writing to Richard Rowntree whose family trust was a long-time supporter of the Liberal Party, asking him to become Coin-a-Matic's agent in the north of England. Bessell would later trade on his partnership to persuade Rowntree to lend him £2000 on another deal which failed. Rowntree only got half his money back.

The laundry venture started brightly enough, but Ray Wolf gradually became disillusioned with his British managing director. Bessell appeared to him to be devoting rather more time to his own interests than to promoting those of Coin-a-Matic. In 1964 they parted company. 'Unfortunately he never got around to making money for us,' explained Wolf. 'He did get the organisation rolling, and I would give him A for effort for that, but here we measure results and they were not up to expectations. I would say he was probably a better politician than a businessman.'

To his potential constituents in Bodmin, Bessell by now epitomised the glamorous world of the 1960s whizz-kid, immersed in a life of fast money, property speculations, and

60

trans-Atlantic deals. The local newspaper would often regard his long-distance business travels as worthy of a news story: 'Mr Bessell Travels by Jet and Train to Saltash Meeting', ran one headline. The deals themselves, mostly put together with his American associate, Eliot Steuer, certainly sounded impressive: the sale and leaseback of shoe shops in America; negotiating development capital for Safeway supermarkets; building a hotel and conference centre near Looe; a loan scheme with Rothschilds Bank ('the chance of a lifetime', wrote Bessell); setting up a Swiss finance group to channel South African funds into the second-mortgage business in America. The figures bandied around were equally grand: £5 million here, £1,500,000 there. None of them came to fruition, though Bessell was never inclined to blame himself. He would inevitably find fault with some third party, or attribute failure to outside factors like a credit squeeze.

It was an expensive life, but Steuer helped out in New York at least. 'You must be sick of me telling you how grateful I am,' wrote Bessell after one visit.

'My impression was that the guy was loaded,' says Steuer. 'He would show me pictures of this big house he said he had in England, but he was limited to the amount of dollars he could bring on his visits because of the austerity programmes in England. I guess I picked up every tab from 1960 on.' The 'tabs' included statutory expenses like nightclubs – and girls. There was 'The Unique Monique' and 'Bubbles' among many others.

None of this, of course, got back to Cornwall, but one scandal almost threatened his election chances. Bessell's wife Pauline, and their children Paul and Paula lived in their new home in Looe while Bessell spent much of his time in London. By the end of the 1950s he was living in London during the week with a young woman law graduate he had met while campaigning, returning to his wife at weekends. Bessell finally told his girlfriend that Isaac Foot had learned of the affair and had warned him that if he ever brought the young woman to the division then he would withdraw his support and Bessell's candidacy would be finished. Bessell made certain that gossip about the affair was hushed up, and certainly not a whisper had reached the voters of Bodmin by October 1964 when they came to choose their new MP.

It was a dramatic and spectacular triumph for Bessell. As news of his victory came out, a 3000-strong crowd outside Liskeard Town Hall kept up a deafening chant: 'We want Bessell . . . We want Bessell.' Finally the familiar slim figure appeared, to be hoisted shoulder-high and carried off to make his victory speech as the first Bodmin Liberal MP for nearly thirty years. For some the emotion of the day was too much. At Liskeard Liberal Club men and women wept.

For Bessell himself there were now other rewards to consider, for, as he was later to explain to a creditor: 'The letters MP are worth more than stocks and shares.' His new status, while affording him the right to impress foreign contacts by writing to them on House of Commons notepaper, did not, however, have any dramatic effect on his financial position which began instead to deteriorate. By the spring of 1965 when he first broached the delicate subject of Thorpe's private life, his debts were piling up alarmingly, and he was looking for alternative sources of revenue to help him out of his difficulties.

Within a few weeks of Jeremy Thorpe asking Peter Bessell for his help in dealing with the problem of Norman Josiffe, there was to be a quid pro quo: Bessell would turn to Thorpe for assistance in staving off the certainty of bankruptcy and political ruin. The vulnerability of both men formed a unique bond between them.

5. 'Diana Darling'

In March 1965, a few days after the Ritz lunch, Peter Bessell was comfortably seated on an Aer Lingus flight to Dublin. His briefcase contained a draft of a legal letter – written by Thorpe – threatening Josiffe with a libel suit. It was a stern document which set out to rebut the 'damaging and groundless charges' made by Josiffe in his letter to Mrs Thorpe. It warned him that there was undoubtedly a 'prima facie case of blackmail' to be made against him, and that if he continued to make his allegations there might well be grounds for proceeding with an action for criminal libel. The action, however, was never to be carried out.

In Dublin Bessell booked into the Intercontinental Hotel and set about finding Josiffe. First he called on Father Sweetman and informed him that there was no truth in Josiffe's allegations. Sweetman was sceptical, for if that were so, he thought, why then had this MP travelled so far to see him? Bessell, however, was satisfied that Sweetman would do his best to help. Next he went to see Josiffe himself, leaving a note at his lodgings when he was unable to track him down.

Josiffe telephoned Bessell at his hotel at 3 am and a meeting was arranged for just after breakfast. Bessell's first impression of him was favourable. Although Josiffe was obviously nervous, he seemed polite, well-spoken, and tidily dressed – a quality Bessell particularly appreciated. They had a brief conversation in the course of which Josiffe repeated his claims against Thorpe, then Bessell told him he had a plane to catch and asked him if he would drive to the airport with him. He warned him to refer to Thorpe in the taxi only by his initials.

During the journey Bessell told Josiffe that he had been wrong to write to Thorpe's mother, and that if he persisted in that kind of thing he could find himself in serious trouble; indeed he might well be charged with blackmail and extradited from Ireland. Josiffe understood Bessell to mean that he had an extradition warrant with him, and surprised him with his reply: 'Well, that's marvellous,' he said, 'in that case I can go back to England and get the whole thing sorted out.'

As they waited for the plane to London Bessell pressed Josiffe to say if he could prove that he had had any association with Thorpe and was shaken when Josiffe replied that if he could only get his luggage back from Switzerland he could provide the evidence, since, he claimed, his case contained letters written to him by Thorpe. Bessell promised he would do his best to retrieve the luggage, and would look out for jobs: he mentioned America as a possibility. Finally he pressed £5 into Josiffe's hand to cover the taxi fare back to Dublin, and hurried to catch his flight.

Back in London, Bessell reported to Thorpe that Josiffe appeared to pose no immediate threat. Josiffe's claim to have letters in his luggage was clearly a worrying development, but otherwise he thought the situation was being 'contained'. Thorpe, however, raised a new matter. He had heard rumours of a further police inquiry in North Devon, and he was anxious to find out what it was about. Bessell offered to help. He would talk to a friend of his, George Thomas, Minister of State at the Home Office who also happened to be a member of the West Country religious society The Brotherhood, whose meetings Bessell attended.

Bessell made an appointment with Thomas and told him the full story of Josiffe, including the Dublin visit, and asked Thomas if he could arrange a meeting for him with the Home Secretary, Sir Frank Soskice, who would have access to any police information on the subject. Before the meeting took place, however, there was another letter from Josiffe. This time the tone was very different: normal, contrite, without any of the hysteria of the first. It is just possible that had Bessell responded in a straightforward manner much of what followed might have been unnecessary. The letter was written from the garden of the Milltown Presbytery:

Dear Mr Bessell,

I have been to see Father Sweetman, and he tells me you were on the telephone to him last Tuesday and had told him that you would endeavour to have the luggage sent as soon as possible to him at Milltown Park – thank you so very much Mr Bessell, I do hope you realised on meeting me that my intention has never been to do Jeremy any harm, regardless of how it may look. But I was so worried and in consequence having tried everything else thought Mrs Thorpe would perhaps have helped – I really did think she knew.

Please try to understand how very complicated my life is with this 'disease' [Josiffe's reference to homosexuality] and also that I would never have written to Mrs Thorpe had things been different. Once again I can only say I am so terribly sorry but unless you know the whole story how can you believe me.

When you had gone I felt so worried about the whole affair and also rather sick as I feel that as I told you, if somebody tells you something viz: that they do care for you (This looks so silly) then it is so much more of a shock when something like this happens. Jeremy once lent me a book called *Giovanni's Room* by James Baldwin – a passage in it reads 'as likened to an electric socket, and a light. Contact and there is light remove the plug and the light goes out. When there is a fuse there is contact but no light. This reads rather oddly but its how I felt on leaving you: For those five years I have *nothing* at all to show at all. My life is so meaningless and when I thought that you were going to take me back to England, I didn't care. I felt that once all the 'dirt' that people have whispered about me for these years was dragged out and given an airing then with a fresh start perhaps I could have made a go of life Which after a doctors help may have been normal and Heterosexual –

I want so much to forget the past. All the things that have happened I must forget or I have no chance. You spoke of going to the States and how you could arrange to get me there. Perhaps a fresh start in a New Country may not be a bad idea. Father Sweetman seems to think that from a basic religious point of view I should be as well off. Though I love Dublin, and all that it has to offer. The one thing it's impossible to get is a job. This is so sad because I know I could have made a success of life here. As you know if one hasn't a degree its almost impossible to get any sort of job – (impossible anyway here and in England) – where one's talents can be usefully employed. The more mundane and ordinary jobs people look at you and say 'Oh but you wouldn't like that' or 'Oh no I'm looking for someone younger or older' when all they really mean is who is this chap and why is he looking for a job like this!!

It's all so difficult. Equity always has the hardy perennial – don't ring us we'll ring you!! So what will happen. I have moved into a flat which only costs £3.0.0. and have therefore reduced my living from £15.0.0. to about £7. If only something would turn up I would be able to manage, I know. Also that things just can't go on much longer in this way, could one advertise in the *New York Times* Educated English Man or what did you have in mind? Also you did say something with regard to a job in Cornwall. Though as I said to you I really would be happier in a 'Catholic' country.

– Mr Bessell. I don't really know what you think of me I know I'm very mixed up but I do so need a help and a start and would really work so hard given the opportunity. Therefore please believe in me and understand that I would never have wittingly caused all this trouble. Please also forgive me for writing on this envelope but I am in the garden at Milltown Park and there is no more paper. I am going to try so hard to find something.

If you do hear of anything please will you let me know. Father Sweetman is still giving me money and I feel so guilty and it is not that at present time is any hope of paying him it back. Also he told me yesterday that he was halfway through the 'Coffers'. – So you see I must get something.

I'm so sorry with regard to all this 'mess'. But don't really know what to do. Please excuse the 'paper' once again.

Yrs sincerely
Norman (L.J.)

Bessell sent a reply that was couched in kindly terms but which was designed to discourage Josiffe. He told him: 'You must cease to talk in such nonsensical terms about your relationship with Jeremy Thorpe. As I have told you, I cannot and do not accept your version of the story.' Some weeks later Bessell received a bill from the Iona Guest House in Dublin which had been forwarded on the instructions of Norman Josiffe. Bessell sent a copy of the correspondence to Father Sweetman with an exasperated note: 'Further trouble over this wretched boy: as you will see from the enclosed, he is now trying to make *me* responsible for his debts. This coincides hideously with Mr Thorpe's experience, and I suppose it is only a matter of time before you or somebody is placed in a similar position. Frankly, I have lost patience, and if you are managing to retain yours, then I think you should be canonized.'

The hoped-for meeting with Soskice finally took place in May 1965. Bessell had a delicate task to perform. He wanted to find out about the state of the rumoured police investigation, and the scope of official knowledge of the Josiffe allegations. Soskice appeared sympathetic. He responded to Bessell's probing with an angry outburst about 'that creature' Josiffe, and it appeared that he knew something about the affair. 'It's a pity about the letters,' said the Home Secretary. Soskice clearly had the impression that Thorpe and Josiffe were still seeing each other. His advice was blunt: 'Keep them apart. Don't allow him to get a hold over Jeremy ... tell him to go to hell. Get rid of him.'

Throughout the meeting, according to Bessell, Soskice had in front of him a manilla file, and Bessell was convinced that it concerned the Josiffe allegations. However, Soskice was a strong advocate for reform of the homosexual laws of the country, and that very month a full-scale debate in the House of Lords had revealed widespread support for change. Soskice appeared to be indicating that he was on Thorpe's side in the matter and that there was no need to worry. He ended the meeting by promising Bessell that if there were any developments then George Thomas would inform him of them.

Bessell was able to report back to Thorpe that it seemed as if the matter were under control. Thorpe was still worried about the mention of the letters, and the existence of a file, but relieved that the matter appeared to be in the hands of the Home Secretary rather than the police. As the months passed and nothing further was heard he grew more relaxed, and there was one more reassuring incident to come. Bessell met Soskice by chance in the voting lobby and thanked him for his help.

'That's all right,' said Soskice. 'It's over.'

Bessell concluded from this, wrongly as we shall see, that the file had been disposed of.

By that time Bessell himself was badly in need of help. With his debts mounting to an uncontrollable level, he asked Thorpe if he could suggest any sources for a loan. The alternative, he said, was ruin. Thorpe approached Timothy Beaumont, later president of the Liberal Party, and told him that Bessell was about to go broke: he was short of liquid cash, but if he could get a temporary loan then he would be in the clear. The alternative was his resignation, disgrace, and possible suicide. Beaumont agreed to lend Bessell £5000, and at the end of June Bessell left for the United States to try and drum up business.

The task of recovering Josiffe's luggage was thus left to his secretary, Diana Stainton. She too had been taken into

Bessell's confidence, and told about Josiffe's claim of an affair with Thorpe. Indeed, Bessell had added colourful embellishments of his own. Miss Stainton was asked to collect Josiffe's trunk which had arrived from Switzerland at Victoria Station, and to take it to Bessell's office. She was also told to look after it extremely carefully since, Bessell explained, it contained evidence which could do great harm to Thorpe.

She fulfilled her task and went home to her flat in Islington. That evening, she received an unexpected telephone call. It was from Jeremy Thorpe, who had never spoken to her on the telephone before. His opening gambit was unusual.

'Diana darling,' he said, 'are you in a gorgeous negligee?' The conversation was soon steered round from small talk to the question of the trunk, and it was clear that Thorpe was trying to establish whether it had arrived at Bessell's office. When he learned that it was there he seemed relieved by the news. The luggage was sent on to Dublin, but when it arrived, Josiffe telephoned angrily to Bessell claiming that a number of things, including letters, were missing. The existence of these letters and what happened to them was to be raised at the Old Bailey trial of Thorpe, but at the time, Bessell pretended to have no knowledge of any incident. In his view the Josiffe crisis had paled in comparison to his own.

In spite of his difficulties, Bessell had kept up the pretence that all his big deals, involving such famous names as Rothschild and Sheraton, were still going ahead. He had borrowed against broking fees on a deal to build a hotel in Knightsbridge, and when, in June 1965, that fell through he was in a desperate position. The Beaumont loan was used to pay back money he owed to his accountant Gerald Whitmarsh, and he had cut back on his expenses by moving a camp bed into his office, selling the Cadillac and cutting his secretarial assistance. He was still over £20,000 in debt.

The sheer enormity of his financial position was spelled

out by him in a letter written in July 1965 to a friend. 'No doubt I could stall for a few days longer, but no more than that ... it was a £22,000 problem. It still is, but it is in immediate terms a £17,000 problem, and I suppose it could be called a £15,000 problem at its lowest possible terms.' He went on:

Do I need to tell you what all this adds up to? Clearly a bankruptcy, resignation from my seat and all the degradation and publicity which affects not only me but the party and my family. I have given the facts to *one* MP who has with great stealth sounded out the party's most wealthy supporters. To no avail. He is still trying but it is a tricky operation, for if he has success (which is now very remote indeed) I regard it as essential that there shall be no leak and no gossip in the party. If he fails then of course it no longer matters.

Meanwhile I have managed (heaven alone knows how) to maintain a calm exterior, have gone about my constituency and parliamentary business as though nothing was wrong. I have said nothing to my family, as I have less confidence in my wife's self-control than I have in my own. But it is almost the end of the road now. As I believe in the power of positive thinking I am still cheerfully booking dates in my diary for next year!

In a bid to convince his bank that there were funds to cover his overdraft, he claimed that a New York firm of industrial bankers had agreed to pay for his office and guarantee his income. They had not. He even invoked a routine reply from the Chancellor of the Exchequer, James Callaghan, to a request for Treasury help on a U.S. banking deal, in an attempt to demonstrate to business contacts that he had friends in very high places. But such efforts could not stave off the crisis for ever.

In August 1965 Thorpe again stepped in to help. He persuaded Timothy Beaumont to lend Bessell another £5000 and then approached Sir Felix Brunner, past president of the

Liberal Party Organisation, for a short-term loan. He explained that he was anxious to avoid a by-election in Bodmin. Sir Felix agreed to lend £10,000 at the usual rates of interest. The money arrived not a moment too soon. Bessell was being threatened with a public court case by Lex Garages for non-payment of a bill due for work done on the famous black Cadillac.

To his business and political associate Richard Rowntree Bessell now told another lie. He said that he had found a long-term solution to his problem by persuading Eliot Steuer, his New York partner, to buy a half-share of Peter Bessell Ltd for £20,000. The point was to persuade Rowntree not to call in his £2000 loan. During these delicate negotiations with the Americans, explained Bessell, he did not want his 'triple A.1.' bank reference disturbed. At the same time he managed to raise another loan, this time from 'Miss Eva' – his eighty-year-old Cornish supporter the Hon. Everilda Agar-Robartes who had been told by Bessell that he might have to resign at the next election because of his financial difficulties. She lent him a total of £15,000 which Bessell says he repaid.

Using these loans he managed to satisfy the most demanding of his creditors. He also took it upon himself to guarantee the bank overdraft of a fellow Liberal MP. In the circumstances his bravura was remarkable. In September he delivered a speech calling for even tougher economic measures to overcome the country's financial difficulties. 'As a nation we have been living on credit for over twenty five years,' he said. 'We have to restrict our expenditure.'

The willingness of Liberals to help Bessell can be explained by the party's parlous political state. With only nine MPs, the loss of one through public disgrace would be acutely embarrassing. Jo Grimond, the party leader, had given him one of the most substantial shadow 'briefs' – seven departments: economic affairs, trade, transport, housing, the Post Office, the Treasury (with Thorpe) and the new Ministry of Land and Resources (with Grimond). In the first six months he had made twelve speeches, tabled forty seven questions, put down three motions and moved one private members bill – on telephone tapping. He was, along with Thorpe, one of the rising stars of the party at a time when its future was about to change course.

With the death of the Speaker of the House of Commons, Sir Harry Hylton Foster, in September 1965, which cut Labour's overall majority to only one vote, it seemed as if Jo Grimond's dream of a 'Lib-Lab' alliance might become reality. His position was not helped, however, by Bessell's intervention at this point. Hearing that the possibility of a Liberal Speaker was being canvassed (which would have maintained Labour's majority) and that Jo Grimond's name was being mentioned, he gave an interview on Westward Television saying that he was '99 per cent certain' that Grimond would be offered the job. He added that if that happened and he himself were offered the job of leader of the Liberal Party he would of course be honoured to accept. The chances of Bessell's being offered the job were approximately nil, and his interview aroused national derision. Grimond, who had not even been offered the Speaker's job, was furious, and the national press enjoyed the sight of a genuine Liberal row. 'I suppose the only hard lesson I've learned is to keep my mouth shut, however much I know,' said Bessell ruefully.

Meanwhile Thorpe had been taking the steps on the party ladder two at a time. His fund-raising abilities had already been recognised by grateful party officials, struggling as usual to raise money for an organisation with no reliable sources of income, and as early as 1962 he had been encouraged to try out a special scheme of his own invention. This was to establish a 'marginal seats fund', controlled and accounted for entirely by Thorpe himself, to channel money into those seats where the Liberals were thought to have a specially good chance of winning at the next election. The fund was kept separate from the party's main accounts, and Thorpe suggested that its transactions should be secret. Although the fund's beginnings were small it gave Thorpe, at the age of thirty three, remarkable control in an important area of party strategy; and as it grew, the fund was to become, in later years, an object of increasing suspicion and controversy.

Then, in 1965, he made a bid for the party treasurership itself, challenging the sitting treasurer, Sir Andrew Murray, a businessman and former Lord Provost of Edinburgh. Thorpe's pitch was that the Liberals should begin tapping the enormous financial resources of private industry – hitherto regarded as exclusive Tory territory. Murray resisted fiercely; if the party wanted 'dirty money', he said, then he wanted no part in it. The party thought about it, then decided it wanted the money, 'dirty' or not. Thorpe landed the job. His first innovation was to bring in no less than four 'deputy treasurers'. Two were old Oxford friends, David Holmes, now a merchant banker living in Manchester, and Stanley Brodie, a rising lawyer. The others were Leonard Smith, the party official who had helped out Josiffe with a job, and Hugo Brunner whose father, Sir Felix, had helped bail out Peter Bessell.

No one to this day is entirely certain just what Holmes contributed to the running of Liberal finances, though he was nominally responsible for raising money in his own area. He did, however, produce some new carpets for the party headquarters, bought cheap, he said, from a business acquaintance of his in the north west. Although the title of deputy treasurer was a purely honorary one, Holmes seems to have found it useful and continued to use it from time to time long after his term of office had ended.

Thorpe's own influence is evident from the party organization's figures which show that money from appeals and donations rocketed by more than 50 per cent during his first full year as treasurer. However, another feature which was always to characterise his periods in office also shows up in the accounts. Expenditure rose by almost the same amount.

His political interventions at this stage were also arousing mixed reactions. In 1966, as the party's official spokesman on Commonwealth affairs, he was asked by Jo Grimond, the party leader, to go on a fact-finding mission to Rhodesia in the wake of Ian Smith's declaration of independence. Thorpe had already taken a hard line on Rhodesia by suggesting that troops should have been flown in, so he faced a hostile reception in Salisbury on his arrival. Nevertheless he succeeded in talking to Ian Smith himself, whom he found obdurate. He returned convinced that drastic action was necessary to end the rebellion, and at the Liberal Party's assembly in September 1966 he stood up and proposed that Britain should bomb the rail links with Rhodesia, thus cutting off her oil supplies without loss of life. Though applauded by the delegates, the idea aroused scorn from the government. The Prime Minister, Harold Wilson, said it would be an act of war, and newspapers quickly coined the phrase 'Bomber Thorpe' which was to stick. Thorpe continued to argue the case for some time, however, and even today there are a number of Liberals who believe the idea was worth more serious consideration than it was given at the time.

Towards the end of 1966 it became clear that the Liberals would shortly be looking for a new leader.

Following the Labour victory of 1966 and the collapse of any idea of a Lib-Lab Pact, Grimond began to lose his taste for the job of leading the Liberal Party. Thorpe was one of those who initially persuaded him to stay on. He had been an enthusiastic Grimond man, though the two were entirely different political animals – Thorpe was never an intellectual. In January 1967, however, Grimond made his final decision, informing Eric Lubbock, one of the now twelve Liberal MPs, rather than Thorpe, 'lest Jeremy try to dissuade me'.

The election for his successor was now on, with Grimond making it clear that he himself favoured Thorpe who would provide the excitement and the campaigning zeal which the party needed. There were two other candidates: Emlyn Hooson, a quietly spoken Welsh lawyer, and Lubbock, whose sensational by-election victory at Orpington five years earlier was a landmark in the party's post-war history. The Liberal constitution required only the party's twelve elected members to vote, and it seemed likely, therefore, to be a swift, sharp election. In the event it was swifter and sharper than most people had anticipated, and several newspapers commented on the haste with which the whole thing was arranged. Liberals in the country were angry that they were being given less than two weeks to discuss the choice confronting their MPs. The Young Liberals in particular wanted to make their voice heard. But there were good reasons for hurrying the election through, as James Margach, the astute political correspondent of the *Sunday Times*, noted at the time. 'If the managers had dallied,' he wrote, 'the party would have been paralysed and torn to pieces.'

Strong words, but well-founded, because the prospect of Jeremy Thorpe as leader of the Liberals had begun to reveal deep divisions within the party. Now that attention was fully focused on him, doubts about his qualities began to crystallise.

Publicly, those Liberals opposed to him complained that he was a light-weight politician, lacking the intellectual depth and gravity of a Jo Grimond. No one denied his dedication to the party or the new drive he would bring to any future campaign, but they hesitated over his 'style'. The wit and elegance which endeared him to political hostesses was lost on down-to-earth party workers. There was, for instance, strong opposition from the north of England. 'We've got to get away from these bloody Old Etonians,' fumed one Yorkshire Liberal.

But behind these public attitudes there were other doubts, more cautiously expressed. Rumours about his private life had begun to circulate, and one man who had helped to give them currency was actually Thorpe's own 'campaign manager', his close colleague Peter Bessell. Indeed, Bessell's activities during this period undoubtedly qualify him for the well-known slogan: 'With friends like this, who needs enemies?'

Several influential Liberals, including Richard Wainwright, the MP for Colne Valley, and Richard Rowntree were recipients of Bessell's confidences about Thorpe's homosexuality. Bessell had also passed on the stories to two Liberal supporters in Bodmin, as well as to a former girlfriend and two of his secretaries. To Rowntree he gossiped that he had had to deal with what he called 'Jeremy's hysterical boyfriends', and Rowntree, while shocked by what he described later as 'these sewer tales', was nevertheless inclined to believe them since Bessell was extremely close to Thorpe and apparently loyal to him.

Wainwright, for his part, found that Bessell's stories coincided with his own worries about Thorpe. Only a few months earlier he had been asked by Thorpe at the House of Commons if he would 'sign in' a guest of his for whom a seat had been booked in the gallery of the House. Wainwright agreed, and duly signed the statutory green chit, without which a visitor may not enter the gallery, before going off for dinner in the members' dining-room. He had scarcely begun his meal, however, when he was approached by an attendant asking him if he would come and deal with his 'guest' who was creating a disturbance. Apparently Thorpe's friend had arrived drunk and had caused a scene in the gallery from which he had been removed. Wainwright, highly embarrassed, piloted him out of the House and returned to his dinner, only to be recalled by another attendant who told him that the man had returned and was now regaling members of the public queuing for their seats with scurrilous claims about Mr Thorpe. This time Wainwright made certain of dispatching his guest by putting him into a taxi and paying his fare home. Next day he told two of his party colleagues about the incident, and then complained to Thorpe himself who laughed it off, though he was clearly annoyed that Wainwright had told others about it. Wainwright was left with a feeling of uneasiness about the friends Thorpe seemed to have. Another Liberal MP, Alisdair MacKenzie, the member for Ross and Cromarty, had even heard indirectly about the Norman Josiffe story. A constituent of his had told him that during a visit to

Dublin he had met a strange young man who had told him that he had had a sexual relationship with Jeremy Thorpe. MacKenzie, a staunch presbyterian, was deeply shocked and confided his concern in Bessell, who hastened to assure him that the young man concerned was mentally disturbed, but that the matter was being taken care of. Another rumour was about an incident involving Thorpe in the course of a visit he had made to the United States.

Those Liberals who heard these stories found themselves in some difficulty. On the one hand, the Liberal Party, with its fragile hold on the political scene, was particularly vulnerable to the damaging effect of a scandal. 'The Liberals have enough problems simply surviving without having to grapple with that kind of publicity,' was how one senior party official put it.

On the other hand, tolerance and freedom from prejudice (a literal definition of Liberalism) lay at the very heart of their political philosophy. The party was firmly behind the Sexual Offences Bill which embodied most of the Wolfenden proposals on homosexuality and which was even then being piloted on its long and hazardous course through parliament by the Labour MP Leo Abse. To be influenced one way or the other by gossip about a fellow-Liberal went against their nature.

Opposition to Thorpe was therefore muted, and neither of the other candidates commanded wide enough support to win, though even here Peter Bessell was able to sow further confusion by confiding in both Hooson and Wainwright that he thought Hooson would make an ideal leader – while continuing to campaign for Thorpe.

In the final days before the vote on 18 January 1967 a 'Stop Jeremy' movement began to take shape, and Gruffyd Evans, chairman of the party executive, was dispatched from Liverpool to throw his weight behind it. Several senior Liberals, including Timothy Beaumont, Thorpe's Oxford colleague, and Pratap Chitnis, head of the party organisation, pressed for a delay in order to boost a compromise candidate in Richard Wainwright, the solid Yorkshireman who might hold the 'northern' faction without alienating the south. But Wainwright inconveniently refused to run, and the election was on.

On the first ballot the vote was split. Thorpe polled six votes, Hooson and Lubbock three each. Since Thorpe had not achieved an overall majority a second ballot was now on the cards, but after hurried consultations both the rival candidates agreed to withdraw and back Thorpe in the final vote, which was therefore unanimous. To the last, Bessell remained true to his uncertain form. An examination of his voting card showed that he voted for Thorpe as first choice and Lubbock as second, dropping Hooson, whom he had encouraged, to third on his list.

Thus, at the age of thirty seven – 'much too young', complained his mother – Jeremy Thorpe was leader of the party of his choice. He moved into the leader's room and ordered a new set of carpets and curtains.

6. An Element of Fear

The year of Thorpe's triumph turned out in the end to be more an essay in survival than a march towards new achievements. It began with a Liberal rally in the Albert Hall where, to the sound of martial music, the new leader, bathed in spotlights and linked by closed-circuit television to audiences in three cities, announced the start of a 'Great Crusade' which would 'set Britain alight for the vision of a Liberal Society'. It ended with the party split and demoralised, as Thorpe himself fought for his own political future.

Few people were aware that Thorpe's battle for survival had a second, private front.

On 20 April 1967 Peter Bessell received an unwelcome communication from Dublin. 'It is with regret that I write to you, for I know you don't want to remember me,' began Norman Josiffe. The letter was in thin, spidery handwriting and it was signed Norman *Scott*, the new surname underlined twice. Inevitably it brought problems:

> The fact is, [he wrote] I am to go to America on July the third and have found that when I was upset over Jeremy etc. I burned my passport. It is so important to me. I cannot tell the passport people here why and how I destroyed it. Also, as you may have heard I have been living here in Dublin, and shall be going to America under the name I have taken when I came out of hospital of Norman SCOTT. This does I suppose confuse the issue, but I am now known and accepted as this person. Also the flight and everything has been booked in this name, so can you help me with regard to changing my name – legally? Its very short notice! But really it is *so*

important. I have been doing very well here in Ireland, of all things as a male model!! Have done several TV commercials and also stills for magazines, also still have a horse and she is going well. Mr Bessell, I am sorry to ask you this for I know you are busy but there is no other way. I hope you are very well.

The letter ended: 'P.S. I am coming to London on 2nd May.'

The letter, and the threat of Scott's imminent arrival back in London, did not come at a good time for Thorpe. He was already beginning to find it hard going to translate his Great Crusade into anything more substantial than rhetoric, and some party members, in particular the Young Liberals, were beginning to grow restless. His speeches in the House of Commons were now couched in a curiously heavy, almost pompous style. 'He felt he had to move away from the image of the sharp, witty debater to being grave,' said David Steel, the party's chief whip. 'It was disastrous.'

Outside parliament, too, he was less than inspirational. There began to emerge a clear distinction between Thorpe the party tactician, rallying a flagging constituency association or mapping out an election campaign, both of which he did with skill and enthusiasm, and Thorpe the party leader addressing the nation as a whole. Here his impact was weak. His speeches – in defence of Israel, pro-Common Market, in favour of United Nations intervention in Vietnam – were impeccably Liberal, but did little to inspire Liberals. Amongst the young firebrands and a number of party stalwarts as well, there was a growing feeling that he lacked any real perception of the long-term aims of the Liberal Party.

There was one place, however, where he was appreciated, and that was at Number Ten Downing Street. Harold Wilson, Labour's Prime Minister (and himself a former Liberal as an undergraduate), had decided that the Liberals, and Thorpe in particular, merited his patronage. In an expansive gesture he made Thorpe a member of the Privy Council within two months of his election as party leader.

The significance of this honour can be measured against the fact that Thorpe's predecessor, Jo Grimond, had not been made a Privy Councillor until five years after he became leader. The appointment meant that Thorpe was now elevated to an elite of the most senior and respected politicians in the land, with access to state secrets and matters of top security. Whatever the extent of Wilson's knowledge about Thorpe's private life, he had certainly been told informally about Bessell's approach to Sir Frank Soskice in 1965. Nevertheless, from now on Thorpe's name would be entitled to the prefix 'Right Honourable', thus proclaiming to the outside world that he had won the full confidence of his Prime Minister – and also of his Monarch. It is a measure of the risks Thorpe was running that in April, only one month after becoming a Privy Councillor, he received a letter written by a young man whom he had met in the King's Road, Chelsea. The man described two 'very pleasant nights' spent with Thorpe and asked for a loan. Thorpe delegated the task of coping with this young man to Bessell who warned him that his letter was tantamount to blackmail. The charge was furiously denied by the young man but no more was heard from him.

Thorpe began to be much in evidence at royal banquets, City dinners, diplomatic functions and at parties at Number Ten where he established contacts with Wilson's entourage, and in particular with his powerful personal and political secretary, Marcia Williams. Thorpe's obvious enjoyment of these occasions became another gripe on the part of his critics in the party who would frequently find themselves being regaled with the latest gossip about who the Prime Minister had been talking to the previous evening, or what the Queen had been wearing, instead of being able to discuss the latest burning issue on the party agenda.

Within the Liberal organisation itself, however, the key word now was efficiency, and those who failed to measure up to Thorpe's exacting standards began to suffer the sharp sting of his discontent. There are two views about the way in which he treated his subordinates. One says that in an

81

outfit as small and as poor as the Liberal Party there are few rewards in the shape of promotion or salary which can be offered for good service, and that the only alternative is to castigate the bad. Richard Moore, Thorpe's political secretary, put it best when he said: 'Jeremy is running a political party with few honours to offer, and no prospect of office to dangle. He hasn't many carrots to hand out. So it's more stick. There *has* to be an element of fear.'

The other view is that Thorpe's treatment of minor offenders, his use of ridicule and sarcasm on subordinates, was overbearing and out of proportion in an organisation as limited as the Liberal Party. One man who felt the full force of Thorpe's wrath on several occasions was the party's press officer, Mike Steele, who was 'fired' by him on at least two occasions for crimes such as altering the wording of an official statement. 'They were gross over-reactions to essentially trivial incidents,' claims Steele, who quietly kept his job each time and waited till the storm blew over.

'Whether my harshness is so excessive is something neither I nor the recipient can judge,' said Thorpe. But amongst the small group of dedicated Liberals who helped to run the party, often for small rewards, the scars were to remain, and when Thorpe later demanded unquestioning loyalty in his hour of need, there were some who found it hard to respond.

The one man whose loyalty was paramount in that summer of 1967 was Peter Bessell who now took upon himself a role whose consequences would be far-reaching: paymaster to Norman Scott.

Bessell's initial response to Scott's letter from Dublin had been to ignore it. His secretary had even told Scott on the telephone that her boss had already done quite enough for him. On 14 July, however, Scott wrote again, and this time there was no escaping the weight of the dilemma he presented. The letter, written this time in a thick and emphatic script, arrived at the House of Commons and was postmarked Maidstone in Kent. It described Scott's experiences

since he had last written. Things had gone wrong. He had
been ill and had spent his savings on hospital bills rather
than on going to America. He had then come to London for
psychiatric treatment and had begun telling his doctor –
Brian O'Connell – all about his experiences, setting them
down one by one in a form which amounted, almost, to a
testament:

Of going to Switzerland to get away. Of the conditions
of coming back begging Jeremy's help to get my luggage
of going to Ireland of writing to Mrs Thorpe for help –
I really thought she knew – of your coming, of that
ghastly taxi ride of your giving me five pounds, of my
fear when you mentioned Sir Frank Soskice, of your
question re: America, of life after that afraid to return to
England, of a gradual decline in nerves, health, of coming
to England and your secretary saying that you had done
enough. I told him – Doctor O'Connell, all this, and he
said that you could never have extradited me, I don't
know about this, all I know is I cannot go into his clinic
because he is full, but that he will see me from time to
time. This means I must have some sort of job. Also
insurance cards and a place in London to live. Alternatively, I should try somehow to get to America where I
have many friends who all feel that I would do very well
there. The situation is serious, the more so because my
brother cannot keep me here very much longer. Is there
anything you can think of. I have no money left now.
I cannot model anymore because my nerves are so shot
to shreds that I soak everything I put on. I can't show up
because I have no riding kit, it's all sold, I have no real
qualifications, I am still on a vast amount of drugs which
means I am not too strong. But wonder, no not wonder,
beg you to try to think of something I need so much to
be doing something. I've had so long to think. Is there no
way of working my way to America? I cannot come up
to London for I have no money so I beg you Mr Bessell
to help somehow. Doctor O'Connell of course will tell

nobody what I said to him but it had to be told don't you understand. It's not been fair to me all these years. I am truly sorry to write but I so need someones help and you said long ago you would.

yours sincerely,
Norman.

Bessell, sensing fresh danger, consulted Thorpe. The obvious course seemed to be to encourage Scott in his plans to go to America. But that would mean applying for a work permit, and there was no guarantee that Scott would qualify for one. Any attempt to get him a job in England, as Scott himself indicated, meant applying for an insurance card, and this would involve contact with yet another set of officials who would undoubtedly be regaled with the whole story again. Bessell suggested to Thorpe that he should, for the time being, pay Scott directly. He therefore wrote to Maidstone and enclosed thirty shillings to cover Scott's fare to London. On 2 August Scott arrived at Bessell's office in Pall Mall, and they sat down to discuss the problems. These seemed to fall into three categories: finding Scott enough money to keep him going without his having to apply for unemployment benefits, arranging for a new insurance card so that he could get work, and securing a passport and visa so that he could eventually go to America.

The first was most easily disposed of. Bessell arranged with his secretary, Sheila Skelton, for Scott to be paid a 'retainer' which would vary between £5 and £10 a week, and would continue until something more permanent could be found.

The second would clearly be more complicated – indeed it was never to be finally disposed of, and it would become over the years a symbol of this deeply entangled relationship. It would have been perfectly easy to apply for a card, and begin making contributions from scratch as soon as a new job was found. There would have been no embarrassing questions. But if Scott wanted to claim unemployment or sickness benefits he would have to explain why there had been no contributions for such a long time. And since Scott had formed the view that Thorpe should have stamped his old card any such explanation could be embarrassing. Bessell therefore impressed on Scott the need for discretion and assured him that he personally would make all the arrangements.

On Problem Number Three, the American visa, Bessell began to see difficulties of a more complex nature, and here he decided that he might have to mislead not only Scott, but Thorpe as well. The havoc which Scott might cause with his story in the United States, where no protection would be offered by the English laws of libel, and where the press's approach to political scandal was a great deal more redblooded than it was in Britain, appalled him. What is more, it might not only be Thorpe who would suffer. Bessell too was a regular commuter across the Atlantic, and rumours linking him with a scandal involving allegations of homosexuality would not exactly help business. 'If it transpired that Scott had talked in America about the fact that he was homosexual, and that I was aware of this, it could have caused me some embarrassment,' he was later to admit. Although that previous month – July 1967 – saw the final passage into law of a new bill, sponsored by Leo Abse, MP, legalizing homosexuality between consenting adults, the stigma attaching to it would not disappear overnight.

He therefore put in hand the process of securing a new passport for Norman Scott, but resorted to delaying tactics in applying for a visa by informing the American Embassy in London that Scott would be unlikely to qualify for 'any job for which work permits are normally provided by the department of immigration and naturalisation.' Rather naturally the embassy turned down the application, but Bessell withheld word of his manoeuvre from Thorpe who would have been furious: he thought the possibility of Scott going to America was to be encouraged at all costs. Scott, too, would have been surprised, since in the course of his conversation Bessell had outlined enthusiastically the possibilities of an American job, such as helping out in a chain of eating houses in which, Bessell vaguely implied, he had a financial interest; he even offered to pay the fare over. Scott, however, had already lost interest in the American trip. For the time being prospects at home looked distinctly more promising. He had moved into a flat in Bexleyheath and was beginning to pick up the threads of his modelling career.

Scott's re-emergence in London coincided with the first public expression of dissatisfaction with Thorpe's leadership. A series of articles in the Liberal magazine *New Outlook* attacked his failure to confront the issues which would win the party support at the next election, and complained about the lack of 'intellectual reinforcements'. It concluded, woundingly for Thorpe, that 'the departure of Grimond is a desperate body-blow.'

Thorpe now made a personal decision which was to have an important effect on both the public and the private conflicts in his life. The time had come, he felt, for the leader of the Liberal Party to get married. He described the decision himself in fairly detached terms: 'I passionately wanted my own children. I decided that this lonely bachelor should get married. A friend and I went on holiday and joined two girls in Greece. One I knew already; I wondered whether I might marry her. I decided I wanted to marry the other. So did my friend. So we said: "Right. Queensberry rules. Whoever wins, the other is best man." I won. He was best man.'

The truth about Jeremy Thorpe's courtship of twenty-nine-year-old Caroline Allpass was both more mundane and, in the end, more romantic than Thorpe's description of it. They met, in fact, at a party in Caroline's Chelsea flat which she shared with a friend; another guest was Thorpe's Oxford friend, David Holmes. Thorpe got on well with her, and they were to meet several times before Holmes suggested that they might all get together in Greece that summer.

Thus it was that on 4 August (two days after Bessell's meeting with Scott), Jeremy Thorpe, wearing a jaunty straw hat and smoking a cigar, left London for Athens, though not without a revealing little interlude. As he passed through the barrier at Heathrow Airport, a sharp-eyed official noticed an alteration in Thorpe's passport. Somebody had added the prefix 'Rt Hon.' before the name.

'Who wrote this?' he demanded.

'My secretary,' replied Thorpe.

'But the only people allowed to make additions and alterations are the passport office.'

'Yes,' retorted Thorpe, 'but they are not always competent.'

By the time reporters had checked back with Thorpe's secretary who, curiously enough, knew nothing at all about the additions, Thorpe was on his way to Athens, and a turning-point in his life.

Caroline, daughter of Warwick Allpass, head of a Battersea chain of furniture stores, brought a completely new and refreshing element into Thorpe's life. Ten years younger than he, her background was uncomplicated, unpolitical, and unquestionably middle-class. 'I come from a very Conservative family,' said Caroline. 'She's a floating voter – we'll convert her,' said Thorpe. Educated at one of Britain's most select girls' boarding schools, Roedean, she had worked in various departments of Sotheby's, the art auctioneers, both in London and New York, before moving to the impressionist painters section. A friend from those days recalled that she was more than just the charming unaffected girl most people saw. 'There was a certain steeliness there. Also a bit of ambition; she would make quite certain before going out with someone that he measured up to her standards, and they were fairly high.'

By the time they had returned from holiday, both had decided that they measured up to each others' expectations; Caroline took perhaps a little longer to make up her mind than Jeremy did. Over the tragically short period of their marriage she was to bring the love and security into his life

87

which had been missing before. One close friend, Michael Ogle, describing her influence, said: 'I saw a man who was emotionally lame pick up his bed and walk.'

For the moment, however, romance had to take second place to some urgent facework on the crumbling edifice of the Liberal Party. By September the Young Liberals, described by one political commentator as 'the most vibrant power in politics today', were challenging Thorpe openly at the party conference. They were clearly a force which, if harnessed, could do wonders for the party at a time when students throughout the world, from the Sorbonne to Berkeley, California, were turning to politics. But Thorpe had no enthusiasm for their attitudes. Publicly he handed them placatory laurels, but in private he was contemptuous of their opinions and their contribution to Liberalism. His hostility was reciprocated, and before long the Young Liberals were joined in their criticisms by members of the party executive, already piqued because Thorpe regarded them, the policy-making arm of the party, as a tedious talking-shop. In November the worm turned; and the executive launched a public attack on their leader. 'Mr Thorpe is too soft on socialists and too fond of socialising,' said one member.

Now the battle was truly joined, with some MPs, notably Eric Lubbock, coming to Thorpe's aid and others turning in desperation to their old leader, Jo Grimond, who remained enigmatic, neither giving support nor withholding it from his successor. By December 1967 Thorpe faced open revolt, and an article in the *Sunday Telegraph* went so far as to ask: 'Can the Liberals Survive?'

The challenge brought out all Thorpe's combative instincts. There was no question in his mind about who would win; it was only a question of how crushing the victory would be. He began planning a campaign to reassert his hold on the leadership, in which the timing up to a crucial meeting of the party executive was to become the decisive element.

On 2 April, having for weeks held at bay rumours of a romance, he announced his engagement in *The Times*, and began preparing a typically glittering celebration. The service itself would be a small one at Lambeth Palace, with the Archbishop of Canterbury giving the blessing, on a date to be kept secret until the last moment. The reception, which would make no concessions to critics of the Thorpe style, would be held in the stately surroundings of the Royal Academy at Burlington House in Piccadilly, where no wedding reception had ever been held before. A guest list of about 750 was drawn up and Thorpe threw himself into the arrangements with as much energy as he was deploying behind the scenes to outflank his opponents.

As the date of his wedding approached there were signs that the attacks of his leadership were abating. The Young Liberals proposed that there should be a new approach to resolving internal disputes within the party. Thorpe, however, seized this olive branch and promptly dashed it to the ground. Two days later, addressing Liberal candidates, he savaged his opponents. They were, he said, 'the small minority in our midst who believe, against all the evidence, that the British electorate wants Marxism in a new dress – what they call non-state socialism.' The speech was written by Richard Moore, but the sentiments were Thorpe's, and the reaction, predictably, was one of outrage. 'Thorpe is talking through his silk hat,' spluttered one Young Liberal. 'The biggest load of hogwash since Macmillan told us we never had it so good,' said another.

Two days later, on 30 May 1968, Thorpe was 'privately' married, with reporters kept just out of reach. Fulfilling the terms of his bet, Thorpe had chosen David Holmes as best man; the only guest was Lillian Prowse, his North Devon agent. The bride's dress – champagne-coloured, matching organza coat, standaway collar – was minutely described from 'secret sources', and Mr Thorpe explained his sudden aversion to publicity by repeating: 'I think there are certain things in one's life that are private. My wedding is one of them.' Next day the happy couple flew to a secret destination – the Mediterranean island of Elba.

Thorpe had thus neatly handed the initiative back to his critics at a moment when they could hardly retaliate. Just to emphasise the point, he left behind him a brief statement for inclusion in the next issue of *Liberal News*: 'My speech to the candidates appears to have stimulated controversy. Splendid. My only comment is that there are different ways of conducting our discussions. One is through tolerant debate; another is through highly personalised attacks . . .'

Nothing could be more personalised than to launch a coup against a man on his honeymoon, but the 'rebels' had been stung into action and could not resist meeting to discuss plans for Thorpe's removal. Inevitably the plans were leaked, and on 11 June the *Daily Mail* carried a story headlined: 'Liberal Move to Oust Thorpe'. The timing could hardly have been more disastrous for them. An angry Thorpe stormed back from his honeymoon armed with a powerful new weapon. 'They wait until I go away on my honeymoon and then attempt the palace revolution. I thought this really outrageous,' he said later. Caroline herself commented: 'What a rotten trick. I suppose in politics they always wait until you aren't there and can't defend yourself.'

On 27 June the lavish wedding reception at the Royal Academy went ahead, with champagne and compliments flowing. Sympathy for Thorpe seemed almost universal. By the time the party executive met next day the tide had turned. Many of the waverers had returned to the fold and the meeting was packed with loyal supporters, including many, like Lady Violet Bonham-Carter, Asquith's daughter, who had not been seen at an executive meeting for many years. Most of them were anxious to pledge undying loyalty to their leader.

'That meeting was one of the nastiest I've ever sat through,' said Mike Steele later. 'Almost fascistic in the way the loyalists attacked anyone who had criticised the leader.'

Thorpe's own comment: 'It certainly wasn't a meeting of the Society of Gentlefolk, distressed or otherwise.' Astutely, he had conceded one motion which called for an element of 'collective leadership' to influence policy decisions, and this took much of the sting out of the revolt. At the same time the opposition had no convincing rival around whom they could rally. By the time the substantive motion of confidence in Thorpe was called, the battle had been won. It was passed overwhelmingly by 48 votes to 2. The revolt was effectively over, and Mr and Mrs Thorpe were able to travel down to Devon to continue the celebration of their wedding by cutting a seven-foot cake in front of a friendly and faithful audience. From that point on, despite occasional cavilling, there was to be no serious threat to Thorpe's leadership until the rumblings of the Norman Scott affair began to surface eight years later.

There is no reason to believe that Caroline Thorpe knew anything about the allegations being made by Scott against her husband in the early months of her marriage, save perhaps for the bare information that he was being pursued, as politicians sometimes are, by 'some maniac', or, as Thorpe would later refer to Scott, 'my madman'. Soon she was to be drawn closer into the unfolding sequence of events, but for now the cover-up was being operated by three people only – Thorpe, Bessell and David Holmes, who was increasingly to play a leading role.

David Holmes had grown up in an environment radically different from that of his friend and mentor Jeremy Thorpe. Born in 1930, he was a working class boy from the Yorkshire mill town of Cleckhampton. But as he grew up he acquired a fastidiousness of style, largely created by his mother, that set him apart from many of his contemporaries. He gained a scholarship from grammar school to Trinity College Oxford where his friendship with Thorpe, and the political and social milieu in which they both moved, smoothed away his northern accent and further refined his laconic manner. After Oxford – where he got a third in modern history – and a short spell of military service, his career led him back to the north of England and into business.

A tall, dark-haired man with chiselled good looks and a

taste for heavy black-rimmed spectacles, Holmes impressed the Manchester business community with his energy, good manners and perfect dress. 'He always knows which shirt and tie to go with which suit,' said a former business colleague. He eventually went to live with a male friend in a tastefully converted coachhouse in Salford outside Manchester. His affluence was reflected in the number of antiques that decorated the house. In London he moved with ease in Liberal, aristocratic society, joining the Reform Club and holidaying in Greece with Thorpe.

He specialised in tax and finance and was at one time or another on the board of twenty four limited companies. He also did voluntary work as a prison visitor. When Thorpe became party treasurer he appointed David Holmes as one of his four honorary deputies. Holmes's specific task was to extract donations from business and commerce. The appointment ceased when Thorpe became party leader in 1967 but Holmes remained a familiar figure to senior Liberals.

He was seen mostly at party conferences, helping Thorpe on with his coat, barring the hotel door to unwelcome visitors or driving Thorpe around on engagements. He was thought of, in the words of one retired party official, as a 'willing pair of legs'. His main political initiative was an effort to form a new political group composed of parliamentary backbenchers and members of the voluntary movement, such as Des Wilson of Shelter, the homeless pressure group, and Tony Smythe of the National Council for Civil Liberties. He organised meetings to set up this group but they turned into long rambling discussions and the proposal faded away.

To an extent Holmes was pushed into the task of monitoring Scott because Bessell had let it be known (in April 1968) that he was going to retire from parliament at the next election to concentrate on rescuing his business interests. Bessell had found himself increasingly out of step with his party on the major issues of the day – the Common Market, hanging, Rhodesia and Vietnam. On Vietnam, which he visited in 1967, he particularly angered the Young

Liberals with his pro-American and pro-Marshall Ky statements. Bessell later hinted that he carried out a mission for American intelligence while in Vietnam.

In the wake of his announcement that he intended to stand down as a Liberal MP, Bessell held secret discussions with the chief whips of *both* the main parties, Conservative and Labour, to see whether he might switch allegiance. Although MPs have from time to time changed from one party to another there can be few precedents for dallying with all three.

By May 1968 the weekly payments made by Bessell to Scott had become systematic, to the point where only a letter signed by Sheila Skelton, or a handwritten note from Bessell himself accompanied the sums of money. In all, the payments were to amount to some £600 or £700, of which Bessell claims he received around £400 back from Thorpe. The passport, number 300283, had arrived in Scott's name, but the visa was still being withheld, though Bessell continued to make encouraging noises about the United States or preferably the Bahamas where he had vague notions of a business deal which, once again, would come to nothing.

Scott meanwhile had modelling plans that called for rather larger outlays, and he now listed his requirements to Bessell. There would be £28 for photographers' fees, 15 guineas for a model book, £40 for clothes, £15 for a bag, £40 for advance rent on a new flat, £37 for food, gas, electricity etc. It all seemed rather excessive to Bessell who ran down the list like a practical husband ticking off his spendthrift wife, reducing each item one by one. ('You can buy very good suitcases cheaply at Marks and Spencers.') The sum he came up with at the end of it was nearer £75 than Scott's £200. He wrote:

Dear Norman,
    My reason for doubt about spending as much as £200 is that it does not guarantee a future and what I am anxious to do is to make certain that your future is secure. However, I think you ought to be able to cut

down your requirements to about £75 and I do not see any reason why this sum should not be advanced instead of your going to the Bahamas. If at the end of the year you are not able to make a go of things in London I would still be prepared to consider assisting you to go abroad.

It is up to you – £75 to get started now in London with no further commitment for twelve months. If you do not succeed then we can talk about the Bahamas again.

Ever sincerely,
Sheila Skelton.

Dictated by Mr Bessell and signed in his absence.

Bessell was over-optimistic. It would be less than seven months before money was again changing hands. But long before then, according to Bessell, Thorpe was once again expressing concern about the threat which Scott posed to his career. In particular, he wanted to find out whether Scott had any letters which might embarrass him, and some time was devoted to a discussion of how this might be achieved. The bizarre (and unsuccessful) method which Bessell says they adopted, though his story was challenged in court, involved David Holmes posing as a reporter in order to persuade Scott to reveal any letters he might still have. The episode was described in great detail by Bessell in the course of Thorpe's trial.

But more contentious was the story he then went on to tell. It was to be the cornerstone of the prosecution case.

Towards ten o'clock in the evening on those days when there is an important vote, a distinct change of atmosphere can be observed within the House of Commons. However sluggish the day's business has been, small eddies of interest begin to disturb the surface. Along the corridors there is a drift towards the Chamber where the green leather benches, noticeably empty until now, start to fill as MPs gather to take in the final stages of the evening's debate.

The Ten o'Clock Division, marked by a loud and peremptory bell which can be heard throughout the House, is the usual culmination, though by no means the final one, of the evening's proceedings. Whether it is the Second Reading Local Government Grants (Social Need) Bill, or a motion of confidence which could bring down the government, if the House divides, then those members who are in the building will troop into the 'aye' or the 'no' lobby to record their vote in answer to the summons of the division bell.

In early December 1968 the House of Commons was more than usually alive with excitement in the wake of a major currency crisis which had caused the Chancellor of the Exchequer, Roy Jenkins, to bring in a savage £250 million tax squeeze, to the fury of big business interests. Rumour, fomented in the City of London, suggested that the Prime Minister, or his Chancellor, or both, were on the point of resigning, and the Labour government was reacting angrily by blaming speculators for causing a crisis of confidence.

One man who was always eager to be on the inside track of such events was Jeremy Thorpe. His love affair with parliament had often kept him late at the House discussing tactics or 'taking the breeze', as the serious business of politics is called in Westminster. It was on just such an occasion that Peter Bessell called in to see him in the Liberal leader's office, to talk about the affairs of the day and, inevitably, to discuss the progress of the Scott problem.

The nature of that conversation was to be hotly disputed in the course of Thorpe's trial at the Old Bailey. According to Bessell it was a deeply serious, even gloomy conversation about ways of dealing with Scott. Thorpe's counsel would suggest that it was, at the most, light-hearted banter. It was, however, interrupted by the Division Bell which summons MPs to vote. The word 'division' flashes up on the TV monitors, giving members just eight minutes to get to the lobbies. Bessell and Thorpe walked down the small corridor behind the vote office to record their votes, then returned to resume the discussion, which continued late into the night.

Whatever the true nature of their conclusions, it was to be overtaken by events. Five months later, Bessell learned that Scott had got married – on 13 May 1969. Scott had telephoned Bessell's secretary and asked her to pass on the news. Bessell thought this was an extremely important development – marriage would mean that Scott was much less inclined to bother Thorpe. This view was not entirely shared by Thorpe himself, who thought it unlikely that any marriage involving a man like Scott could last very long.

Thorpe's doubts about the stability of Scott's marriage were to be wholly justified. But it had started promisingly enough. Scott's financial independence had brought him a new life in Chelsea, which, in the late 1960s revolved around a short-lived social phenomenon known as 'swinging London'. Its epicentre was the King's Road, and the male model was part of its elite, so Scott, now living in that very street, was, for once, in the right place at the right time. He became friendly with a rich young man whom he had met at a party, and eventually he moved into his flat in Chester Square. Working regularly for a fashion studio, Scott found himself reasonably well off.

It was through this friend that Scott met Susan Myers, a dark-haired attractive girl whose family lived in Lincolnshire. Sue Myers's mother, when introduced to Scott in his purple velvet suit, was not impressed. Sue, however, fell in love with him, and on 13 May they were married. Two weeks later they moved out of London to live in Dorset in a cottage near Milton Abbas, where the rent was paid for by Sue's sister who was married to the actor Terry-Thomas. One effect of the move was to finish Scott's modelling career which had anyway begun to deteriorate, and though Sue initially continued to work in London, only travelling down to the cottage at intervals, money was short. There was another problem — Sue was pregnant. As the summer wore on and she was forced to stop work, she began to worry about whether she would qualify to apply for maternity benefits which are paid to expectant mothers. Scott, of course, was in no position to claim since he still had no insurance card.

The isolation of the Dorset cottage and the shortage of money began to take their toll on both of them, and the relationship grew increasingly strained. Scott had turned again to Peter Bessell who promised to take up the matter of his card with the Department of Health and Social Security. Time passed, however, and nothing happened, so Scott took more direct action. He telephoned the Thorpes' house in Devon, where he found himself speaking to Caroline Thorpe. It was the first time that Mrs Thorpe had heard at first hand the full ramifications of the affair, and, whether she believed the story she was hearing or not, it must have been an upsetting experience for her. She told Scott that she could not help.

By now Scott was growing desperate. His requests had gone unheeded and his wife's pregnancy was well advanced. On 27 August he rang Bessell again and, in the course of a hysterical tirade, threatened to take his story to a Sunday newspaper and expose the whole thing. Bessell assured him that he was doing everything he could to help but Scott refused to accept his word and slammed down the telephone. Next he rang the Department of Health directly and asked to be put through to the Minister of State, David Ennals, himself. His call was taken by the minister's private secretary who assured him by way of an immediate letter that Bessell had indeed been in touch with Ennals and that 'the matter is being looked into'. Bessell's approach to Ennals had elicited an assurance from him that there was no question of a prosecution for failure to stamp insurance cards in cases like this, especially if it meant going back eight years to prove who had been the relevant employer. But Ennals had added that any direct assistance would have to come from Scott's local branch. Bessell therefore spoke to the manager of the Weymouth office of the Department of

Health and asked him if he could help out. Following Scott's call he dashed off a placatory letter:

> I have done all in my power to hurry matters along, but miracles cannot be achieved in five minutes and it will take all the tact and persuasion of which I am capable to arrange for a card to be issued to you, properly franked so you can obtain benefit for your wife during her period of confinement. It would be a great mistake if you jeopardised this in the way you suggested to me on the telephone, and I hope for your own sake and in spite of your anxiety you will accept my advice and guidance.
>
> I have spoken to Jeremy Thorpe and put him in the picture regarding the present position.

The last sentence is significant since it is the only case in all of Bessell's letters to Scott where he refers directly to Thorpe, yet ironically, on this occasion at least, he had almost certainly *not* consulted him. It was in the middle of the summer recess and Bessell was reluctant to alarm him more than necessary.

The situation was saved for the time being by a visit to the Scott household from a Department of Health official sent along from the Weymouth office, who issued an emergency card by which Mrs Scott at least could obtain her maternity benefits. Scott himself was still without his own insurance cards: but that may have been at least partly due to his own ambivalent attitude towards them. On the one hand he wanted them because they represented a necessary step along the road towards a normal working life. On the other hand by acquiring them he would immediately be faced with the responsibility of paying regular contributions. 'In a way getting them just made matters worse,' he reflected later.

This was finally emphasised by Ennals himself who laid out Scott's prospects in a letter to Bessell dated 21 January 1970. He explained that because Scott had fallen so far behind in paying contributions he would not be entitled to any unemployment benefits until February 1971, and even that would depend on his paying regular contributions for the whole year in between. He could, of course, pay off the arrears at a low rate, and in the last resort he could fall back on 'supplementary benefits', the safety net which the state provides for its neediest citizens.

None of these solutions appealed to Scott. He did not have the money to pay the arrears (and Bessell did not want to be compromised by paying them for him), and to claim supplementary benefits was beneath his dignity. There may even have been a deep-seated reluctance to accept too easy a solution to the problem. Although, in the end, he *was* actually issued with a new card, it quickly lapsed since he failed to pay the necessary contributions.

Meanwhile his marriage was going from bad to worse. After repeated quarrels Sue left the cottage and returned to her mother in Lincolnshire, while Scott went back to London to live in the flat in Earls Court which had originally been Sue's and which they had kept on. On 18 November Sue gave birth to a baby boy which was named Diggory Benjamin Scott. For a few weeks she and the baby returned to London to live with Scott, but relations were not improved when Scott told her that he had been seeing his former boyfriend. 'Naturally I slept with him when she was away, as one does,' says Scott. 'I told her about it because I wanted her to know the truth.'

There are some truths, however, which are harder to take than others, and Sue moved back to Lincolnshire. Scott, to raise money, started selling off some of the contents of the flat, and his wife dispatched relatives to rescue the rest. Eventually Scott found himself with little apart from a bed to sleep in.

The final stages of a brief and unhappy marriage were approaching, with consequences which would once again pose a severe threat to the Liberal leader.

7. A Bit of Spare Cash

Jeremy Thorpe was the Liberal Party's most successful fundraiser, but he was also its biggest spender. His flamboyant approach to politics and his grand designs for the party's future envisaged an income far larger than that organisation had ever contemplated. He was impatient with the petty restrictions of a small budget and irritated by cautious advisers. If he felt that the leader should hold a crusading rally in the Albert Hall, then the Albert Hall it would be, despite mild suggestions that there were cheaper ways of doing it; if campaigning by helicopter was better publicity than travelling by bus, then he would hire helicopters; and if installing closed-circuit television seemed a good way of demonstrating how modern the party had become, then he was certainly not going to be told by any subordinate that the party could ill afford such extravagance.

For Thorpe, the image of the leader was the image of the party – the two were indivisible. The trouble was that projecting both cost money, and the Liberals, unlike their rivals, had no reliable source of income. Whereas the Conservatives traditionally drew their funds from private industry, and Labour could look to the trade unions, the Liberals had always experienced difficulty in raising revenue. From almost as far back as the days of Gladstone there had been grumbles about money, how to raise it and how to spend it. In 1891 a row blew up over a £5000 donation from the great imperialist Cecil Rhodes, which somehow never showed up in the party accounts. Sir Henry Campbell-Bannerman, later the party's leader, was convinced that the party secretary, Francis Schnadhorst, had 'trousered' the money, but it was more likely that it had been spent on the party at Schnadhorst's discretion entirely, without the consent of officials (a high-handed approach to finance which Thorpe was to make almost systematic under his own leadership).

After the break-up of the Coalition which saw Britain through the First World War at the expense of a disastrous split in the Liberal Party, Lloyd George set up a fund which he was to control himself on behalf of his faction of the party, and which he used unashamedly in his campaign to regain the leadership. The fund was a constant source of controversy, partly because it was heavily founded on revenue raised from the sale of honours – a scandal of which Lloyd George himself was undoubtedly aware – but also because no one within the Liberal hierarchy had access to its accounts or knowledge of its scope. Lloyd George withheld contributions from it at times when the party was almost desperate for money, in order to increase his hold over the rival camp of H.H. Asquith, and in doing so helped ensure that the Liberals suffered humiliation in the 1924 election. Once he was again leader, Lloyd George poured money into the party but continued to control the fund. The very fact of its existence put off many would-be contributors who often seemed to think that its resources were infinite.

The history of Liberal finances after 1931, when the last contribution from the Lloyd George fund was made, is summed up by Dr Roy Douglas, a historian of the party:

After ... 1931 the Liberal Party was thrown wholly on its own resources. Some individuals were able to give considerable sums. Most of that money seems to have been paid with pure altruism, often anonymously, and with no possible prospect of reward or recognition These contributions have on several occasions rescued the Liberal Party from imminent disaster; but although they have seemed large to Liberal treasurers, they have represented what for both other parties was a negligible sum. The Liberal Party has contrived to exist, and to maintain a national organisation, on sums which are less than some Constituency Conservative Associations receive.

Jeremy Thorpe inherited at least one of Lloyd George's qualities: a deep conviction that he was the best judge of how the party should spend its money; and increasingly he was able to control the resources. One further characteristic which his great Liberal predecessor would have recognised was the irritating absence of any personal fortune. The few directorships he had taken in the course of his career had never yielded more than modest salaries, and although a doting Liberal supporter had once left him a legacy of £17,000, he had seldom had more than the party leader's normal expenses to supplement his MP's salary. Only later, however, was he to take the road, which the young Lloyd George had tried before him, into the murky world of speculative capitalism.

From his early days Thorpe was a master of the gentle art of charming money out of rich people on behalf of the Liberal Party. One donor, who gave considerably more than she had intended, ascribed his success to an ability to persuade would-be benefactors that the whole process was going to be 'the most tremendous fun. He absolutely convinced me that by giving money to the Liberals I would become one of a select few on the inside track of something new and tremendously exciting. I was never entirely clear about what it was, but it sounded a lot more enjoyable than most things one contributes to these days.'

Until 1970 the sums given were relatively small, but they mounted up. Donors tended to be rich Liberals like Timothy Beaumont, or the Rowntree Trust, an organisation founded by the Quaker Joseph Rowntree, which made regular contributions in pursuit of its aim to broaden the political base of the country. In Thorpe's period as treasurer money from appeals and donations doubled, with the result that the Liberal Party Organisation's income in 1966 was transformed. Mounting expenditure, however, virtually extinguished the gain.

By 1969 the situation was desperate. The party's overdraft of almost £90,000 was more than its annual income. John Pardoe, the new party treasurer, made drastic cuts in staff and moved the headquarters from its premises in Smith Square in the heart of Westminster to more modest quarters off The Strand. Pratap Chitnis, head of the party organisation and a man who had always believed that a more careful husbandry would have prevented the crisis in the first place, decided to resign. Thorpe himself launched an ambitious fund-raising drive aimed at persuading 8000 people to contribute £25 each, thus raising £200,000, but the response to this was hardly more encouraging than the famous Liberal Million Fund, set up in 1925 to raise £1 million, which petered out at around £100,000.

The problem of raising money was a constant source of anxiety for Thorpe. Long evenings were spent in his office at the House of Commons discussing different schemes, different approaches to industrialists, bankers, charities. Endless bottles of whisky were consumed as extravagant ideas were floated about what might be achieved if only the money could be found. One senior Liberal recalls the period with some awe: 'Jeremy fantasised. It was impossible to discuss real political issues with him, because he was only interested in his dream about the achieving of power. He would convince himself that given the right money he could change the face of politics and bring the Liberals back to power. He believed that money was the key to it all.'

At these times scepticism was not encouraged In fact those amongst Thorpe's colleagues who were imprudent enough to raise objections or point out flaws in the argument were accused of disloyalty and not encouraged to participate again. Increasingly he turned to a small circle of friends, including Peter Bessell, who were happy to go along with the fantasy. 'If only we could find just one millionaire who would open his purse' became Thorpe's watchword, repeated to Bessell at regular intervals.

Then, in May 1969, he found one. Jack Arnold Hayward's

wealth was based on the engineering business built up by his Wolverhampton-born father, Sir Charles Hayward, into the giant Firth Cleveland group of companies. Jack Hayward had helped to expand it in America before moving with his family to Nassau in the Bahamas where he was quick to spot the potential for large-scale investment. In Freeport an American millionaire called Wallace Groves had permission from the Bahamian government to live in a tax-free haven of 50,000 acres of leased Crown land in return for a promise to build a deep-water port and encourage industrial development. Hayward joined him in 1956, persuaded his father to commit £1 million and helped construct the Freeport boom. International companies, drawn by tax advantages, the tourist potential, and the healthy proximity to the United States, poured in money to make it the fastest growing industrial centre in the Caribbean.

As well as being an investment genius, Hayward was a British patriot on an almost eccentric scale. His love for the mother country was nurtured by the fact that he lived 3000 miles away from it. His motto for the Bahamas – a former British colony – was 'Keep all things Bright, Beautiful and British'; he drove a Rolls Royce and a second-hand London taxi around Grand Bahama Island; he introduced London red double-decker buses; and he insisted that portraits of the Queen should hang in Freeport offices. 'He is a man who cannot bear to see a flag flying from a building unless it is the Union Jack,' said a colleague, and his patriotism won him the title 'Union Jack' Hayward.

He was also a keen supporter of causes. Some of Hayward's donations were eventually to be deployed in ways that he had never intended. But the first contact between Hayward and Thorpe was straightforward enough. In April 1969 Hayward read in the *Daily Telegraph* about an appeal, launched in Britain by three West Country MPs including Jeremy Thorpe, to save Lundy Island, an isolated bird sanctuary in the Bristol Channel, which was in danger of being bought up by foreign interests. 'I had a bit of spare cash', said Hayward, 'so I telephoned Jeremy Thorpe and offered it to him.'

Hayward's call came through to the Thorpes' London home late one night and was answered by Caroline.

'I always said to Jeremy', recalls Hayward, 'that if I had got a snooty reply, which I might have done from certain English women, especially at that time of night, I would have called the whole thing off. But Caroline was so sweet. I said, "You don't know me from Adam, Mrs Thorpe, my name is Jack Hayward, I live in the Bahamas and I wonder if I could help about Lundy." She probably thought I was a nut-case, but she was very nice and asked me to phone back, however late, because Jeremy was out at a dinner.'

By the time Hayward did call back the Thorpes were in bed but wide enough awake to consider the extraordinary offer that was being made by this unknown benefactor.

'My dear fellow,' said Thorpe cautiously, 'how very nice of you . . .' As he outlined the problem facing the island, Caroline was passing him notes across the bed, with scribbled warnings like: 'How do you know he isn't an agent for the Scientologists?'

Finally, Hayward asked the key question: 'How much do they want for it?'

'Well,' said Thorpe, taking a deep breath, 'I think we could get it for £125,000.'

'OK,' said Hayward, 'count me in.'

'Do you mean the whole amount?' asked Thorpe incredulously.

'Yes. If you can get it for that I think it's worth it.'

Thus, three months later, Jack Hayward, the saviour of Lundy (at a final price of £150,000) found himself sitting in a small church on the island surrounded by grateful inhabitants celebrating its reprieve. The service of thanksgiving, relayed to the crowds outside, had been organised by Thorpe who was sitting with Caroline in the pew behind Hayward.

Hayward, impressed by the smooth organisation of the day's events, leaned back and whispered: 'God, Jeremy, you've done a super job, this is fantastic. You really should be Prime Minister of this country if you can do a job like this.'

'It's on the cards, my dear fellow,' came the whispered reply.

Next morning Thorpe enlarged on his thoughts about the prospects and potential of the Liberal Party – provided, of course, it had the funds. 'Are you interested in supporting us?' he asked finally. Hayward hesitated, and said he would have to think about it, so Thorpe suggested that Peter Bessell, who was in New York, might meet him there to discuss the matter further.

In the end it was Bessell, armed with figures showing how various amounts could help the party out of its difficulties, who convinced Hayward that the Liberals were another great British tradition worth preserving.

'I went for the top amount,' said Hayward. '£150,000. The figure 150 seems to have haunted me.'

By March 1970 word had reached the headquarters of the Liberal Party that a big donation was on its way. By that time the party had a new treasurer, Sir Frank Medlicott, a distinguished former MP for the National Liberals who had resigned on principle from this Tory-orientated group after the Suez fiasco in 1956 and joined the Liberal Party proper. He was determined to bring some method into the party's tangled finances, having already been shocked at some of the things he had found. In the first place there were at least three different funds within the party, only one of which the party treasurer controlled. At General Elections these funds grew to four or even five, and money was transferred from one to another at a bewildering pace.

The existence of these funds, and the way they were handled under Thorpe's leadership, was to be a central issue in later events. It is important therefore to distinguish between each and to identify who controlled them in the election year of 1970.

The Liberal Party Organisation, which banked with Coutts & Co. in The Strand, was the main administrative arm of the party and was run by the treasurer, Frank Medlicott, who was responsible for paying staff, maintaining the party headquarters and strengthening links with the grass-root organisations of the party up and down the country. Permanently short of money, it was low down on Thorpe's own list of priorities.

The Liberal Central Association was the oldest of the party's funds, dating back to the beginning of the century, and was the responsibility of the chief whip's office. It financed candidates and MPs, and was the 'executive arm' of the parliamentary party. In 1970 its treasurer was an accountant, Sidney Hope, who reported directly to Thorpe.

The marginal seats fund/direct aid committee was Thorpe's own invention, his personal property, and a perennial source of envy, irritation and controversy amongst fellow-Liberals. Thorpe's claim to run it himself was undisputed since he raised most of the money for it. His insistence that its accounts should be kept secret was less generally accepted, but he argued successfully that publicity about its allocation of resources would only arouse jealousy and gossip, as well as alerting the opposition to where the Liberals were making their big push. In 1970 only one other man, Edward Wheeler, a party official, knew which constituencies the money went to, and his knowledge was only partial. He did not know, for instance, how much money was coming in, and did not have regular access to the two direct aid committee bank accounts at the National Westminster Bank in Victoria Street which recorded its transactions. The mystery surrounding this fund was further compounded by the fact that it was also known as the *direct aid fund*, the *winnable seats fund*, or occasionally a combination of both.

The party leader's fund was a small account at Lloyds Bank, Finsbury Circus, used, mostly during an election, to handle incidental expenses. It was Thorpe's responsibility.

The General Election fund, at Coutts, was run by the party organization which handled the thousands of small donations sent to any political party gearing itself up for a major campaign. This was Medlicott's responsibility but he did not always have full control over what was charged to it.

The Liberal general fund, also at the Victoria Street branch of the National Westminster Bank, was set up to cater for the Hayward money. Controlled by Thorpe, it was to witness some dizzying transactions in the course of a short but spectacular life.

It was Medlicott's ambition to bring order to this proliferation of accounts. 'I think it is essential for all money to pass through the party's bank account under the jurisdiction of the party treasurer,' he wrote to Thorpe. 'If not, we run the risk of the party having as many treasurers as it has bank accounts.' It seems a modest proposal, but it was to founder on the rocks of Thorpe's outright hostility to any such notion. The first sign that he would oppose it came early in 1970 when two donations amounting to £12,500 were diverted from the party organisation to the central association without Medlicott's knowledge. They were followed by two further donations, £25,000 from a Scottish Liberal, Simon Mackay, later Lord Tanlaw, and £15,000 from a successful arms dealer, Geoffrey Edwards. Both gifts were anonymous. But the crunch came with the arrival, in May, of Hayward's cheque, made out to Jeremy Thorpe.

It was clear from the outset that a gift of this size would transform the party's finances, but opinions about how it should be spent differed sharply. Medlicott felt that the first priority was to clear the party's debts, then to set up a fighting fund for the election, and finally to establish a solid investment for the future. He suggested setting up a trust to deal with the money and put forward a short-list of suitable trustees. Thorpe was not impressed.

On 15 May, he, Peter Bessell and Frank Medlicott met in the Liberal leader's office at the House of Commons to split up the £150,000. Thorpe immediately suggested opening a fresh account – the Liberal general fund – with himself as main signatory. Medlicott and Bessell would also be entitled to sign cheques, but Thorpe would control it. The decision ran directly counter to Medlicott's own ideas, and as if to demonstrate how Thorpe intended to use the money, the first pay-out of £50,000 was to the direct aid fund, with its two accounts, both handled personally by him. It was agreed in addition that a £40,000 reserve should be set up (to Medlicott's relief), and that the rest should be distributed amongst the various funds. Less than half of the amount needed by the party organization to pay off its debts was granted and a mere £10,000 was earmarked for the organization's election expenses. When Medlicott asked Thorpe for a slightly larger contribution to the election fund, the reply was a curt refusal: 'Within one week of us agreeing that the £40,000 reserve was to be sacrosanct, you now wish to raid it!' wrote Thorpe. His impatience had perhaps been sharpened by the announcement that a General Election would be held on 13 June.

A summer election was unusual for Britain, but Harold Wilson, after agonising over whether his Labour government should hang on until the autumn, had finally decided to take advantage of the opinion polls which were running in his favour and stage a Presidential-style campaign. It was to prove, as Joe Haines, one of his advisers, has remarked, 'a massive miscalculation'.

Thorpe flung himself into the campaign, working up to sixteen and a half hours a day to barnstorm the country. He was determined that his first General Election as leader should be a stunning success, and he was delighted when Liberal supporters presented him with what they considered an election-winning slogan: 'Faith, Hope and Jeremy'. Two helicopters were hired, and telex equipment installed. His themes were traditional Liberal ones: attacks on the two main parties for running Britain into debt, the offer of a 'third force' in politics, and the conviction that a Liberal Revival was just around the corner. His style was anything but traditional, and for the press, starved of glamour, it was a bonus. Thorpe was photographed bounding in and out of his helicopters and plunging into astonished crowds without a trace of the embarrassment normally shown by the British politician confronted by his electorate *en masse*. On television, too, Thorpe continued to be impressive.

It was all to no avail. Defying the polls, the Conservatives led by Edward Heath were returned with a healthy overall majority of thirty seats. The Liberals' representation in parliament dropped from thirteen seats to six, and even those six MPs barely clung to power. Thorpe's own majority in North Devon fell to a mere 396, only seven more than his slender victory in 1959 had won him. The result was a severe blow to party morale and Thorpe's self-esteem.

After the defeat came the reckoning. Leafing through his mail Thorpe found a letter from his treasurer announcing that, according to the National Westminster Bank, Thorpe's two direct aid accounts, once buoyant with Hayward money, were now overdrawn by more than £4000. The election in all had cost a record £103,000. Thorpe's reaction was to dispatch a furious letter to Medlicott accusing *him* of being personally responsible for the financial disaster. He then commandeered the whole of the remaining balance in the general fund account and transferred it into the direct aid fund and the central association. Medlicott was bewildered by the outburst. 'I do not know what reason you have for writing to me as you are doing,' he wrote sadly. Surveying the wreckage of his careful plans for the secure future of the party, Medlicott concluded that resignation might be the only course open to him. 'It is highly unsatisfactory that the party leader should insist on personally handling such a large part of the party's finances . . .' he wrote to his deputy Philip Watkins who chaired the finance and administration board. 'I am not prepared to continue as party treasurer unless the present division of finance and responsibility is brought to an end.'

On 24 June he wrote to Thorpe asking for a full explanation of the election figures, to be presented at a meeting of the finance and administration board the following week. But five days later tragedy struck and blew aside any question of a detailed discussion of the affair.

Caroline Thorpe had spent the grim days following the election looking after her husband and their baby Rupert in their Devon cottage. On 29 June they made preparations to leave for London and piled the family luggage into a Ford Anglia estate car. Because there was so little room left in the car, it was decided that Jeremy and Rupert would go by train while Caroline drove on her own. After seeing her husband and son on to the train, Caroline returned to the cottage, picked a large bunch of white carnations from the garden, and set off on the four-hour drive. As she neared the Venture roundabout on the A30 Basingstoke by-pass some two and a half hours later, her car veered suddenly across the white centre line. It struck a lorry travelling in the opposite direction, then collided with a car immediately behind it. The Anglia somersaulted into the air, crashed on to its roof and skidded to a halt. Luggage and clothes were thrown everywhere. The first things that a passing motorist saw were the white carnations, scattered across the road. Caroline lay trapped in the car until she was pulled free and carried unconscious to an ambulance. By the time she reached hospital she was dead. Thorpe, who had just finished a speech in the House of Commons, was told immediately. He drove to Basingstoke to identify the body, then travelled on to his Devon home.

The driver of the lorry, Brian Knock, reported at the inquest into Caroline Thorpe's death that as her car had headed straight towards him he could see that Mrs Thorpe was 'looking down at the inside of the car'. The coroner suggested that some of the luggage might have been dislodged and that she was trying to replace it. However a passenger in the lorry, Stephen Blythe, told another story: Mrs Thorpe, he said, 'seemed to be looking straight ahead of her. She did not seem to know where she was going. I said at the time that she was day-dreaming.' The conflicting evidence was never explained.

In later years a certain mythology grew up around the death of Caroline Thorpe and played an important part in the subsequent war of words between Jeremy Thorpe and

Norman Scott. Friends of Thorpe contend that during Caroline's journey to London she was haunted by the memory of an appalling confrontation that had taken place the day before. Norman Scott, runs the story, had turned up at the Thorpes' cottage, Higher Chuggaton, and insisted on talking to her. He had made accusations against her husband, and had told her, for the first time and in lurid detail, about the homosexual relations which he claimed had taken place between them. The experience had so preoccupied her as she drove back to London that she allowed the car to drift over the central divide and smash into the oncoming lorry.

There is not a shred of direct evidence that this happened. Scott himself denies it – 'a wicked lie' is what he calls it – and there are no independent witnesses to testify to his presence in Devon on that day. Scott maintains that he never left London. He does confirm that he had telephoned Thorpe's cottage some six months earlier, in 1969, when his marriage was beginning to crumble, and did in fact speak to Caroline. He claims that he was under the impression that Thorpe had already told her about his homosexual past, but he accepts that this call may have marked the first occasion on which she became aware of the nature of his allegations. But he is insistent that this was the last time he spoke to her.

The death of his wife had a profound effect on Thorpe. For more than a year he remained obsessed by her memory, unable to talk for any length in private without recalling her. Some years later he told the journalist Susan Barnes about his experience during those months: 'After Caroline died,' he said, 'I forgot about the electoral disaster. It just blurred. I suppose that for a year, while I did everything I had to do – took party meetings, did all my constituency work, laid the wreath on the Cenotaph – I did it all mechanically.' And speaking on a religious programme on BBC radio, he said: 'Unless you believe in the resurrection I think the whole of this life is a very bad joke . . . Separation in this life, compared with eternity, would be like a postage stamp on Cleopatra's Needle. People are not just snuffed out. There must be a further purpose.'

He conceived the idea of erecting a monument to Caroline in Devon, a column of Portland stone to stand 600 feet up on a hill overlooking the Taw Valley near Barnstaple – a very public memorial. 'When people see it rising into the sky they will think of Caroline Thorpe and the sunshine she brought with her during her tragically short stay in North Devon,' he said. He asked the Welsh architect Clough Williams-Ellis to design it, and the Archbishop of Canterbury to officiate at the service of dedication. His grief was given public expression in July of that year when he made a speech in honour of the Tory minister, Iain Macleod, who had just died. Those who heard it say that it was the finest he had ever made, and it provoked spontaneous admiration and sympathy in a packed House of Commons.

For more than a year the Liberal Party, in public at any rate, was virtually leaderless, and it was not until John Pardoe decided that it was necessary to write him a letter of brutal frankness reminding him of his responsibilities to the party that Thorpe snapped out of his period of mourning.

Caroline's death brought an unwritten truce between the party leader and his treasurer. Thorpe agreed to release more money from the Hayward account and Medlicott dropped his plans for unifying the finances of the party. But peace lasted barely three months before Thorpe again accused him of neglecting the interests of the party. ('Really, Frank, you don't make life easy,' he wrote. 'Discussing finance with you is becoming almost as time-consuming as raising it, and I don't find it half so productive!' To which Medlicott made the spirited reply: 'You complain that I cause you a lot of trouble, but I am bound to say, as party treasurer, that you are causing *me* a lot of trouble.')

This time the row became public. Press speculation about the source of the Liberals' new-found finance had heightened in the course of the party's annual conference that autumn, and Medlicott was asked to confirm the name of the donor.

Medlicott admitted that Hayward, whose name had already been mentioned in *The Times*, had given the money, and he publicly expressed gratitude to him. The announcement infuriated Thorpe. That evening, as Liberal delegates attended a reception given by the BBC, Thorpe turned on Medlicott and gave him a humiliating dressing-down in front of astonished guests. He said that Hayward had requested anonymity and had particularly insisted that no publicity be given to his donation. Sir Frank was deeply hurt. He and his wife left the reception immediately, and drove home to consider his future.

Hayward had not, he says, asked for anonymity, but there were almost certainly more complex reasons for Thorpe's anger. For one thing he regarded Hayward's money as very much his property; it was he, Thorpe, who had found him and conjured the funds out of him. But at the same time he saw in Hayward a source of finance for the future. That summer he had visited the Bahamas and had delicately mentioned the possibility of further donations. Any publicity had to be carefully orchestrated so as not to poison what could turn out to be an almost bottomless well.

None of this was comfort to Medlicott. He had been publicly insulted by a man twenty five years his junior over a matter in which he considered himself innocent. At the same time he was far from well, and had already had to take time off to recover from illness. But he was by no means defeated. 'I simply will not accept a situation in which the party leader subjects the party treasurer to lecturing and hectoring as though I were a defaulting bookkeeper,' he wrote to Philip Watkins. 'It is clear that the party leader has no longer any confidence in me as an office holder and this raises considerable doubts in my mind as to whether I ought to continue as treasurer.' He also wrote a long letter of apology to Hayward who replied that he was not in the least upset.

In the end Medlicott concluded that his loyalty to the party overrode his loyalty to Thorpe, and he stayed on. Extremely popular with rank-and-file Liberals, he was enthusiastically re-elected next year. But the bickering with Thorpe, which continued through 1971, did little to improve his ailing health. In November he developed a tumour of the brain, and in December of that year he resigned. Barely three weeks later he was dead. One of the ugliest features of the whole affair was a rumour, circulated amongst the party's hierarchy following Medlicott's death, that his constant complaints about finance had been caused by his illness, rather than by the existence of any genuine grounds for concern.

The truth is that Sir Frank Medlicott was a treasurer who was prepared to stand up to Thorpe and argue with him about the way party finances were run. He would have been shocked, for instance, by the fact that his successor, Philip Watkins, was not only willing to accept the status quo, but was to combine the role of treasurer (whose task is to husband the resources of the party) with that of chairman of the finance and administration board (whose job it is to spend it). He also became treasurer of the Liberal Central Association.

As time went on, Thorpe was able, through his growing control of funds donated to the party, and the secrecy he maintained in handling them, to argue that Hayward's payments were actually made to him personally, rather than to the party, thus justifying in retrospect the system he had built up. When interviewed by police in June 1978 he gave this explanation of £20,000-worth of Hayward money which was central to allegations made against him:

I . . . resolved that, since Mr Hayward had made it quite plain to me that, not being an adherent to the Liberal Party, he was not making these monies available to the party, but to me personally, I would not cause them to be paid into the Liberal Party funds where they would be soon defrayed. I therefore made arrangements for the sum of £20,000 to be deposited with accountants and to be held as an iron reserve against any shortage of funds at any subsequent election.

115

This was, of course, a precise articulation of the very doctrine that Medlicott had spotted early and had attempted, unsuccessfully, to neutralise. For if the party leader were actually to keep to himself large sums of money of which the rest of the party was ignorant, to insist that only he were the proper arbiter of how it should be spent, and to regard the organisation as merely a 'defrayer' of useful money, then what was the point of having a party budget at all?

It is worth pointing out that despite what Thorpe maintained, as far as Hayward was concerned, he was giving the money to the Liberal Party, certainly not to Thorpe personally. Yet although the grand total of his donations over the years was to approach a quarter of a million pounds, only that first £150,000, given in 1970, ever showed up on Liberal Party accounts. And one donation of £40,000, made by Hayward in May 1974 specifically for help in a General Election, was not even paid into an account bearing the word 'Liberal'. As Hayward somewhat plaintively told the *Sunday Times*: 'If you send a cheque in all good faith at the request – instructions, directions, call it what you will – of the leader of the Liberal Party to an account that is called the Liberal Party General Election fund, if you think that it is going to help the Liberal Party in a General Election, and then the bank involved says "there is no account of that name" ... it's perplexing.'

Thorpe, as we shall see, was to take steps which would conceal from most members of the party organisation not just the source but the very existence of money given. In the meantime, however, there had been another party casualty. Towards the end of 1970, following the public dispute between Thorpe and Medlicott, Lord Beaumont, president of the party, decided to raise the matter of secret funds and the need to subject the marginal seats account to regular audit. He informed Thorpe that he would be mentioning the matter in the course of his presidential speech, only to find himself on the receiving end of another tirade. 'If you bring that up I will tear you into little shreds,' announced Thorpe bluntly. Beaumont, not relishing the prospect, withdrew his comments and resigned the presidency instead.

There is little question that Thorpe was under considerable strain during this period in the wake of his wife's death. But once again his treatment of distinguished colleagues was losing him friends at a rate he could ill afford. Then, in October 1970, his gloom deepened further when Peter Bessell approached him with the kind of news he had learned to dread: Norman Scott was being sued for divorce by his wife Sue, and wanted to defend the case. The implications were stark: once allowed to stand up in a court of law, protected by the privilege which court proceedings allow, Scott might seize the opportunity to rehearse in public the litany of his accusations against Thorpe.

The nightmare had begun again.

8. A Pleasant Place to Die

Peter Bessell's handling of the Scott affair over the next few months was to bring Thorpe close to the very calamity he had been attempting to avert. Far from defusing the threat, Bessell succeeded only in rendering it even more unstable, with the result that by mid-1971 Thorpe was exposed to the risk of disastrous publicity.

Bessell's immediate aim, in the autumn of 1970, was to take a firm hand in controlling the progress of Norman Scott's divorce. It was just possible, he and Thorpe agreed, that if Scott wanted to save his marriage, or at least win regular access to his son, then even he might accept that to make allegations of a homosexual affair in court could only harm his case. But Scott's unpredictability made it important that the progress of the action should be closely monitored. On 29 October, therefore, with Thorpe's agreement, he wrote to Scott: 'Dear Norman, I have heard indirectly of your latest problems, and I am very sorry indeed to know of these troubles ... I will do anything I can to help you.'

What he proposed was that Scott should see a solicitor called Leonard Ross, who had a small but thriving practice in Dorset Square, London. Ross was known to both Bessell and Thorpe, having served as solicitor to the two companies of which they were directors – Manhattan Equipment and Drinkmaster – as well as acting for Bessell's own company, Peter Bessell Ltd. But his relationship with Bessell was more than simply that of solicitor and client. He had been involved as a business partner in yet another of Bessell's ill-fated ventures, an attempt to set up a hamburger and fast-food franchise in Britain as an off-shoot of a New York company. The deal had foundered in 1970 through lack of capital and the absence of suitable sites, leaving a number of disgruntled associates; but Ross, who had been to New York in the course of negotiations, was still on close terms with Bessell. He agreed to help with this latest problem, and Bessell explained to him some, if not all, of the special circumstances which would attach to the Scott divorce case. He trusted that Ross would share his opinion that Scott's damaging claims against Thorpe were irrelevant to the proceedings in court.

Scott had already been in touch with another law firm and decided to contest his wife's divorce action on the grounds that she had deserted him and removed their baby son. However, at Bessell's prompting, he agreed to see Ross instead, and made his first visit to Dorset Square in early November 1970. It was quickly clear that relations between them would be strained. Scott lost no time in telling Ross his version of the relationship with Thorpe, and made plain that he considered it to be central to his defence. When Ross asked him why, he said that Thorpe's failure to stamp his insurance card was a direct cause of the poverty in which he and his wife had had to live, and which had undermined their marriage. Ross said he would do what he could to help, though he doubted whether raising the matter would help in court; he mentioned the possibility of Scott's applying for legal aid to help with costs.

It was apparent to Ross that this was to be no ordinary divorce case. It was one in which a number of reputations, including, possibly, his own, would be at risk. His next step therefore was to consult the man who seemed to have most to lose – Jeremy Thorpe. He called on him at his flat in Ashley Gardens near Victoria Station and told him about the interview he had just had. As far as he himself was concerned, he explained, nothing that Scott had told him about Thorpe was relevant to the case; but whether the allegations came out in court or not depended on the way the other side in the action intended to handle it. He therefore proposed that he should travel to Skegness in Lincolnshire to consult the solicitors who were handling

Sue Scott's petition. Thorpe thanked him warmly and agreed that he should go ahead.

In Skegness, Ross discovered that his opposite number was already well aware of the allegations against Thorpe, having heard from Mrs Scott that her husband might well bring them up in court. Quite separately he had reached the same conclusion as Ross – that Scott's claims about Thorpe had nothing to do with the divorce. He certainly did not intend to allude to it. Ross reported back to Thorpe that as far as both sets of lawyers were concerned, his name would not be mentioned publicly.

On 1 December Ross again saw Scott. He told him that the grounds for divorce being put forward by his wife were cruelty, and the main evidence would be his homosexual relationship with two men – neither of them Thorpe. There was thus absolutely no reason for him to bring Thorpe's name up, and if he did it might well affect his chances of winning the right of access to his child. Scott was furious. Not only did it seem as if he were going to lose the action, but he was also going to forfeit the opportunity of publicly accusing the man whom he now blamed for so much that had gone wrong with his life. He accused Ross of working for Thorpe and Bessell rather than for him, then stormed out of his office. Later he telephoned Ross and withdrew his instructions. This alarming twist galvanised Bessell into further action. He spoke to Scott's mother and begged her to persuade her son to reconsider. Ross was a fine lawyer, he said, and would certainly do his best for his client. Mrs Josiffe agreed to pass on the message.

In the end a suspicious and reluctant Scott was persuaded to change his mind. Ross, for his part, wrote to him on 13 January 1971 promising him that he would do what he could to ensure that Scott won access to his son. He also mentioned another important matter: 'Please let me know whether you wish me to obtain legal aid on your behalf. There has been some talk of your costs being paid by those who are interested in your future, but this is obviously a decision which you would like to make yourself.'

Ross's casual remark is an acknowledgement of the way in which Thorpe's fate was still bound up with the life of Norman Scott. Ten years after their first meeting, and seven years since they had last seen each other, Thorpe was still accepting a measure of financial responsibility for Scott. Yet this was not the impression given to outsiders: just a few months later a Thorpe aide was to write tersely to one of Scott's friends that the Liberal leader was 'under no obligation to this gentleman'.

The next time Scott went to see Bessell, later that month, Bessell's manner towards him had changed. The firm but friendly father-figure had begun to resemble Uriah Heep. He began by commenting on how wretched Scott looked, and by sympathising with his predicament. He announced that Thorpe had behaved 'abominably', and suggested that the time had come to make amends. He himself had several proposals to make which would help Scott make a new start in life . . . .

Behind Bessell's new attitude lay an extraordinary episode in his business career which had brought him to a new financial and emotional crisis. Some eighteen months previously he had been approached by an old business partner, Norman Graham, who had become the owner and chairman of a company called the Plastic Carton Corporation of America, manufacturing plastic egg-boxes at a factory in New Jersey. Graham said that he wanted to expand his business and asked Bessell whether he was interested in joining him. It was just the kind of deal Bessell liked – a big U.S. corporation looking for an outlet in Britain. He and Graham quickly formed a British subsidiary to build and operate a factory, and, using his prestige as a local MP, Bessell persuaded the Liskeard Rural District Council in Cornwall to purchase compulsorily ten acres of land outside the town and to rush through planning permission for a new factory. The cost of building it was to be £825,000 and it would house £5 million-worth of imported machinery. Speed was essential, he said, otherwise the Americans might be tempted to set up their European operation in France instead. The prospect of the factory and 800 jobs in an area of high unemployment speeded the transaction through, and by August 1970 contracts had been placed, designs drawn up, and levelling work on the site begun.

Only the most minimal checks were made on the American parent company. If they had been more thorough they would have disclosed that it was already close to bankruptcy and that the Liskeard venture was a last desperate effort by Graham to pull his business out of trouble. Within two months of the contractors moving on to the site, work had to be abandoned because neither Bessell nor the Americans could meet the bills. The vacant site was called 'Bessell's memorial' by local Liberals. Bessell himself calculated that the eventual debts would approach £250,000, and within a short time the American company went bankrupt, owing some £4 million. It was a complete disaster for Bessell who, as a twenty-per-cent stockholder in the British company, was a target for irate creditors.

Bessell says that he repaid, voluntarily, between £30,000 and £40,000 over the next few years, covering debts for which he had no legal liability, because he felt he was morally responsible. The creditors remember it slightly differently, one in particular recalling long arguments between solicitors before Bessell's legal debt was established. Even that turned out to be unenforceable when Bessell finally left for America.

Bessell told later of the despair he felt at the collapse of the scheme:

Everybody had done things on my word, and I was very concerned that it would really do me great harm in business ... at that time I was about to leave the House, and I didn't want to go back into business with that kind of mess, but the fact was that I saw no way out of it. I saw my political life at an end, my personal life was in a mess, and my business, which I hoped to pick up and bring back to the standards of the early 1960s was in a state of total disaster. I had had enough. I was physically and mentally exhausted, and I was quite ready to kill myself.

Even in the contemplation of death, however, Bessell was able to perceive the chance of turning a fast buck. He had taken out a life insurance policy, but insurance companies are notoriously reluctant to pay out on suicides. He decided therefore to kill himself by staging a car crash. This would not only save his wife and children the agony of having a suicide in the family, it would yield them considerable insurance benefits.

He decided that he would carry out his plan in America where he was due to go in early January 1971 for business talks in the wake of the Plastic Carton debacle. It occurred to him that Florida would be as good a place as any in which to stage his own violent death – he had always wanted to end his life in the sun, and Florida seemed to him a pleasant place in which to die.

In New York he met up with David Holmes, his Liberal colleague, who was in the United States on holiday, and the two men had lunch together at the Algonquin Hotel. The conversation they held, and their subsequent movements, were to be the subject of some dispute at Thorpe's trial, since the prosecution were to contend that they revolved around the Norman Scott problem and were concerned with ways of relieving Thorpe's obsessive concern with it. But whatever the true nature of their discussions, Bessell's morbid plans seem to have begun dissolving.

His morale was further restored by a meeting in New York with the Liberals' benefactor, Jack Hayward, to whom he poured out his troubles. Hayward reacted sympathetically. 'Peter was desperate,' he recalls. 'He was facing his creditors. He was thinking of taking his own life. He had a wife and two children, and a girlfriend in New York. I felt sorry for him.'

The girlfriend was Diane Kelly, a young divorcee, whose father, Fred Miller, a businessman, was to play an important role in the rehabilitation of Peter Bessell, and on this occasion offered him a loan which would help set him up in business again.

Jack Hayward's sympathy took the form of a guarantee for a £10,000 overdraft at Bessell's bank in Plymouth, and a further £25,000 loan. Armed with both these generous offers, Bessell not only forgot his plans for suicide, but felt sufficiently encouraged to open a new company, registered in New York – Peter Bessell Inc. – which would be involved in some remarkable deals before its final demise.

Since confessions seemed to be the order of the day, Bessell confided in Hayward that Thorpe too had his problems, though they were of rather a different nature. There was a young man whom Thorpe had known in his youth who was now threatening to make public claims which would endanger his career. It would help if he could be got out of England for a time and Bessell wondered whether there might be a job for him in the Bahamas – perhaps at a riding stable where he could use his skill with horses. Hayward genially replied that he would do anything to help, and even telephoned Leonard Ross in London to offer his services. But he regretted that riding stables were not a feature of life in the Bahamas.

By the time Bessell next saw Scott in London, he was in a better position to be magnanimous. He suggested that Scott might like a holiday in the Bahamas while he waited for the divorce action to come up. Alternatively, Hayward would probably be able to find him a job out there (this in spite of Hayward's doubts on the subject). Or, if neither of these ideas appealed to him, they might arrange a world cruise, with himself, Thorpe and Hayward all chipping in. Scott, far from being overwhelmed by these offers, was highly dubious about the whole idea. He did, however, agree to consider the offers while continuing to contest his wife's divorce action.

So far Thorpe's name had been kept off any legal documents, despite Scott's efforts to include it. Scott had sent

124

Ross a long statement about the Thorpe connection to go with his application for legal aid, but Ross had edited it down, 'omitting those matters which I do not consider to be relevant to an application for legal aid.' Scott wrote back angrily accusing Ross of suppressing evidence; he threatened to write to the Law Society complaining about his conduct. Ross replied calmly that he was certainly entitled to do so, but that 'if you continue to disregard my advice, it inevitably throws a doubt upon whether or not I can continue to act for you.' He insisted that any mention of Thorpe was irrelevant to the application. 'How can your relationship with J.T. affect that issue?' he asked.

But the chances of Scott accepting Ross's legal advice were now slender, and by June Ross had ceased to act for him, forwarding the file to yet another firm of solicitors. He also sent Scott a bill, for £77.55p, which was not to be paid for a very long time. Not until Ross had reminded first Scott, then Bessell, did he eventually receive settlement of the account, two years later. On 27 April 1973 the bill was paid with a cheque – signed by Jeremy Thorpe.

The divorce itself – in September 1972 – was, in the end, uncontested by Scott. At the access hearing he was granted a maximum of four hours visiting every year, in the presence of the other parent; there was no mention of Thorpe.

In the meantime, however, Scott had been pondering Bessell's offers to help him get away from it all. He had quickly rejected any idea of going to America or the Bahamas, but he had spotted something rather nearer home. A small cottage called Mill House in the village of Talybont in Caernarvonshire, North Wales, had been advertised in *The Times* at a rent of £12 a week. At the same time the owner of Scott's London flat wanted to buy the tenancy and was offering £1000. Bessell encouraged Scott to go, and told him to keep in touch with Ross who would advance him funds to pay the rent. In order to cover this he sent Ross a cheque for £25, of which Scott received £15 immediately and £10 a few weeks later. On 5 February 1971 Scott left for Talybont together with two friends, and an Afghan hound called Apple, two whippets named Emma and Kate, and a cat.

The villagers were generous in their welcome to this exotic invasion, and Scott was quickly befriended by the local garage proprietor, Keith Rose, and his wife. For a time he settled down well, but soon the isolation from events in London, and his inability to control the build-up to his divorce action, became too much for him. He attempted suicide by taking an overdose of sleeping tablets and walking out on to the mountain behind the village. It was not a successful bid, and he was found and taken in by the Roses. Soon he was telling them the full story of his troubles. What he related seemed shocking to them, suggesting as it did that powerful interests were being protected while an innocent man suffered.

Their suspicions deepened when Peter Bessell made his next intervention. Scott had telephoned him in London to complain about the rent money which had run out, and had been invited to visit him so that they could discuss matters. Bessell explained that Thorpe was going through a very difficult period and was in need of compassion and understanding, while he himself was extremely short of money. Scott replied that he too was in need of compassion, but more immediately needed money. He had begun thinking of how he could start a new life in North Wales, which he liked. He might perhaps begin schooling some horses again. Bessell asked him if that would be expensive, and Scott said he thought the initial cost might amount to several hundred pounds including rent and transport for the horses. Bessell replied that they could probably manage that, and even more. He pressed some money into Scott's hand to cover his return ticket and told him not to worry.

Scott returned to Talybont in a state of some excitement, and told the Roses of his new prospects. The days went by but he heard nothing more. Finally he called London from Keith Rose's garage premises and, in the presence of Rose and his mechanic, talked to Bessell. Rose listened in as Bessell reassured Scott he had not been forgotten. In fact he had managed to scrape together as much as 'five' to cover everything. Rose got the impression that this meant £5000. Bessell intended it to be £500, though the ambiguity was probably deliberate. Scott simply wanted it to be paid immediately to cover living expenses, and extracted a promise that Bessell's secretary would send some money right away.

A few days later, however, the deal – whether £500 or £5000 – was off. In a letter dated 7 April, Bessell announced abruptly that he had been unable to raise the money and was leaving for a business trip in the United States. He advised Scott to keep in touch with Leonard Ross. The withdrawal of the offer infuriated Scott, and led directly to a dramatic escalation of the whole affair.

On 4 May, Keith Rose wrote to Thorpe at the House of Commons telling him of Bessell's action and concluding: 'Mr Scott's financial situation is now critical. He is not without friends who are willing to help him, but obviously the situation must be resolved. It must surely be in your interest to resolve it.'

The reply was short and succinct. The return letter, signed by Tom Dale, Thorpe's personal assistant, read:

As far as [Mr Thorpe] is aware, he does not know Mr Norman Scott. However, he believes that Mr Van de Brecht de Vater knew a Mr Norman Josiffe who may be the same person. Mr Thorpe asks me to say that he is under no obligation to this gentleman.

This was certainly a very literal response to Sir Frank Soskice's advice to 'tell him to go to hell', but it had the effect of leaving Scott in a mood of despair and anger – a dangerous combination.

The double rejection – thoughtless on Bessell's part, deliberate on Thorpe's – was now to subject the affair for the first time to the scrutiny of a wider public.

9. 'Dear Reggie . . .

In May 1971 the let on the Mill House in Talybont ran out, and Scott was forced to live in a caravan. By now some of the villagers who had befriended him were beginning to doubt his stories and to give this desperate and obsessed young man a wider berth. He had, however, made another friend, a widow called Gwen Parry-Jones, formerly the sub-postmistress of the village. She offered Scott accommodation and became a sympathetic audience to his story. More than this, she became convinced that his depression was a direct consequence of his troubled relationship with Jeremy Thorpe.

She therefore decided to take matters into her own hands by writing to Emlyn Hooson, the Liberal MP who represented a neighbouring Welsh constituency, Montgomeryshire, and whose father she knew. Her letter did not name Thorpe, but it urged Hooson to look into the affairs of a Liberal colleague who, she claimed had ruined the life of a young man, and, in concealing the affair, had damaged the Liberal Party itself. She hoped that Hooson would bring his influence to bear to see that justice was done and the young man rescued from his predicament. On 19 May Hooson replied asking her to meet him and tell him more about her allegations. An appointment was arranged for the following week at the House of Commons.

Hooson was a lawyer and a Welshman, soft-spoken but extremely firm. His views about homosexuality were fairly reactionary, and he certainly did not want to see homosexual allegations being bandied about within the party; but his first instinct on receiving Mrs Parry-Jones's letter was the lawyer's: to test the evidence. He had gained the impression

3

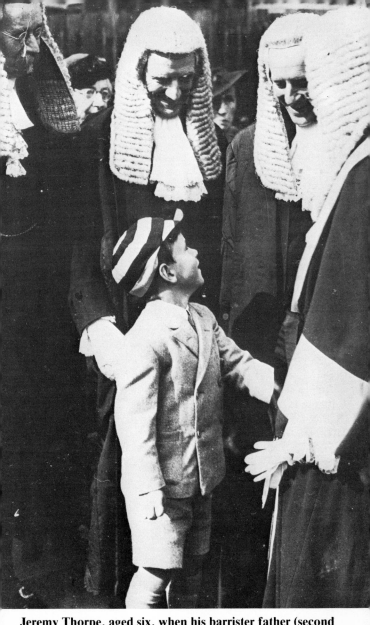
Jeremy Thorpe, aged six, when his barrister father (second from right) became a King's Counsel in 1935.

Jeremy Thorpe at Oxford in 1951 as president of the Union.
Back row, left to right: H.E. Shuman (secretary),
M. Summerskill, I. Yates (treasurer), O. Kerensky, J. Lucas,
W. Rees-Mogg (ex-librarian), M. Barrington-Ward,
G.N.L. Dalzell-Payne (librarian), Hon. D. Wedgwood-

Benn, H.H. Dubber (steward). Front row: Robin Day (ex-president), the Rev. Canon Claude Jenkins (senior librarian), Dingle Foot (ex-president), Jeremy Thorpe, Michael Stewart MP (ex-president), Asa Briggs (senior treasurer), Uwe Kitzinger (ex-president), Godfrey Smith (ex-president).

Thorpe's first marriage (above) in June 1968 to Caroline Allpass. The best man, on left of the picture, is David Holmes. Right: Thorpe cradles his son, Rupert, after the christening ceremony in the Palace of Westminster, July 1969. Rupert's mother died in a car crash the following year.

Thorpe married again in 1973. His second wife, Marion, was originally a concert pianist. She is pictured (above) at the London home of her first husband, Lord Harewood, and (left) with Thorpe and his son after their marriage.

Jeremy Thorpe with his mother, Mrs Ursula Thorpe, at a luncheon in his honour held at the National Liberal Club after he had been elected Liberal MP for North Devon in 1959. Thorpe (insert left) flourishing telegrams of congratulation at a press conference after his election as Liberal Party leader in 1967.

Peter Bessell, Thorpe's closest political friend and confidant through the 1960s, on the stump in his West Country constituency. Thorpe holds the umbrella. -

that the MP involved was Peter Bessell himself, and this did not particularly surprise him. He had not held a very high opinion of Bessell ever since the days of the leadership contest back in 1967 when Bessell had pretended to back him while continuing to campaign for Thorpe. He regarded him as 'an odd fish'.

Hooson showed Mrs Parry-Jones's letter to the Liberal chief whip, David Steel, and told him about the interview he had arranged with her. On the day in question Hooson was called away to an urgent legal conference, and when Mrs Parry-Jones, accompanied by Scott, arrived at the House on 26 May, they were met by his secretary who apologised on his behalf and asked them if they would mind seeing Mr Steel instead. She said that Mr Hooson had really wanted them to see the party's leader, Mr Jeremy Thorpe, but unfortunately he was abroad. Scott said that they would be perfectly happy to talk to Mr Steel, and he murmured that the matter did in fact touch on Mr Thorpe so perhaps it was just as well that he was absent. The interview took place in the Liberal chief whip's room. Steel was immediately impressed by Mrs Parry-Jones whom he took to be an honest and straightforward person, but he was sceptical about Scott; he diagnosed him as a man who had either just gone through a nervous breakdown or was on the brink of having one.

The bombshell came when Scott revealed that the MP involved was not Bessell but the leader of the Liberal Party, Jeremy Thorpe himself. Steel had always been a Thorpe man; he had supported him in the leadership election and had generally approved of his policies. He had heard vague rumours about his private life over the years but had dismissed them as insubstantial and irrelevant, the sort of thing often heard and ignored about fellow-MPs. But as he studied the letters which Scott had brought with him, including those which detailed Bessell's payments, he grew increasingly uncertain. Scott's story seemed to have substance, and if it were true, the implications were horrendous.

As he offered whisky to his two guests, he concluded, half to himself: 'Jeremy will have to go!'

Steel brought the bad news to Hooson next day. Ashenfaced, as Hooson recalls it, Steel told him that the MP involved was not Bessell but Thorpe. They decided that they must interrogate Scott more closely, and an interview was arranged for the following afternoon, 27 May. This time Scott was alone, since Mrs Parry-Jones, having made the introduction, had gone back to Wales.

The second interview took the form of a cross-examination, with Steel and Hooson challenging Scott on crucial points in the narrative while Hooson's secretary took notes. Scott seems to have stood up well, though on one point, at least, he over-dramatised. He felt it was important to establish early on that the police had already taken a statement from him, but he exaggerated the circumstances. He said that he had arrived at the House of Commons armed with a gun, intending to shoot Thorpe, and had been arrested in the central lobby. He even mis-dated events by two years, saying that they had happened in 1964 or '65. The incident, as he had described it, certainly added colour to his account, but it was easy to disprove and was an invaluable weapon in Thorpe's defence later when it was shown to be inaccurate.

Another difficulty in Hooson's mind was the strength of the documentary evidence. The letters which Scott produced and Hooson photocopied gave ample evidence of Bessell's involvement in paying Scott and helping him in his various contacts with officialdom, but there was only one actual mention of Thorpe's name, and that was at best ambiguous: in one of Bessell's many letters to Scott, a single paragraph read, 'I have spoken to Jeremy Thorpe and put him in the picture regarding the present position.' That proved nothing. Scott insisted there were other letters, personal letters written to him in affectionate terms by Thorpe himself, but these had been taken from him by the police when he made his statement. Scott was maddeningly vague about this, changing the date several times, and saying the police station had been 'somewhere in Chelsea', possibly Cale Street. Hooson asked him the name of the detective who had interviewed him, and Scott said he thought it had been Smith. 'That's an easy enough name to make up,' replied Hooson. Scott said that there were other letters which would help his story, but he had left them with a Major and Mrs Shute who lived in Gloucestershire. Hooson suggested that if he wanted to give his case any substance, he should get hold of them.

At the end of a long session, Hooson remained unconvinced. 'I formed the strong impression', he told reporters later, 'that Norman Scott had a definite fixation about Jeremy Thorpe, somewhat in the manner of a jilted girl. I remember saying to Scott: "Supposing Thorpe did treat you badly: what right have you to be maintained by him?"' The reply took them back full circle to the insurance card which, Scott claimed, had been withheld by Thorpe.

Steel, too, was uncertain, and deeply worried. He realised that without further evidence Scott could simply be dismissed as a 'nut-case'. The trouble was, he could see for himself that although Scott was highly strung, he certainly was not mad. While it was impossible therefore to dismiss his story out of hand, raising as it did such serious questions about the behaviour of their leader, it might prove just as difficult to investigate the allegations: both MPs, by merely pursuing the evidence, might be accused of disloyalty. Hooson in particular, no friend of Thorpe's and a former contender for his job, would be regarded automatically as prejudiced in any inquiry.

Nevertheless, both men felt that the matter must be followed up. They asked Scott to stay in London for the time being.

It was the Whitsun recess, when MPs are normally absent from Westminster, and Thorpe was not expected back from a trip to Zambia until the following week. He had been helping the firm of Indeco Morrison, a general trading company of which he was an alternate director, in negotiations with the Zambian government, and at the same time renewing his acquaintance with Kenneth Kaunda, Zambia's President. Hooson, therefore, began to make his own discreet inquiries. He soon discovered that rumours about Thorpe's earlier homosexuality were not entirely unfamiliar amongst a small circle of Liberals, though there was little firm information about it. He managed, however, through Scotland Yard, to trace 'Inspector Smith', formerly of Chelsea police station (which was actually in Lucan Place, just *off* Cale Street). Edward Smith was by now a detective chief inspector at Southwark. He confirmed to Hooson that Scott had made a statement back in 1962 and that the police had taken some letters from him, but he added that Scott's claim to have taken a gun into the House of Commons was inaccurate. No weapon had been involved.

Hooson said that he would get back to him. His next step was to telephone Bessell who was in Cornwall, having just returned from another trip to America. For once Bessell was disastrously slow on his feet. He admitted he had been 'deeply involved' in the affair, and had made payments to Scott. Then he added, fatally: 'It was bound to come out sooner or later.'

Hooson's reply brought him up short. 'In that case,' he said, 'Jeremy will have to go. He'll have to resign as leader, and he'll probably have to resign his seat as well. I'll be asking David [Steel] for a meeting of the parliamentary party so we can discuss the whole business.'

In that instant Bessell realised that he had completely misjudged the situation. He had assumed, without thinking, that Hooson would be just as anxious as he was to keep the matter quiet, and he was shocked to learn that he had no such intention. Nevertheless, he remained calm enough to ask whether Hooson was quite happy to sacrifice Thorpe's seat at a time when the Liberals had only six MPs. If Scott's story was true, was the reply, then there was no choice in the matter. Who then would succeed Thorpe as leader? asked Bessell cautiously. That, replied Hooson, was a matter for the party.

As Bessell put the telephone down, he realised that by his response he had put at risk Thorpe's future career. His first instinct was one of relief – perhaps it was as well finally to bring the matter to a head. But Hooson's inflexibility had angered him, and he decided that at the very least he would try and warn Thorpe before anyone else got to him. First he called Thorpe's mother in Surrey and established that her son was due back from Africa the next day. He asked her to make sure that as soon as Thorpe returned he should telephone him; he would be at the flat of Susanna Hoe, his researcher, who was also his girlfriend. Then he booked himself on to the London train.

Next day Thorpe arrived back at Heathrow Airport and went to his flat in Ashley Gardens where he received Bessell's message. He asked both Bessell and Susanna Hoe to come round to agree tactics. The first thing to do was telephone Steel and find out whether his attitude was the same as Hooson's. Bessell decided to deny the substance of his replies to Hooson. The subsequent telephone calls were to be tape-recorded by Miss Hoe, in order to ensure that there was a record of what was said.

Steel proved hard to track down, and Thorpe spoke first to Hooson. He accused him of jumping to conclusions about Scott without giving him a chance to put his side of the story. The tension rose as Hooson began challenging Thorpe on different aspects of the story, but Thorpe managed to control his anger. He admitted that he had met Scott years earlier, but he denied that there had been anything improper in the relationship. He had merely befriended him briefly because he felt sorry for him. Why then, asked Hooson, had Scott been able to describe accurately the interiors of both Thorpe's flat in London, and his mother's house in Surrey? Because he had visited them both, replied Thorpe, and he had then used this knowledge to build a complete fantasy about the extent of the relationship. Did Hooson not realise, he asked, that Scott was an unbalanced character who had actually had treatment in a mental hospital? Anything Bessell had done, he insisted, had been carried out without his knowledge. The conversation ended with Hooson grimly insisting that there would have to be an inquiry.

The conversation left Thorpe in a state of high nervous tension. Exhausted by his long trip, yet with the adrenalin still coursing through his body, he paced up and down the flat talking with fierce intensity of his determination to fight for his future. Bessell, impressed, decided that he too would carry on in Thorpe's support. A meal, which they ate together, restored their confidence.

David Steel had himself been trying to reach Bessell, to confirm what Hooson had told him. But his first conversation was with Thorpe, who repeated his denials. Steel's attitude was a great deal less harsh than Hooson's. He agreed that there would have to be an inquiry, but he thought it was premature to talk of Thorpe's resignation. He arranged to meet Thorpe at the House.

When Steel finally talked to Bessell he was amazed to hear a version of events very different from the one which Hooson had recounted. The only independent witness now seemed to be backing rapidly away from his story, leaving Hooson uncomfortably exposed as a biased prosecutor without supporting evidence.

But if Steel was baffled, Hooson, supported by his conversation with Bessell and his knowledge of the police inquiry, was convinced that Thorpe had not told him everything. When the two men met in Thorpe's room at the House of Commons there was a blazing row, with Thorpe telling him that if he pursued the matter he would see to it that his legal career was ruined. Hooson, for his part, said that Thorpe was either innocent, or a mixture of Oscar Wilde and Horatio Bottomley. Later, Steel, Hooson and Thorpe argued the matter over together. Thorpe, when he had calmed down, was bitter about the fact that Hooson had been in touch with the police. If anybody was going to talk to them it should be he. He intended to ask the Home Secretary and the Commissioner of the Metropolitan Police by what law the police were entitled to give out information of that kind to anyone who asked them. At one stage he even suggested that he was prepared to sue his colleagues if they took it any further.

Steel and Hooson, however, were firm. They pointed out that as leader he was particularly vulnerable to blackmail. An inquiry would clear the air, and, though it should be small and self-contained to prevent any leaks, it must be thorough. In that case, said Thorpe, there must be a senior and responsible Liberal to chair it, and he suggested Lord Byers, leader of the Liberals in the House of Lords. Byers would be in a position to consult the Home Secretary if any further information were needed from the police, and for his part he would draw up a long memorandum setting out everything that he knew about Scott.

Both MPs agreed with this suggestion. Byers, as an elder statesman of the party, was above any suspicion of harbouring ambitions for the leadership, and he was one of the few men with the authority to be able to tell Thorpe what to do if he disagreed with the findings. In this sense Frank Byers was a natural choice. But for a delicate inquiry like this one, in which tact and patience would be necessary to elicit the truth, it might perhaps have been better to select a man whose manner was a little less brusque. Liberals are fond of telling stories about Byers's lack of social finesse, most of which suggest that tact and patience were not the qualities which came most naturally to him.

Byers made it clear that he intended not only to take part in, but to lead the inquiry. Thorpe promised that he would give him all the information he needed; 'I'm going to write you my story,' he told him.

Hooson now went back to Detective Inspector Smith and asked him to come to the House of Lords to answer questions about Scott and to give his views on the weight of the evidence. He also rang Scott's mother – as did Steel – who supported her son's account.

All this time Norman Scott had been waiting in the flat where he was staying with his friends Jack and Stella Levy. Frequent calls from Hooson and Steel had kept him in touch with developments, and he was finally told that the inquiry would be held on the afternoon of 9 June. It was to be a testing day for everyone involved, but for Scott in particular it was to be an ordeal.

The three interrogators, Steel, Hooson and Byers, held a preliminary meeting with Detective Inspector Smith at which it was established what they would want to know. He informed them that he would have to come back with a senior officer. It would be up to him to give them any answers he felt able to provide, after they had seen Scott. There was just a hint in Smith's reply that the process of eliciting those answers would not be a straightforward one.

At two o'clock that afternoon, Norman Scott was ushered into Lord Byers's office in the House of Lords – spacious by Westminster standards, with its conference table and leather-backed chairs – to face the three-man inquiry. Each of those who took part in this extraordinary confrontation remembers it slightly differently, but for all it was a tense and even emotional affair. Scott, inevitably, was overawed by the surroundings and extremely nervous. 'I felt these men were incredibly powerful,' he recalled later. He quickly sensed hostility on the part of Byers and grew increasingly flustered at the tone and direction of his cross-examination.

Hooson, who was more disposed to believe Scott than were the others, began by asking him a few preliminary questions, and then Byers took over. He asked Scott about his early years and his first meeting with Thorpe. When Scott mentioned the treatment he had received from various doctors Byers pressed him for names and hospitals. Scott mentioned the Littlemore Hospital near Oxford which Byers noted down. He then pursued Scott on the matter of his letters. He pointed out that they contained nothing to prove that Scott had had an affair with Thorpe and asked him the whereabouts of the love letters which he had mentioned. Scott was forced to admit that he had not succeeded in retrieving them and Byers suggested that he had invented their existence. Scott snapped back that he was not a liar.

Byers is adamant that he did not set out to browbeat Scott.

As the story took shape, however, he formed the distinct impression that blackmail lay behind it, possibly aimed at Bessell, but spelling ruin for Thorpe as well. At the same time, everything about Scott offended him – his manners, his motives, the aura of self-pity which hung over him; there was something almost malign, he felt, about this man and the threat he represented.

Steel, for his part, was looking at it more dispassionately. He realised that evidence to sustain Scott's allegations was missing. 'We didn't have the extra dimension,' he recalled later. He thought that Byers's approach was too aggressive, but he knew that whatever happened at the inquiry itself, in the end it came down to a question of believing Scott or Thorpe. The outcome of that choice could not be in doubt.

The exchanges between Byers and Scott now became more heated. Scott demanded to know where his insurance cards were, and insisted that Thorpe should be held responsible for them. He told Byers at one point: 'I'm not impressed by the fact that you've got a title. I remember you as plain Frank Byers! I remember seeing you several times at the Reform Club with Jeremy!' That was an exaggeration, but it provoked Byers into expressing what he had been wanting to say for some time, which was that Scott's motive was blackmail.

Scott had had enough. Gathering up his papers, he prepared to leave the room. 'It is I who have been morally blackmailed,' he announced. 'I kept quiet because of my loyalty to Jeremy over the years. I did nothing. I have no insurance cards and I have lost everything!'

Byers ushered him out of the building and suggested that his best course of action would be to seek treatment for what was clearly a problem of mental stress. Scott's parting shot – that he intended to take his story to Fleet Street – confirmed Byers's worst impressions about the man.

It had been a highly unsatisfactory inquiry, neither proper courtroom investigation, nor reasonable discussion of a problem. But all three Liberals agreed that there were elements of Scott's story which involved the police. They therefore asked Smith to meet them next morning at the House of Lords. Smith was accompanied by a more senior officer from Scotland Yard, Detective Chief Superintendent John Perkins.

That meeting was scarcely more productive than the last. Perkins made it clear from the outset that he considered the Liberals' inquiry to be an internal political matter in which the police had no direct involvement. He would reply to specific questions but he would not volunteer information. The Liberals, for their part, put questions which were far too general to elicit the crucial facts. They wanted details of the episode which Scott had described involving a threat to shoot Thorpe; Perkins told them it had been only a minor incident and no weapon had been used. They asked whether there was a case to proceed with, and Perkins announced simply: 'There is no case ... there's nothing to worry about.' They questioned Perkins about the statement Scott had given to the police, but he told them that it would be against regulations to produce it. However he could assure them that there had been no prosecution because there was no corroborative evidence. 'The case would have been laughed out of court,' he added.

The police response was guarded and unrevealing, and it left little room for further action. Hooson was to go so far as to say later: 'Clearly we were being misled ... but I fail to understand why.' He felt, with some justification, that if the police had been more forthcoming about Scott's statement, and had told them precisely what his claims against Thorpe had been, they would have been in a far better position to arrive at an informed judgement on the whole affair. As it was, the three Liberal investigators were required to reach a verdict – the consequences of which would be far-reaching and which would be cited on numerous occasions in the future in Thorpe's favour – on the basis of evidence that was unreliable, unsupported and disclaimed by the police.

To understand the police attitude and the way they reacted

to the Liberal inquiry, it is necessary to explain precisely how they had handled the allegations made by Norman Scott against Jeremy Thorpe from the outset. We have traced the progress of the police file on Scott from 19 December 1962, the day he first walked into Chelsea police station to make his statement alleging serious charges against a member of parliament, to its culmination at the Old Bailey trial of Thorpe on 8 May 1979.

There is no evidence that there was a deliberate police cover-up, or a concerted attempt from the outset to protect Thorpe. But there were two key decisions, one on the part of officers investigating the Scott allegations, the other on the part of MI5, which explains why there was no follow-up to accusations of criminal conduct which raised potentially an issue of national security. There was also a notable readiness on the part of a former Commissioner of the Metropolitan Police, Sir John Waldron, and a former Home Secretary, Reginald Maudling, to back up Thorpe's explanation about Scott. (In discussing the security services we have used the familiar terms MI5 and MI6 to describe the two arms of the service, rather than the new titles, DI5 and DI6, by which they are now technically known.)

Scott's 1962 statement was made to two officers, Detective Inspector Robert Huntley and Detective Sergeant Edward Smith. In the course of a long and detailed account of his association with Thorpe, Scott alleged that a criminal act had been committed. The allegation could hardly have been made at a more sensitive time: only two months after John Vassall had been convicted of spying as a result of homosexual blackmail. In the light of this the police inquiries can hardly be described as exhaustive.

Scott's statement was taken down by Smith, and Scott was medically examined by the police doctor. The police took possession of the two letters written to Scott by Thorpe. Scott was then allowed to leave, but was asked to stay in touch. Smith did in fact maintain contact with him for some time, visiting him on several occasions.

Huntley, who took charge of the investigation, had several

lines of inquiry that could have been pursued. Scott had mentioned four locations, in the West Country and in London, where, he alleged, homosexuality had taken place. He had also mentioned the names of various people, including the Colliers, his former psychiatrist Dr Anthony Willems, and Ann Gray, who had recently accused him of stealing her coat, all of whom might be able to throw light on his claims. Finally, there was, of course, Thorpe himself. Huntley decided against contacting any of these people, believing there was insufficient corroboration for Scott's allegations. Huntley and his superiors assessed that Thorpe if questioned would simply deny Scott's story. Instead, he asked the Barnstaple police to carry out a number of checks. In his memorandum to the Devon police, Huntley mentioned the existence of letters to Scott which 'appear to suggest that there is something to his allegation'. At the end of his summary, Huntley commented: 'The association was more than just friendly.'

The Devon police failed to come up with anything positive but managed to trace another man, whom Scott had named as an independent source of corroboration for Thorpe's homosexuality, to the Cambridge area. But this potential witness dismissed Scott's claims as fantasy.

In the meantime Huntley had checked Scott's criminal record file and had turned up the report on the Ann Gray incident, as well as the earlier larceny offences. He traced Detective Constable Raymond Whitmore-Smith, who had interviewed Scott in Thorpe's room at the House of Commons about Ann Gray's coat, and asked him for an assessment of Scott. Whitmore-Smith's report is interesting, because it is the first police confirmation of an association between Thorpe and Scott (or Josiffe as he still then was). It concluded:

During the interview with Josiffe in the presence of Mr Jeremy Thorpe, it was patently obvious that Josiffe was a rather weak personality, apparently labouring under considerable mental strain, and completely domineered by Mr Thorpe who was acting in an advisory capacity to Josiffe. During the period when Josiffe was writing his statement, Mr Thorpe left his office to attend a Division in the House of Commons, and during his absence Josiffe was noticeably relaxed and more talkative. Soon after Mr Thorpe's return the interview terminated, and I left the office.

Although Whitmore-Smith's information confirmed that Scott did actually know Thorpe, his conclusions about his character coincided with those already reached by Huntley who considered Scott to be unreliable and unstable. In the absence of firm evidence to corroborate his story there seemed little point in pursuing it; Chelsea was a busy enough station as it was without having to follow up such wild allegations, and short of confronting Thorpe himself, who would certainly deny the charges, there seemed little more that he could do.

Huntley therefore wrote a report on the incident which recommended that no further action be taken. He attached the two letters from Thorpe and the Whitmore-Smith report, and sent it on for confirmation.

It went first to Huntley's immediate superior at Chelsea, who counter-signed it, then to the officer in charge of the division's criminal investigation department. Because the matter involved an MP it was judged wise to pass it further up. The next stage took the file beyond the station and division level into Scotland Yard itself where it was given a correspondence number, noted in the registry department, and passed on up, through the hands of two more senior officers until, on 29 April 1963, four months after Scott's complaint had been lodged (and in the same month in which the Vassall Tribunal made its report), it landed on the desk of the Assistant Commissioner (Crime), Richard Jackson.

Up to this point the case had been a purely criminal investigation. Any broader issues, such as the vulnerability to blackmail of a young MP, could only have been pursued by Special Branch, that arm of the police force whose role is to work alongside MI5 investigating threats to the security of the state and the murkier area of political crime. Special Branch could have been called in at any stage (it was they, for instance, who handled the main Profumo inquiries, and who passed on their findings to the security services). But there is no evidence that in this case they were consulted at all. Once the file reached assistant commissioner level, however, it entered the province where matters of crime and state security can, if need be, come together.

The Commissioner of the Metropolitan Police has access to security as well as to criminal records and can liaise with MI5, the domestic arm of the security services. The Commissioner at that stage was Sir Joseph Simpson, now dead, and Jackson would almost certainly have shown him the Thorpe file, at which point Simpson would have checked its findings with any corresponding security report. Thus, for the first time, the Bacon report of 1960, which had reported the suspicions about Thorpe's homosexuality, ought to have been matched up with a police inquiry.

Neither, however, was judged sufficiently disturbing to merit further action. The then Home Secretary, Henry Brooke, now Lord Brooke, was not told of either inquiry, though as the police force's political boss he was ultimately responsible. Brooke does not even recall the matter being mentioned informally during the routine twice-weekly meetings which the Commissioner generally has with the Home Secretary of the day. Instead, the Scott file was carefully locked in the assistant commissioner's large old-fashioned iron safe, where it joined some thirty others judged too sensitive to be returned routinely to the registry. The police were thus – in spite of Huntley's circumscribed inquiries – recognising the problems posed by the file's contents. Any police officer making inquiries which affected it would now have to apply to the Assistant Commissioner for permission to study the file, and would presumably be ordered to report back on the progress of any investigation.

The security services also took no action, and this attitude must be open to question. Less than a year later, Lord Denning, reporting on the Profumo affair, criticised them for failure to take action after 'the conduct of Mr Profumo disclosed a character defect which pointed to his being a security risk.' Naturally, Thorpe, being merely a junior MP, did not come into the same category as Profumo who was Secretary of State for War; but as he progressed towards Privy Councillor status there were grounds for a far closer look at the implications of Scott's allegations which might have been investigated by the Special Branch. This was not done.

Both police and security services had now independently decided that action by them was unnecessary. These decisions were to have far-reaching consequences, since they would determine official responses to any questions about Thorpe for years to come.

The next time the matter was raised was early in 1965 when Peter Bessell, acting on Thorpe's behalf, went to see Labour's then Home Secretary, Frank Soskice. Bessell refers to the fact that Soskice had some kind of file in front of him, and he speculated that this was 'the Scott file'. When Soskice concluded that there was 'nothing to worry about', Bessell deduced that the file would henceforth be handled by the Home Office, or might even be destroyed altogether.

The reality was rather different. If Soskice had anything in front of him, it is likely to have been a summary of the police file rather than the file itself; there would have been a digest of the security file, and Soskice would have noted its tentative findings. Faced with these equivocal findings, he saw no reason for pursuing the matter, though his attitude clearly indicated that Thorpe should watch his step and see to it that all connections with Scott were severed. There was no question of the Home Office assuming responsibility for the file, as Bessell, and subsequently Thorpe, imagined they might. It remained at Scotland Yard.

By 1967, when Thorpe became leader of the Liberal Party, and later a member of the Privy Council, the response from the security services seems merely to have been a repeat of their cautious findings. There was certainly no attempt to make further checks on Scott, although, as we have seen, he was by then a growing threat to Thorpe's reputation.

This, then, was the background to the Liberal inquiry of June 1971. Scotland Yard first learnt of the Liberals' interest when Hooson's request for help was passed back by Detective Inspector Smith and filtered upwards. Very soon, however, they were to hear about it in a more forcible manner from an entirely different direction – the top. Thorpe had meant what he said when he demanded to know by what right Smith had given out police information in response to Hooson's inquiries. He had complained to the Home Office, who had passed the complaint to Sir John Waldron, the new Commissioner of the Metropolitan Police. He in turn alerted the Assistant Commissioner and insisted that any help the police afforded to the Liberal inquiry should be closely supervised by a senior officer who should not exacerbate Thorpe's complaint by giving out more than minimal information.

There is, at any given moment, a 'pool' of senior officers at Scotland Yard, ready to help out on any unexpected inquiry. The man on duty at that time was Chief Superintendent John Perkins of the criminal investigation department. It was agreed that there was no question of his showing the Liberals Scott's statement itself, nor the accompanying letters from Thorpe. To do so would, technically, be a breach of the Official Secrets Act; more important, there was no glory for anyone – and, in view of Thorpe's complaint, only trouble in store – if the details of the case were now to be raked up.

Interviewed several years after the event, Perkins was enigmatic about his reasons for holding back. He confirmed that he had read Scott's statement himself, and he was under the impression that it must at some stage have been sent to the Director of Public Prosecutions to consider whether action should be taken (in this he was, however, mistaken). Asked if he had come under pressure from higher up, he simply grinned and said: no, not that he knew of. 'I was called to see the Commissioner,' he said. 'He told me Mr Thorpe had laid a complaint against police with the Home Secretary. He had complained that police would be acting improperly if they divulged information gathered in a police inquiry. I was ordered to attend the meeting with Lord Byers and ensure that he was not given such information. That is what happened.'

He added, however, that the questions he was asked were not probing enough to elicit detailed information in any case. These comments on the affair were the last he was to give – within a few weeks Perkins suffered a heart attack, and died.

Detective Inspector Smith shared Perkins's view that the Liberals had simply failed to ask questions that were sufficiently precise to elicit the information they wanted. They were, in his view, 'totally naive'. In the circumstances, it is difficult to see how they could have been anything else.

Jeremy Thorpe, at this stage, can himself have known little of the police background. His only information – and, as we have seen, it was inaccurate – had come from Peter Bessell following his conversation with Frank Soskice six years earlier. Now, however, in June 1971, he made a direct intervention himself by speaking to the current Home Secretary, Reginald Maudling, whose help was to be invaluable.

Maudling was a genial and likeable *bon viveur*. Once tipped as a future Conservative Prime Minister, he was now, at the age of fifty four, past the peak of his political career, though his intellectual qualities and his acumen as a politician were still widely admired. He was also, however, a man whose public reputation was vulnerable. Less than a year previously, in 1970, the first rumours had begun to appear in print of a massive web of corruption involving a north of England architect called John Poulson who was said to have paid bribes to win local government contracts. Maudling, it emerged, was a business partner of Poulson's. At the same time the affairs of an 'off-shore fund' called the

Real Estate Fund of America were causing far graver concern. Maudling had been the fund's first president and had remained a major shareholder until the fund crashed in December 1970 owing its investors some £4 million. Just one month before Thorpe came to see Maudling, news had come from New York that Jerome Hoffman, the fund's founder and the man who had recruited Maudling as president, had been indicted by a Federal grand jury on thirty two counts of mail fraud over a £400,000 mortgage swindle.

The combination of these two scandals was to lead to Maudling's resignation as Home Secretary and deputy Prime Minister just a year later; he was, therefore, in talking to Thorpe about the threat caused by Scott's allegations, only too conscious of the need to preserve intact the reputation of a man in public life – if he is to survive. More than this, the two men were friends. Both were members of an exclusive political institution, founded by Winston Churchill, called 'The Other Club'.

Thorpe told Maudling about Scott's appearance at the House of Commons and about the story Scott had given to Steel and Hooson. Thorpe explained that he was preparing a statement for Lord Byers which would set out his own account of the Scott affair, and he would like this to be forwarded to Maudling for his information and advice. In the meantime he needed to know whether the police had any further background on Scott. Maudling, who was sympathetic, suggested he should get in touch directly with Sir John Waldron at Scotland Yard.

There are two interpretations of what happened next. One view is that the events of the following few weeks came as close to a 'cover-up' as any subsequent episode. The other is that Thorpe was merely asking the Home Secretary and the Commissioner to provide essential facts so that a fair decision could be reached.

The truth is that Thorpe used both Maudling and Waldron to protect his reputation in front of his own party-members by presenting an incomplete account of his relationship with Scott. By endorsing this account they were helping to give him a clean bill of health. Both Maudling and Waldron were well aware of the assistance they were giving Thorpe, but their rationale was simple: officially, their only concern was whether Thorpe had broken the law. The events concerned were now eight years out of date. There was no suggestion of any new crime so the police were not involved. If, therefore, Thorpe restricted himself to asking questions simply about criminal matters, then they could indeed assure him that there was no cause for concern.

Whether Maudling, who died in 1978, warned Thorpe privately about what he was doing is another matter. As one senior civil servant commented: 'I think you can take it that Mr Maudling, who was an extremely shrewd politician, would have pointed out the risks that Mr Thorpe was taking. But what he said to him in private about the consequences was between the two of them.'

This, at any rate, is how Thorpe enlisted the backing of these two powerful allies: following Maudling's advice to contact Waldron directly, Thorpe telephoned the Commissioner and asked two questions: Had there been a 'gun incident' involving Scott in 1964 or 1965? And did the police have any details of Scott's psychiatric background? Waldron called back to say they had no knowledge of either, though in 1962 Scott had *talked* of wanting to kill Thorpe. Thorpe then forwarded to him part of the statement which he intended to give Lord Byers. It mentioned the gun incident as one of Scott's wilder allegations, then added: ' ... on which occasion he [Scott] alleges, incriminating letters written by me to him were taken from him by the police.' Thorpe asked Waldron to vet the statement so that he could be sure it was accurate.

Waldron was unhappy about the sentence referring to 'incriminating letters'. As his file showed, the letters had been considered inconclusive evidence when they were first taken in 1962, and if they were now to be described as 'incriminating', questions might well be asked about why the police had failed to act on them. He therefore returned this first draft of Thorpe's statement, asking for the sentence to be deleted. Thorpe did so.

By 13 July Thorpe was confident enough about his statement to send the following letter to Maudling:

Dear Reggie,

I am very grateful to you for your interest and help in the case of Scott. As far as Byers, Steel and myself are concerned, the matter is closed.

To the intense annoyance of all three of us, Hooson, whose motives are not entirely selfless, is intent to go on rummaging around, seeing if he can't stir up something. He's already suggested that I should have resigned from the leadership and possibly Parliament as well!

Frank [Lord Byers] feels the only way to convince him that he is really muck-raking to no purpose is to set out the facts in a confidential letter from me to Frank, of which he would keep the letter but which Hooson should be shown.

The enclosed is the letter which I propose to send Frank. Before I do so I would want to be certain that it accurately reflects your own recollection of our exchanges and that of Sir John Waldron.

In short, I would like to append to my private letter to Frank, a short note from you, and one from Waldron, or one from you on behalf of both, saying that its contents are a fair summary. No more is required. Needless to say it would remain in Frank's files and be treated as totally confidential.

I am sorry to be a bother. But the first lesson in politics is that no one can be as disloyal as one's own colleagues!

Yours ever,
Jeremy

The letter which he enclosed began by apologising for the trouble Byers had been caused by Josiffe (as he referred to him). Thorpe said he had not set eyes on him for eight years. 'My recollection of him,' he continued, 'which I put to you, Emlyn and David in the Lords, is that he is a "nut" case.' Thorpe went on to say that since Byers had taken charge of the matter, he thought he should tell him in confidence that he had consulted the Home Secretary.

My object was two-fold. First, I was a little surprised to say the least at the ease with which information could be obtained from a police officer by an MP without any verification of the call by the former, about an individual case.

Whilst in this instance we had cause to be grateful for the very helpful co-operation given to us, there is no doubt that even here, information such as this transmitted to anyone who might be prejudiced, indiscreet or unable or unwilling to act judicially, could be very dangerous indeed ... the allegations made were in my view so serious that the police are really the only proper people to investigate these matters.

Indeed, this did not seem to me to be a job which one ought to ask one's colleagues to carry out, nor is it one which it is their job to discharge. Fortunately Scott himself visited the police and made a series of allegations ... the Home Secretary subsequently told me that Scott had visited the police, that frankly they didn't really know why he had gone to see them; that there was nothing which called for action on their part arising out of the whole affair; that there was no evidence on which to prosecute for blackmail, since Scott didn't appear to be making any threats or demand.

Further, I was quite free, with his agreement, to contact the Commissioner, Sir John Waldron, direct, and discuss the matter with him. As a result I rang Sir John and indicated that I was familiar with the background. I asked him whether there was any record of the 1964 or '65 incident when Scott alleged he had been arrested when entering the House armed with a gun with intent to murder me.

Sir John telephoned me to say that there was no record of the gun incident at the time and that one might safely conclude that it had never happened.

The letter ended:

As far as I am concerned, apart from the possibility of periodic and neurotic eruptions, this tiresome matter is closed. I know this is your view. I conclude that both our other colleagues think likewise.

The letter was misleading. Anyone reading it would conclude that the so-called 'gun incident' was the main focus of the allegations concerning Thorpe and Scott, and once that had been dismissed there was no further cause for concern. But the real circumstances in which Scott had originally given his statement back in 1962 are never mentioned. Even the date is omitted, and by stating that the police said they 'didn't really know' why Scott had been to see them in the first place, Thorpe is investing the incident with a vagueness which is at odds with what really happened. Scott had, after all, been questioned by police who had been called to his hotel after hearing that he had been making threats against Thorpe; he had been taken to the local station; and he had made a full and detailed statement. All this information would have been extremely helpful to the Liberal inquiry team. All of it was not available to them.

This, then, was 'the whole story' which Thorpe had promised to Byers, and this was the version which was passed on to Maudling himself for his official response. At that point Maudling held Thorpe's political future in his hands, knowing as he did the full contents of the police file. The reply he sent to Thorpe and which finally buried the Liberal inquiry, can be seen in retrospect as a masterpiece of ambiguity:

Dear Jeremy,

Thank you for showing me your letter to Frank Byers. I have shown it to the Commissioner. Neither of us see any reason to disagree.

R.M.

The reply was hardly surprising in the light of the earlier police response and the assurances already elicited personally by Thorpe. But the readiness of Waldron (now dead) to limit himself to answering only questions framed by Thorpe; for Byers to accept those answers as relayed by Thorpe; and for Maudling to accept Thorpe's evidence, all suggest a remarkable willingness to help.

Byers, already hostile to Scott, was further convinced that he was a liar when a colleague whom he had asked to check up on Scott's medical treatment with the Littlemore Hospital found no trace of either Scott or Josiffe (the explanation may be that Scott was in fact a patient at the Ashurst Clinic, part of the Littlemore Hospital group, but not the main centre). Byers also spoke to Maudling and received an assurance that there was no police interest in Scott's allegations.

Thorpe felt that he had been fully vindicated, although he told Hooson that he would resign if a scandal ever blew up.

As for Hooson, he was left with the uncomfortable feeling that nothing had been finally settled. He confided in one other MP, Richard Wainwright, at that stage chairman of the party, and told him about the inquiry some two weeks after it had ended. He was convinced that they had not heard the end of the matter, and he was right.

One other person, of course, was more than unhappy. Norman Scott, who had left the House of Lords in despair after the June inquiry, telephoned his mother and told her about the reception he had had. As he talked to her he became convinced that the only way to help his case was to secure the letters which Thorpe had written to him.

151

He also wrote a long and despairing letter to Gwen Parry-Jones whom he told about the inquiry. Byers, he wrote, had called him 'a common blackmailer', and all of them, he felt, were 'as bad as Jeremy'.

'I see the meths drinkers in Hyde Park,' he continued, 'and see how slender the thread is between their life and mine. Suicide seems the only way. . . .'

He was aware that the letters he really needed were those in the hands of the police, so he telephoned the Yard and asked where he could find Inspector Smith. Like Hooson before him, Scott traced Smith to Southwark and made an appointment to see him. At 3 pm on 10 June – immediately following the Liberal inquiry – Scott found himself being interviewed by the same two men, Smith and Perkins. Perkins said he was very doubtful about the prospects of Scott retrieving the Thorpe letters, but extremely interested to be able to examine those which Scott had received from Bessell and to question Scott himself (whom he still suspected as a possible blackmailer). Scott went over, yet again, the details of his story. It was not, however, an unguided monologue. Examining his thirteen-page statement, it is possible to deduce that Smith and Perkins were deliberately probing for evidence of blackmail. They could find nothing, however, to substantiate the charge. Scott's statement was merely passed on to Scotland Yard where it was attached to the existing file.

That file was by now beginning to be uncomfortably bulky.

Hooson felt one final obligation, and that was to Mrs Parry-Jones who had originally raised the whole matter with him. He wrote and explained that it was hard to establish a legal case against 'Mr T' without additional evidence. 'That there would be a moral obligation if the story is correct is undoubted,' he wrote. 'However, it is vitally important for me and my colleagues to clear away any suspicion of blackmail, and this we are proceeding to do.'

Mrs Parry-Jones was satisfied that Hooson had done what he could, and her reply reveals that she, too, like other friends of Scott who had lived at close quarters with his obsession, had begun to have her doubts about him. On 16 June she wrote:

Dear Mr Hooson,

Thank you so much for your letter received this morning. I too was sorry that I did not meet you in the House of Commons, but your secretary was charming, also Mr David Steel was most cooperative.

You have by now had time to study the case of Mr Norman Scott. However charming he was, you realise it was necessary for me to bring his case to your attention. I fully realised that it was serious; none of this might have got to light if I had not reported it to you, but for the party's sake I thought you should be informed.

If he has been threatened with suspicion of blackmail that is in itself punishment enough for him. From my opinion, with all the trouble of his divorce etc. the added worry of a blackmail case against him would only make matters worse for him – he needs medical attention, so that he will get out of his fantasy world and that each of us must have a purpose in life and a purpose to work.

The village at first accepted him, but later they all became suspicious and avoided him; as I do a lot of voluntary welfare work I felt it was my duty to try in my small way to provide him with a meal and sit and listen to his troubles. At all times he was a perfect gentleman towards me and I saw no sinister motives, only in his mind about his guilty past, and it was a constant battle to him to try and prove that he wanted a more normal way of life – therefore no one can help him except himself to grow up and be a man.

Don't if at all possible bring a case against him – he will not trouble you again.

Thank you so much, sorry to have added more work to your already busy life.

Yours sincerely,
L.G. Parry-Jones (Mrs)

153

Nine months later, Mrs Parry-Jones was dead. She had a 'high level' of alcohol in her blood. Scott would claim that she had been driven to suicide by what he called the corruption of Westminster politics, which she had witnessed at first hand. Her letter, an obituary to a generous and sensible woman, lends no support to that theory.

10. Mr 280 per Cent

The atmosphere in Gordon Winter's Belgravia flat was faintly oppressive – what had begun as an interview was rapidly turning into an interrogation. Lean, blonde and fit, Winter seemed at times more like a policeman than a journalist, and as he fired off one question after another, Norman Scott's anxiety communicated itself to his pet whippet, Emma, who trembled in sympathy as she crouched at his feet. Finally Winter broke the tension by offering Scott a cup of tea and thoughtfully providing a saucer of milk for the dog.

The interview was Scott's first direct contact with the press. In the aftermath of his rough treatment at the hands of the Liberal inquiry team, Scott had poured out his story to friends visiting the flat of Jack and Stella Levy with whom he had been staying. It had been passed back to a reporter on the *Daily Mirror* who had in turn arranged for Winter, a freelance journalist working mainly for South African newspapers, to see Scott in person. For two weeks Winter had taken Scott through his account, and in the course of this marathon and often emotional session, had pressed Scott to explain what lay behind the venomous tirades he repeatedly launched against Jeremy Thorpe.

'I was deeply in love with Jeremy,' said Scott tearfully. 'I thought our idyllic relationship would last forever. But he discarded me .... That's why I loathe him now.'

Scott's story, as was so often the case when he felt he had to justify himself, was sometimes fanciful and exaggerated. His allegations took in not only Thorpe, but also what Winter describes as 'top British VIPs and members of foreign royal families'. But it was the character and background of

155

his interviewer, Gordon Winter, which were later to encourage the even wilder speculation that sinister foreign forces were at work in the Scott affair.

In the late 1950s Winter, a British citizen, emigrated from London to South Africa and joined the reporting staff of the *Johannesburg Sunday Express*, covering a beat which included crime, society scandals and the odd political story. In the mid-1960s he found himself in the middle of a nasty scandal. A prosperous Johannesburg mine-owner had been shot and murdered, and the gun used in the killing turned out to belong to Winter. When police arrested Lawrence 'Johnnie' Bradbury, a Londoner who had driven the killers to the scene of the crime, some surprising links between the murder and London gangsters were uncovered. Winter's wife, it transpired, had left him to become the lover of gang-leader Charles Richardson, and served with Richardson on the board of one of Bradbury's companies. The Richardson brothers ran an empire of protection rackets and fraudulent companies in London, enforcing their will with mock 'trials' and 'sentences' of torture. They were also engaged in deadly rivalry with the equally brutal Kray twins. To escape the death penalty Bradbury told all he knew to the British police, and the gangs were broken up. Winter, despite being the chief state witness against Bradbury, was held in detention for two months, and then deported from South Africa in 1966.

Back in London, Winter began filing stories for South African papers, specialising in detailed coverage of the British anti-apartheid movement. He cultivated the acquaintance of Peter Hain, a Young Liberal and an outspoken opponent of the South African regime, and became a familiar figure at anti-apartheid demonstrations in London, enthusiastically photographing the participants.

Winter's collection of photographs came to light when they were used in the private prosecution of Peter Hain who had been charged with conspiring to disrupt South African sporting events in Great Britain. Winter – reluctantly, he

156

said – became a star witness against Hain, but the prosecution failed.

More curious were his direct and indirect contacts with various intelligence services. One outlet for his journalism was Forum World Features which used a number of bona fide journalists but which had been founded in Britain indirectly by the Central Intelligence Agency as a propaganda vehicle. He also became friendly with a man called Lee Tracey, a former MI6 (British Foreign Intelligence) agent who ran a business selling electronic and surveillance equipment, and who would later become a 'postbox' for the Scott dossier.

Winter insists that he encouraged Scott to talk, initially at least, for therapeutic reasons. 'I felt that he desperately needed to pour out his troubles,' he recalled. 'He said to me: "I'm so terribly grateful to you. You'll never know the strain I've been under. Nobody will listen to me, everybody thinks that I am lying or mad. If I hadn't met you I think I would have had a nervous breakdown."'

But Winter the journalist – as opposed to Winter the therapist – was wary about using information from so biased and volatile a source. Scott's story verged on blackmail, and it presented grave libel risks for any newspaper who published it. Nevertheless it was, as Scott told it, a sensational tale, complete with sexual allegations against a leading politician, a cover-up, hush-money, and episodes involving senior serving government ministers. Scott says that Winter told him it could make a best-selling book worth at least £60,000. Regardless of the problems, Winter was resolved to follow it up, but from the start his reasons seem to have been more than purely journalistic.

'I don't care if it's true or not,' one acquaintance recalls him saying. 'It will topple the Liberal Party and help me get back to South Africa.' What seems to have been in Winter's mind was the prospect of publicly embarrassing a party which was considered an enemy of apartheid, and thus getting back into the South African regime's good books. Winter was to claim later that he had been an agent of

South Africa's Bureau of State Security (BOSS) all along. He also claimed that it was on BOSS's instructions that he did not try to break the Scott story immediately, preferring to hold on to it until its impact could do most damage to the Liberal cause.

In late 1971, Winter stalled Scott by saying he had to do more checking, so Scott returned to North Wales. He did not go back to Mrs Parry-Jones's house at Talybont; instead, he moved to a house in a nearby village and established a small pony-trekking business. In March 1972 Mrs Parry-Jones died of alcoholic poisoning. Her body lay undiscovered for two weeks.

Scott gave evidence at her inquest and stunned local reporters and the coroner by describing his visit with Mrs Parry-Jones to the Commons, and by claiming that he had had a homosexual relationship with Jeremy Thorpe. The coroner returned an open verdict and the reporters filed the extraordinary story to Fleet Street. That night senior Liberals, and Thorpe himself, were asked for their comments. The answers were uniform: Scott's claims had been fully investigated and there was no truth in them; Scott was a lying trouble-maker with a long history of mental trouble. The story was spiked.

The sad circumstances surrounding Mrs Parry-Jones's death further estranged Scott from the local community, and he left to take a job with the Woodend Stud at the foot of the South Downs at West Ashling in Sussex. It lasted only a few months until he moved to stay with his old friends Jack and Stella Levy who had bought a house at South Molton – in the very heart of Thorpe's Devon constituency.

One day, on a visit to London, Scott met Gordon Winter again and told him about the inquest. He also gave him the correspondence between the Talybont garage proprietor, Keith Rose, and Thorpe's office, as well as Rose's statement about the telephone call to Bessell. This seemed to give Winter enough evidence to go on.

Thorpe, meanwhile, had been embellishing his reputation

as a doughty opponent of apartheid. On a visit to South Africa in May 1971 he told an academic audience in Cape Town that the policies of the government were pushing the country towards totalitarianism. At Witwatersrand University in Johannesburg he called on students to resist official 'tyranny'. After a visit to the African township of Soweto, Thorpe said he would mount a campaign to force British firms in the Republic to improve the conditions of African workers. On his return to Britain in June, he was quoted in a newspaper describing the Nationalist government in South Africa as 'Nazi'.

Gordon Winter decided to try and sell Scott's story to the *Sunday People*, a paper with a robust reputation for muck-raking. The *People*'s editor, Geoffrey Pennington, was unimpressed. He thought the evidence slender and the story in its present form unpublishable. His view was endorsed by the chairman of the Mirror Group who own the *People*, Sidney Jacobson (now Lord Jacobson). 'It consisted of the incoherent ramblings of a man with a vendetta against Jeremy Thorpe,' said Jacobson. 'I never read it myself, but I was told about it by Pennington, and I agreed with his decision.' Winter tried it out on the *People*'s stablemate, the *Sunday Mirror*, but rather naturally their attitude was the same.

Winter's dossier did, however, find another home – in the files of MI5, who added it to their growing stock of information on Scott. Its route to MI5 was via Winter's friend Lee Tracey, to whom he gave a copy. Tracey 'skipped through it' and saw that it 'apertained to Thorpe and made allegations'. He passed it to his old employers in MI6. 'I didn't have anything to do with where it eventually went to,' explains Tracey, 'but I was told that it had been handed to the internal security people (MI5) and that they had had the information on file for years. I think Gordon thought there was some kind of official cover-up and that by using me as a postbox he would let the service know that he knew the story. He was using every route he could to expose it, and I think his motive was financial. If questions were asked, say in the Commons, newspapers would feel free to buy the story. In my view Gordon Winter was the best agent BOSS ever had in London.'

Ironically, it was the 'South African connection' rather than the Scott affair itself which would later surface most dramatically in parliament. But for the time being, Winter locked Scott's papers away, convinced that an opportunity would occur to use them in the future.

Meanwhile, in South Molton, Scott had begun to drink heavily and to take large quantities of tranquillisers. He slipped into a mood of stupefied quiescence which meant that for a time the danger to Jeremy Thorpe had receded.

On 24 February 1973, Jeremy Thorpe announced his engagement to Marion, Countess of Harewood, at a meeting of constituency workers in Barnstaple. Thorpe, then aged forty three, was three years younger than his bride-to-be. The local Liberals greeted the news with a standing ovation. Thorpe's mother was also delighted. 'They have been so lonely and have been through a lot,' she said. 'I admire her so much in the way she has made her life her own, and her dignity.'

Marion was the former wife of the Earl of Harewood, who is a cousin of the Queen and eighteenth in line of succession to the throne. Her life had had more than its share of unhappiness. She was born Maria Stein, daughter of an Austrian music publisher who fled from Vienna during the war and brought his family to Britain. She became a successful concert pianist and in 1948 was introduced to Lord Harewood, a patron of the arts, by the composer Benjamin Britten. Their marriage was considered controversial by royal standards – as a foreigner, a commoner, and half-Jewish, Marion was not considered an ideal choice for a cousin of the Queen – but her charm, beauty and intelligence quickly won over the doubters. The Harewoods had three sons. Then in 1962, Lord Harewood deserted Marion to live with a thirty-four-year-old Australian model and five years later, in 1967, they were divorced, with Buckingham

160

Palace closely concerned in working out the details. Marion kept a cottage that the couple had bought near Aldeburgh in Suffolk, and an imposing house in Orme Square, Bayswater. She also won custody of her three sons, all of whom were beginning to discard their parents' conventions, being more interested in pop culture and the hippie way of life than in classical music.

Early in 1972 Jeremy Thorpe was invited to dinner at Lady Harewood's London house. He had been asked there by Moura Lympany, also a concert pianist, following a performance of Beethoven's violin concerto at the Festival Hall to which he had escorted her. On the way to Orme Square, Miss Lympany told him that Marion would make an ideal wife for him. Thorpe laughed and dismissed the idea, but in the course of the evening Miss Lympany noticed that he seemed to be paying great attention to his hostess.

'Coffee was brought in, and Marion got up to serve it,' she recalled. 'Jeremy went over and asked if he could help. Uh-huh, I thought.'

The marriage took place on 14 March 1973, in Paddington registry office, attended by Thorpe's three-year-old son, Rupert, Marion's sons, Robert, James and Viscount Lascelles who was one of the witnesses. Other witnesses were Thorpe's mother, Mrs Ursula Thorpe, and his great friend and financial adviser, Robin Salinger. A special guest was the 'matchmaker' Moura Lympany. The couple celebrated Holy Communion afterwards at Westminster Abbey.

In marrying Marion Harewood, Thorpe was choosing a woman of a very different nature to that of his first wife. Where Caroline Thorpe had always displayed to the world – particularly the political world to which she was suddenly exposed – a light-hearted and open disposition, Marion Thorpe was less easy to get to know. She was protective of her private life, and shrank almost visibly from the role of the political wife. When, later, she was to campaign alongside her husband, she had to disguise from local constituents the distaste she felt for the glad-handing and the cheerful back-chat which is an essential part of canvassing.

Nevertheless, Marion Thorpe was to devote herself to helping her husband in his career, and later was to exhibit a tenacity and determination in his defence which was to astonish even her friends.

The wedding was a muted affair by Thorpe's standards but the reception proper, which was to follow that summer, more than made up for it. Undaunted by the criticism which had followed the last one, Thorpe began to plan a glittering party at the Royal Opera House, Covent Garden. It took place in the famous crush bar and was followed by a concert. Once again there were grumbles that the lavishness of the affair was bad for the party's image, but a good time was had by all those who managed to secure an invitation.

Thorpe could rise above criticism of his spending habits with apparent effortlessness. He was, however, to experience much greater difficulty in combatting those who faulted his methods of making money. Despite the sentiment engendered by his second marriage, 1973 was to be the year in which the first serious public doubts about Thorpe's financial acumen were voiced.

They arose initially as a result of Thorpe's position as a non-executive director of London and County Securities. The London and County Group was dominated by a barrister with professed Liberal sympathies called Gerald Caplan, who had taken over a defunct hire purchase company and turned it into a small banking house, and, as a result of an agreement with the United Drapery department store chain which held a bank licence, had gone into the 'secondary' banking business. Caplan's empire extended to property, 'second mortgages', finance, pharmaceuticals and building.

Thorpe found himself under serious attack for the company's operations after a judge had criticised a London and County subsidiary for charging a punitive 280 per cent rate of interest to a defaulting second-mortgage borrower. A Liverpool postman complained that the company charged him nearly £840 in interest on a £700 second mortgage which he had held for four months. At the start of 1973 Thorpe was attacked in parliament for his directorship. Some Labour MPs derisively labelled him 'Mr 280 per cent', and others shouted: 'Watch your pocket!' and 'Give him a second mortgage' when he tried to put questions during a debate. These parliamentary wounds were aggravated by newspaper headlines that constantly referred to 'Thorpe's Bank'.

Throughout his political career Jeremy Thorpe, like many other MPs, had had to boost his salary with outside work. The leader of the Liberal Party received no extra grant for carrying out what is a national rather than a constituency job, and in 1971 Thorpe complained about doing a 'minister's job on a backbench MP's salary'. By then he had supplemented his parliamentary pay with directorships in ten companies, mainly in banking and finance. His choice hardly demonstrated business acumen – three of the companies he was involved in were eventually wound up. On the other hand, the salaries he was paid were usually extremely small.

What Thorpe's directorships up to 1971 do reveal, however, is that even the tiny Liberal Party could yield good business connections. Both Thorpe and Bessell were helped in their business careers by Gerald Whitmarsh, an influential West Country Liberal, chairman of Devon County Council and a local money baron. His principal company had been Western Credit, a money-lending and credit operation which he had co-founded in 1935. Western Credit, based in Plymouth, had a strong Liberal-Methodist slant. After the war, Isaac Foot became a shareholder and, later, chairman, while the Methodist Newspaper Company, as well as the UK Temperance Institute, held shares. Later, Isaac's son Lord Foot became a director. By the 1950s, group profits were averaging £100,000 per annum, and Whitmarsh had built up a network of finance companies. He, Bessell and Thorpe first collaborated in business when they set up Manhattan Equipment and, later, Drinkmaster which, were reasonably successful. Bessell became a director of Whitmarsh's Cornish Developments Ltd, which was later sold to Guinness Morrison International, in whose subsidiary, Indeco Morrison, Thorpe was an alternate director. In the takeover, one of Thorpe's friends from Oxford days, Michael Ogle, became a director.

Thorpe became a director of another of Whitmarsh's finance companies, Capital Securities Ltd, as well as joining the board of Hensher (Furniture Trades) Ltd, in which Whitmarsh's wife held 2700 shares. Another business with a Liberal tie-up was the Liberal Insurance Bureau. It was founded by Mark Willies, an insurance broker and Liberal candidate for North Somerset. The idea was that a percentage of the insurance brokerage fees would go straight into party funds. The Liberal Party nominated a director – Thorpe was the first – but the scheme did not work out. Willies's record did not improve with time: in May 1979 he was convicted in a Chicago court of swindling American clients out of 800,000 dollars by falsely promising to obtain loans, and pocketing the advance commissions. The Liberal insurance scheme was later revived by another of Thorpe's entrepreneurial acquaintances – George de Chabris, whose activities were later to become the subject of a Scotland Yard investigation – but it was never destined to be one of the world's great commercial successes.

Liberal connections also brought Thorpe on to the board of Rediffusion (South West), a TV rental chain, and of Industrial Leasing and Finance. This company was run by a Liberal supporter, John Ellis, while a Liberal peer, Lord Ogmore, was also a director. The company, using funds from the Moscow Narodny Bank, provided capital at fixed rates of interest to clients wishing to purchase industrial equipment. Industrial Leasing was caught by the rapid rise of bank interest rates in the mid-1970s and eventually went into voluntary liquidation.

These business interests were by no means unusual for a member of the House of Commons. Until recently the view has been that the wider the range of MPs' interests, the better: it means that they are in touch with the real world which exists beyond the perimeters of Westminster and can therefore bring an expertise to parliamentary debates which would otherwise be lacking.

But the commercial boom in Britain in the early 1970s revealed another, less attractive aspect of this easy-going relationship between politics and business. Some companies, expanding feverishly as the brakes were taken off the economy, saw the recruitment of an MP to their board of directors as a means of establishing a useful respectability. The more senior the politician, the better it was for the image. It was up to the MP himself to judge whether the enterprise to which he was lending his name was sound or not. But not all of them checked as thoroughly as they ought to have.

Gerald Caplan's London and County Securities was very much in the market for respectability. Once the money supply was eased by Edward Heath's Tory government, London and County went through an explosive period of growth. In one year turnover went from £2 million to £10 million. Yet this fast-growing group was run virtually out of Caplan's own office and had lamentable accounting procedures. Its deposit base was not enough to generate the profits it claimed. However the 'in-store' secondary banking outlets did provide a veneer of respectability, and with minimal inspection from the Bank of England, it enabled Caplan to expand and prosper.

Thorpe became a director as the result of the intercession of his City friend, Robin Salinger, who was to become one of the most significant members of Thorpe's 'inner circle' and a crucial supporter when things began to go badly wrong later on. Salinger was what is known in the City as an 'attaché', deriving most of his living from commissions on business introduced to stockbrokers. His advice to Thorpe did not stop at business. To the fury of Liberal Party officials he would frequently be seen at Thorpe's elbow during party conferences at a time when access to the leader was at a premium. He further enraged them by marrying the secretary to the Liberal peers, thus depriving the organisation of one of its most attractive workers.

It was early in May 1971 that Salinger telephoned Gerald Caplan to invite him and his wife Valerie to dinner at the extravagant Empress Restaurant in Mayfair. In the course of the meal Salinger asked Caplan whether he would like Thorpe to join the board of his company.

'Within ten seconds I said "Yes",' recalls Caplan. 'Then I asked why Thorpe wanted to join us, and he replied that he was Thorpe's best friend and he wanted to help him make some money.' Caplan says Salinger explained that while Thorpe was not short of money he needed to improve his income. As leader of the parliamentary party, he had only his salary of £4500 a year, out of which he had to pay £2000 to run his office with two full-time secretaries and two part-time personal assistants.

Caplan immediately realised the value that Thorpe could be to him. 'At that time we were opening bank branches in department stores and I realised that if Thorpe performed the ceremonies there would be good publicity for him and for us,' he says. Over dinner the terms were worked out. Thorpe would get £5000 a year, a company car and motoring expenses, expenses on company business, 10,000 one-penny shares under a share option scheme and another 2000 paid-up shares at 25 pence.

'In my view Thorpe was making considerable progress at that time,' explains Caplan. 'I thought one day he could become Prime Minister. He was young, he had political clout, and the Liberal Party was starting to go from strength to strength.' The admiration was mutual; Thorpe later said that he thought the success of London and County was due solely to the 'genius and drive' of Caplan.

A week or so after the Empress dinner, Caplan took tea with Thorpe at the Commons, assured him that the board wanted him and that their decision was unanimous. Salinger, for his part, received a 'modest fee' of £10,000. Thorpe plunged enthusiastically into opening bank branches. At one time he said: 'I look forward to the time when London

166

and County Investments will operate a national network, extending their services to the whole country.'

Thorpe was used to provide window-dressing and respectability for a business in which both were essential. By the summer of 1972, Thorpe's shares in London and County were worth a notional £40,000 for the outlay of a few hundred pounds. He, nonetheless, felt free to comment on the probity of other MPs' business interests. On 7 July 1972, he introduced a parliamentary order paper in his name entitled 'Allegations of financial corruption in public life' over John Poulson's construction business which had, among other public officials, involved the Home Secretary, Reginald Maudling, the man who had so recently helped Thorpe out over the Scott affair. It prompted the *Sunday Telegraph*'s City editor, Patrick Hutber, an old Oxford contemporary, to sound a warning to Thorpe.

'London and County is not the National Westminster,' wrote Hutber. 'It is not Lloyds. It is not Barclays. It is not the Midland. It is not Warburgs. It is not Hill Samuel . . . If I were leader of the Liberal Party, conscious, as perhaps Mr Maudling should have been conscious, of the value of my name to a business, these are the calibre of names I should regard as giving me as much dignity as I lent them.'

Hutber's implied criticism of the standing of London and County was justified. Inside the group, albeit unknown to Thorpe, matters were in disarray as money was shuffled around in a bewildering fashion.

When the group's problems began to surface early in 1973, Thorpe pleaded with Caplan to close down the second-mortgage side of the business which was attracting such bad publicity. Caplan initially refused. There were long angry meetings with Caplan, some involving other Liberal MPs trying to lend their weight to Thorpe's argument; but the business stayed in operation. Finally Thorpe issued a statement saying that he had investigated the matter, and was satisfied that only 14 per cent was charged on second mortgages. Relations between him and Caplan deteriorated.

At one point, Caplan says, Thorpe announced: 'If I get one more headline my political career will be at an end.'

By early 1973 London and County was already on the road to collapse. The group was borrowing short and lending long, a classic recipe for disaster. To get business it had to lend on a more speculative basis than other banks, and the property market, imperceptibly at first, started to decline.

An increasingly desperate Gerald Caplan was engaging in all sorts of bizarre practices to prop up his shaky empire. He used money from the company's twenty three banking branches in order to buy shares in his own company and keep the stock market valuation up. Caplan's style of company leadership was described by a co-director as evoking an atmosphere like the medieval court of Edward II – 'the barons persisted in regarding his fault as bad advice, when it was the king that was at fault.' Severe criticism at the London and County annual general meeting led Department of Trade inspectors to start inquiring into the companies' affairs. Then in November 1973 the threat of a Monopolies Commission investigation forced Caplan to back out of a takeover bid for the assets of Inveresk Paper in Scotland. Thorpe and the other directors issued a joint statement saying that London and County had enough capital for the offer. They did not, and with the property market slipping as well, City confidence in London and County ebbed and the share price dropped. There had been an attempt by one disgruntled shareholder to vote Thorpe off the board but Caplan had rejected it. Privately Thorpe had been sent a message by Patrick Hutber, warning him that the companies' affairs were attracting growing concern. Nevertheless, as late as October 1973, Thorpe was still opening bank branches in department stores.

Just over a month later, on the last day of November 1973, the storm started to break. A respected banker from Hill Samuel resigned from the board of London and County and the shares collapsed from 138 pence to 39½ pence. Attempts to keep going with massive overnight loans from the London money market failed and a major rescue operation, involving two big banks, was set up. Thorpe declared that he would stay on the board to ensure that the £15 million invested by 12,500 small depositors was secured. Within a few days a consortium of banks and institutional investors in London and County put up £35 million to secure the small depositors. Thorpe played a leading role in the negotiations, first with Eagle Star Insurance and United Draperies, who held huge investments in the group, and then with Caplan's great rivals, First National City Finance. The rescue could not revive the company, however, and it crashed, ultimately leaving a deficit of £50 million.

There was a domino effect. Large depositors in other 'secondary' or fringe banks started to withdraw their funds just in case. The Bank of England launched a 'lifeboat' to rescue other fringe operators who were perilously close to drowning. Together with the major clearing banks (who had approximately £5000 million invested in property and fringe bank companies) it created a billion-pound fund to be made available to twenty six secondary banking companies. The governor of the Bank of England later explained why. It was not to save stockholders and shareholders, he said, but to secure depositors and 'avoid a widening circle of collapse from the contagion of fear ... had the rapidly escalating crisis of confidence passed into the banking system proper, had a major established bank defaulted, I do not know how we would have stopped the course of collapse.' From the wreck of London and County had arisen the spectre of a banking crash on a par with Wall Street in 1929.

Jeremy Thorpe managed to escape the worst consequences of the collapse. The Department of Trade inspectors who later investigated the group found that he had been unaware of the improper accounting practices within the company. In giving evidence before the DTI inspectors Thorpe said he had been advised by his solicitor Lord Goodman throughout most of the affair. But of Gerald Caplan, the man once hailed as a 'genius' by Thorpe, the inspectors wrote in severe terms, thought they acknowledged the extraordinary persuasive power of the London and County chief. Their report said. 'Before us most of his fascination was gone. There was only left his inherent deviousness, a capacity amounting almost to genius not to give a straight answer to a straight question. He had less regard for the truth and a lower standard of integrity than is reasonably to be demanded of a chairman and managing director of a public company.' Caplan decamped to the French Riviera and then to Los Angeles where he is now fighting attempts to bring him back to England to face £2·4 million theft charges.

Thorpe formally resigned from London and County and all his other directorships on 17 December 1973. He said that he was doing so in order to devote himself fully to the Liberal Party leadership. The Young Liberals, arch critics of the leader in the past, publicly welcomed Thorpe's 'courageous move'.

By the end of the year, with Ted Heath's Conservative administration running into fraught difficulties over its confrontation with the miners on pay policy, it seemed that another General Election might not be long delayed. Thorpe would go into it with hands that looked commercially clean. Yet before the election he was to become involved, albeit unwittingly, in an attempt by Peter Bessell to swindle the Liberal Party's chief benefactor, Jack Hayward, out of half a million dollars.

11. Bay Street Blues

The origins of Peter Bessell's plan to swindle Jack Hayward were innocuous enough. Sometime early in 1973, Thorpe learned that Hayward was not entirely happy with the operation of the Grand Bahama Port Authority Ltd, in which he owned a 25 per cent stake, and was vaguely considering other uses for his fortune.

'Jeremy asked me if I would like to sell out,' recalls Hayward, 'and I said yes. I told him that he would not be able to sell my small share, he would have to sell the lot. He said he might be able to help and I said good luck. I thought it was a sort of favour he was doing me because I had done favours for his party. As I heard it from Jeremy, he then approached Bessell, who he said had the contacts to try and find a buyer.'

The total value of the company, which owned most of Freeport as well as other assets, was estimated at around 100 million dollars. Not everything was for sale, but enough to put a top price of 90 million dollars on the deal. The package included the Freeport utilities – power, water, gas, the harbour and the port – the development company, the shopping centre, the profitable casino as well as approximately 80,000 acres of land on Grand Bahama Island and another 26,000 acres in California. If the top price could be found, brokerage commissions could reach 2.5 million dollars. Bessell's idea was that the commission should be split three ways – 700,000 dollars to himself, 700,000 dollars to another broker whom he would involve in the deal, and the balance to Thorpe. This was a perfectly legitimate aspiration in itself though it was to involve the Liberal leader in a more rough-hewn business world than he had previously experienced.

To understand why this should be so, it is necessary to detail some of the history of the Freeport company which revolved round the man who still held the majority shareholding, the American Wallace Groves.

Groves was a modern Caribbean Croesus. He had originally built his fortune on the American stock exchange, buying and selling companies at colossal speed. He suffered a temporary setback when he was imprisoned for mail order fraud but a deal with the old white Bahamas government of Sir Roland Symonette in 1955 set him back on the road to wealth. Members of Symonette's United Bahamian Party were known as the 'Bay Street Boys' because so many of its ministers had their business offices on Nassau's main commercial thoroughfare, Bay Street (Bay Street had also been a popular pirates' lair centuries before). One of the leading 'Boys' was Sir Stafford Sands, a lawyer and member of the assembly. He went to work for Groves and simultaneously helped draft the Hawksbill Creek Agreement under which Groves bought 211 square miles of virgin land on Grand Bahama Island for less than three dollars an acre.

Groves initially wanted to create an industrial centre for American companies eager to avoid high taxes, and obtain cheap labour and land only 76 miles from Florida. Groves established the Grand Bahama Port Authority Ltd to construct and administer a Freeport in which imports and exports moved duty free. The Authority was virtually the government of a country within a country: it took on state and municipal responsibilities and even had the power to deport people. As it developed, Freeport became a complete company town.

Groves's operation was questioned by a politically explosive report published by the Bahamas Governor in 1967. It was the result of a commission of inquiry into the business and operation of casinos in Freeport and Nassau, conducted by Sir Ranulph Bacon who had retired as Assistant Commissioner at Scotland Yard. The report revealed that Groves's

172

lawyer, Sir Stafford Sands, then Minister of Finance in the United Bahamian Party government, had been paid €200,000 by the Bahamas Development Company, a subsidiary of the Port Authority, to help obtain gambling exemption certificates for casinos. The report noted that he had sold his services as a politician, not as a lawyer.

On top of that, Sands had been paid nearly 2 million dollars in legal and consultancy fees by the Grand Bahama Port Authority. Five of the six members of the Bahamas Executive Council – the Islands' cabinet – were paid off by the casino interests. The Port Authority also paid 10,000 dollars a month to the government party, supported a Nassau newspaper and the Prime Minister and a leading senator. There was also evidence linking some of the men who ran the day-to-day gaming operations with famous Mafia mobsters including Meyer Lansky.

This saga of Caribbean intrigue effectively finished off the electoral chances of the United Bahamian Party and Sands was forced to leave the Islands. Groves, however, prospered. The original agreement for an industrial development was amended to allow private residential building and greater tourism. Apart from the beaches and azure sea, the main tourist attraction was still gambling.

While Groves and his empire seemed capable of surviving the money allegations they were more seriously threatened by the changing political climate of the Bahamas and the rise of black aspirations through the nationalist opposition party, the Progressive Liberal Party. When the PLP, led by Lyndon Pindling, took power in 1967, Groves and his fellow directors, among them Jack Hayward, began to fret about the possibility of nationalisation.

Hayward had bought into the Grand Bahama Port Authority Ltd and its subsidiaries in 1956 and initially had been impressed with Groves's vision, and content to leave him with almost complete executive control. Later, relations soured as Hayward became increasingly dissatisfied with Groves's methods. By the 1970s the only things the two men had in common, it seemed, were their neighbouring mansions on the beach at Lucaya. Even that did not last as Groves took himself off to a private island inhabited solely by himself, his servants and his pilot. Nonetheless, Groves, like Hayward, was interested in the possibility of selling out if a suitable buyer could be found.

Thorpe began serious work on the project during his honeymoon with his second wife, Marion. Over Easter 1973 Mr and Mrs Thorpe flew to the Bahamas where they spent ten days with Jack Hayward at his expense, enjoying a round of barbecues, parties and days on the beaches of Grand Bahama Island. Hayward's partner, Edward St George, then offered them his apartment near the United Nations Plaza in New York where they spent a week. Their time in America, however, was not quite as relaxed as their stay in the Bahamas, for Thorpe was able to combine his honeymoon with some serious and highly confidential negotiations.

In New York, Thorpe linked up with Peter Bessell and the third potential broker, George Lawrence, a financier with whom Bessell was already heavily involved in a property sale in the affluent New York suburb of Bronxville. Lawrence thought he could interest the giant Mobil Oil Corporation in the Freeport deal. On 26 April, they gathered in Washington to explore the idea further.

All three men wanted to find out whether the American government would provide insurance guarantees for any American corporation which bought Freeport so that investment would be protected in the event of nationalisation. They met in the White House executive office with an aide of President Nixon's special assistant for international economic affairs. Although it was a low-level meeting, it did act as useful preparation for Peter Bessell when, three months later in August 1973, he sat down with senior property men of Mobil Oil to start discussing the multi-million-dollar deal.

Bessell at that time appeared to have achieved the prosperity that had eluded him for so long. He had a pleasant apartment and smart office in New York – set up with the help of a loan from Jack Hayward – and seemed to be the epitome of a man who could deliver. The appearance, however, was deceptive; all that had been achieved was a super-inflation of the old facade.

The first of his acquaintance to perceive that this was the case was Bessell's erstwhile great friend and associate in New York, Eliot Steuer. Early in 1973 Bessell had told Steuer that a considerable amount of U.S. dollars – 85 billion – was sloshing around in European banks as a result of dollar-support operations. Bessell said that through a friendship with the merchant bankers Hill Samuel he could get some of these dollars re-invested in the United States at low rates of interest – 4 or 5 per cent.

Steuer readily approached General Electric, Union Carbide, General Foods and Goodrich Tyres to see if they were interested in these long-term cheap funds. Goodrich were interested in borrowing up to 500 million dollars and the tyre corporation chairman was set to fly back from Malaysia to meet Steuer and Bessell. Steuer asked him to wait until Hill Samuel confirmed the loans. At the last moment Bessell telephoned to say that the scheme was a 'disaster'. Bessell said that the man he thought he was dealing with from Hill Samuel was in fact an impersonator. 'Would you believe this,' Steuer recalls Bessell saying, 'the impersonator was calling from an insane asylum.' Bessell denies that his informant was in an asylum: 'I think I said he was fit for an asylum because that is the place for anybody who feeds that kind of information. It was authenticated, no, it wasn't authenticated but it sounded so convincing and he was dropping names so widely that I concluded that it was true. I had no reason to doubt it, I should have taken more care.' The abortive deal ended Steuer and Bessell's business relationship.

Bessell hoped for greater rewards from his collaboration with George Lawrence. The road to the Lawrence family had been suitably bizarre. It started through a friendship that Bessell had struck up with Guy Richards, a New York writer drawn to exploration of the story about the alleged escape of Tsar Nicholas and his family during the Russian Revolution. Bessell appeared to share the writer's enthusiasm for revising history and impressed Richard with his range of contacts. Richards duly became a stockholder in Peter Bessell Inc. and introduced Bessell to George Lawrence's uncle, William, with whom he had been at Yale. The Lawrence family, it transpired, was considering disposing of 6 million dollars of family property in Bronxville; Bessell was naturally eager to offer the services of his brokerage firm. When George Lawrence produced Mobil Oil as a potential buyer for Freeport their intimacy deepened.

Thus, by the spring of 1973 Bessell found himself immersed in three major projects – Freeport, Bronxville and the historical resurrection of the Romanoff dynasty. The first to bite the dust was the Tsar, though the story had a fair run for minimal outlay.

On his return to London, Thorpe had tabled a parliamentary question to the then Foreign Secretary, Sir Alec Douglas Home, asking for information and confirmation about the so-called 'Hardinge' letter. Thorpe had been put up to it by Bessell who had claimed to him and Richards that a secret contact, a 'Mr Miller', had shown him a letter from Lord Hardinge of Penshurst, a permanent under-secretary at the Foreign Office during the reign of King George V, which purported to confirm the escape of the Tsar and his family. To Guy Richards, Bessell had claimed to know Presidents Johnson and Nixon and Secretary of State Kissinger.

It is true that Bessell had been introduced to Kissinger, when he was National Security Adviser, by Nelson Rockefeller. Kissinger had been impressed by Bessell and found his story about a 'secret' State Department file on the Romanoffs convincing enough to ask for inquiries to be made. Kissinger's inquiry drew a blank. Bessell, however, claimed that one of Kissinger's aides had discovered secret documents, code-named 'Chivers', in a White House safe and that these documents included wireless messages from a secret agent chronicling the 1800-mile escape route used by the Russian royal family. An exhaustive investigation into the Hardinge letter by Tom Mangold and Anthony Summers for their book *The File on the Tsar* showed the letter to be a clumsy forgery.

Bessell's story about the Hardinge letter and the secret 'Chivers' documents attracted publicity for him despite the fact that it was, in Dr Kissinger's word, 'crap'.

The substance of the Bronxville deal was also proving sticky. It had started promisingly enough with Bessell setting up an American company, Twentieth Century Securities, for a sale and leaseback deal which would be funded by a 'secret' British investor. But because of currency and investment restrictions by the Bank of England, the deal had not been consummated. The Lawrence family naturally became frustrated at the lack of progress, and to secure his options Bessell issued two post-dated cheques as deposit on the sale. One, on his personal account at the National Westminster Bank, was for £106,834; the other, on a Twentieth Century Securities account with Chase Manhattan, was for 225,000 dollars. When the cheques became due on 29 June 1973 he asked for a further extention and paid 25,000 dollars for it. It was agreed that the money would be lost if he defaulted.

From Bessell's point of view the Bronxville deal went through three stages. After his 'secret' investor had dropped out, Bessell tried to buy the properties himself using the National Westminster Bank for funds. He was keen to do so because he calculated that the value of the property would double within a few years. Bessell says he also talked with Western Credit and Whitmarsh's company, Capital Securities, of which Thorpe was a director, about funds. The third stage, in August 1973, again saw Bessell as broker, advertising the properties in the *Financial Times* and setting up a possible deal with Grosvenor Estates. It was a deal in which he hoped to participate, as well as being the broker.

It still looked possible but Bessell's problem was time, and time was fast running out. The Freeport deal with Mobil had also stalled. There had been a meeting at which the oil corporation's property chiefs had expressed great interest but they wanted, and got, a long, exclusive period to consider the offer. The president of Mobil Oil Estates paid a private visit to Freeport to look over the place but nothing was heard from Mobil for several months. Bessell, on the brink at last of becoming a rich man, had gambled that he could buy enough time to complete the Bronxville deal by depositing the worthless cheques with George Lawrence's company. If either deal came off he would be all right, but as the months passed and nothing happened it became clear to him that he was heading, inexorably, towards a terminal business crisis.

In December 1973, a desperate Bessell arrived in London hoping to speed up the property deal. He was now dealing directly with the chairman of Capital and County Properties and a director of Grosvenor Estates. Gerald Grosvenor, now the Duke of Westminster, and director Jimmy James had visited the Bronxville suburb the previous month and had decided that they could only take 10 per cent of the deal. Capital and County were to take the rest. When Bessell held this meeting with the property men on 14 December he was faced with a serious shortage of cash, and considerable debts. His New York creditors were expecting him to come back from the meeting with the deal completed and a large deposit cheque. He put pressure on James and on Capital's chairman to close the deal, but they would not be rushed.

Bessell had run out of time but bought himself a few more weeks by telling his New York creditors that the deal had been finalised and that the deposit money would reach him by 16 January. That weekend he retreated to Cornwall to plan his next move. He saw an old friend, a psychiatrist, and confided to him that he was going to commit suicide. He was thinking of his old car-crash plan. The psychiatrist, worried by the suicide threat, telephoned Jeremy Thorpe. Thorpe arranged to see Bessell the next day.

Monday 17 December was a tough day for Thorpe. In the morning he resigned from London and County and his remaining five directorships. That evening Peter Bessell arrived on his Orme Square doorstep with apparent good news of the Mobil deal.

This was the starting point of Bessell's plan to prise 500,000 dollars out of Jack Hayward, the amount he needed to pay his debts. Hayward would be told that an advance commission of 700,000 dollars, later reduced to 500,000 dollars, had to be paid to an 'intermediary' in order to ensure that the United States end of the deal went ahead. This would be the legitimate commission that the Bronxville property owner, George Lawrence, expected for introducing Mobil, but only *after* the deal was complete. To pull off this double fraud on Lawrence and Hayward, Bessell needed to exploit Thorpe's authority. Thus, the purpose of his visit to Orme Square was to convince Thorpe that the Mobil deal was on, so long as an advance commission was paid to an American intermediary, and to persuade him to telephone Hayward with this information. Thorpe did so and told Hayward that the advance commission should initially go to Bessell. Hayward at first agreed to the transfer but was already sceptical. He decided to string Bessell along until the situation was clarified.

Thinking that the money was on its way, Bessell spent a frantic day organising its method of payment. He called Hayward's solicitor and told him that the money should go to Chase Manhattan's City branch in London and then hurried down to Chase's Berkeley Square office to discuss the handling of the money. The blow fell when Bessell got back to his office. Hayward, en route for Freeport, had left a message saying that the money was delayed. Bessell finally got through to the Bahamas; Hayward told him that he could not, as a minority shareholder, pay the money, and suggested that Bessell talk to another director in New York. On Christmas Eve Bessell arrived in New York and went to see the other director who promptly turned him down. Bessell still did not give up. He persuaded Thorpe to join him in the Bahamas after Christmas to talk to Hayward and the other directors of the Grand Bahama Port Authority.

179

Thorpe and Bessell arrived in Freeport, on board Hayward's private plane, on New Year's eve.

Soon after their arrival Thorpe and Bessell flew with Hayward and his business associate Edward St George to Wallace Groves's private island. Thorpe said that he had discussed the project with the American Secretary of State Henry Kissinger who had said that he approved of the plan. Bessell pretended that the Mobil deal was going ahead and repeated his claim for the advance commissions to ensure its success.

Groves's acute nose for a rat sniffed trouble in Bessell. He told Bessell: 'Produce the people. You know, we would have thought that they would have made some contact, come and seen the place.' Bessell told Groves that he wanted to put the deal together first, before he brought them down. He stressed that he had to pay the commissions if he wanted any more work done, but Groves and his fellow directors were unmoved. 'What have they done?' Groves asked Bessell. 'You seem to have made all the contacts.'

Bessell said that he did not need the money himself but wanted to be sure that he would receive a commission at the end if the deal went through. Groves told him, 'We'll reward you beyond your wildest dreams,' and then, turning to Thorpe, added grandly: 'Mr Thorpe, the Liberal Party will be the richest party in Great Britain and you can have champagne for breakfast, lunch and dinner for the rest of your life if you pull this off.' For Thorpe, who had so recently sacrificed all his directorships in order to safeguard his political career, Groves's apparent euphoria must have been encouraging – it did not, however, hold out any immediate prospect of relief for Peter Bessell.

Back in Freeport, Edward St George privately told Hayward: 'This is a confidence trick. Peter Bessell is really trying this on, I don't believe there is anything in it.' Hayward agreed, but was convinced that Thorpe himself had been duped. Hayward later explained his feelings: 'Poor old Jeremy, he'd been sucked in. I said to Edward St George, "He's got a lot on his plate, he just hasn't done his homework on this job, he's too involved with constituency affairs. He's the leader of the Liberal Party. He just flew out with Peter Bessell." '

Thorpe had, however, assured Hayward and St George that he had never had any reason to distrust Bessell and would have staked his life on him. It was, in the light of what Thorpe knew about Bessell's earlier business crises, a remarkable testimonial for the leader of the Liberal Party to give.

Bessell returned to New York and set about organising his own disappearance. His debts were over half a million dollars, his companies were bankrupt, and, as he later wrote to Thorpe, he 'deserved to be behind bars'. He wrote a series of other letters and left for the West Coast and Mexico telling his son and daughter that they were to open certain letters and post some others if he failed to return within a week. A week later, Peter Bessell, accompanied by his future wife, Diane Kelly, was hiding in a dusty motel in Encenada, sixty miles south of Tijuana. When his son and daughter opened the letters they discovered the business was finished. His son returned to London to deal with the office there, while his daughter tried to salvage things in New York.

To George Lawrence, with whom he had spent eighteen months negotiating and whom he eventually tried to swindle, Bessell wrote: 'I am sorry to have to tell you all my plans have come to naught ... I will not go into all the details now. It is true to say that I made a terrible error over the Bronxville properties ... At least you had 25,000 dollars and I hope that everyone will keep their heads ... my sincere regrets. I hope and believe it will all turn out well in the end ... sincerely Peter.'

As soon as he got the letter Lawrence presented one of Bessell's cheques, for £106,834, to see if it would bounce. It did.

Bessell had left his power of attorney with his fiancée's father, Fred Miller, a businessman from whom he had also borrowed money. In Bessell's absence Miller and another old friend, Dr Cooper, who had become involved with

Bessell's companies since leaving his medical practice in Cornwall, visited George Lawrence to secure a brokerage fee if the Bronxville sale went through. Lawrence made a deal with them: he would not prosecute Bessell for the dud cheques provided Bessell relinquished his claim for a commission. The Bronxville sale, for 5.25 million dollars, eventually went through in June 1974, too late to be of any assistance to Peter Bessell.

Bessell also wrote to Jeremy Thorpe and Jack Hayward apologising for his actions. The letters were models of Bessell explanations, so riddled with ambiguities that Bessell, when later cross-examined on them at the Old Bailey, had to draw up four categories to guide the unwary reader through: true; false; partly true and partly false; or unable to say whether true or false.

None of this rich material surfaced in the press at the time. Indeed, most of Thorpe's Liberal parliamentary colleagues were unaware of the fact that their leader retained any business association with Peter Bessell. They were, however, curious about the reasons for his temporary absence from the British scene at a time of national crisis. The quadrupling of oil prices after the 1973 Middle East war had caused a U-turn in the Tory government's economic strategy. From printing money as fast as it could, the government slammed on a credit squeeze. Then, when their pay policy was being challenged by the miners, a three-day working week for 1974 was declared. The air was thick with talk of class war. 'Is Britain governable?' was the question that dominated the political debate.

When Thorpe arrived back in London after his six-day trip to the Caribbean with Peter Bessell he found a party row waiting for him. Liberal MP Cyril Smith criticised him for lack of action on the industrial crisis. He wrote an open letter to Thorpe asking, 'When the hell are we going to do something?' Thorpe went on radio to say, 'If Mr Smith had made inquiries he would have found out that I had been away having private and political talks in the Caribbean and America.' He then wheeled out a new Liberal plan for solving the crisis, by a huge productivity bonus for the coal industry.

There was also another, more familiar problem waiting to be dealt with. It involved Norman Scott.

12. A Hypnotic Experience

Norman Scott's life in South Molton had followed a predictable pattern. He was suffering from nervous anxiety and inability to sleep, and his friendship with Jack and Stella Levy was strained. Early in 1973 he became a patient of Dr Ronald Gleadle at the South Molton Health Centre. He told Gleadle about Thorpe and showed him the Bessell 'retainer' letters. Gleadle treated Scott for his nervousness, prescribing large doses of the tranquilliser Librium and the sleeping drug Mogadon. One evening when he was particularly low Scott slashed his wrists with a razor blade and then scored the word 'incurable' down his arm.

Gleadle patched him up but the drama meant that he had to move from the Levys' house. He took a small isolated cottage near Simonsbath on the edge of Exmoor. Life there was grim. He did some work with horses but apart from his social security payments he had no income. Shortly after he moved in, he started a dispute with his landlady over the rent. He fed himself on a subsistence diet of vegetables, mainly swedes.

As a way out of his cycle of despair, Gleadle suggested to Scott that he might benefit from a course of hypnotherapy with the vicar of All Saints Church, North Molton, the Reverend Frederick Pennington. Pennington also used to perform occasional exorcisms, in an upstairs room at the Health Centre. Scott visited him in autumn 1973 and in the course of six tape-recorded sessions told Pennington his life story. Pennington thought it was a story that merited outside attention.

When one day in November 1973 he met Thorpe's Tory opponent in North Devon, Tim Keigwin, and his agent,

Robin Nelder, he told them about the allegations. Pennington did not mention Scott by name but nevertheless Nelder thought the story serious enough to tape record an account of it.

The combined attention of Gleadle and Pennington did induce some sort of calm in Scott, but it was clear that he was not going to stop talking about his obsession or change his character (he would later, when being questioned in court, suggest that Dr Gleadle was trying to poison him by prescribing such large doses of Librium and Mogadon).

Like Pennington, Dr Gleadle also thought Scott's story warranted further investigation. He therefore passed on the essence of it to an old friend, Lord Banks, who had once been president of the Liberal Party. They had been members of the same church when Gleadle had lived in Harrow. Gleadle told Banks that a young patient he was treating, whom he did not name, had claimed to have had a homosexual relationship with Jeremy Thorpe. Gleadle thought the Liberal Party should also know that the young man appeared to have letters to support his claim.

Banks was disturbed by the call and decided to consult another Liberal peer, Lord Wade. He was reassured when Wade told him that something similar had cropped up in 1971 and was found to have nothing in it. Wade, however, told Thorpe who also saw Banks. Thorpe said that he was being pursued by a man and a woman, and had spoken to the Home Secretary, Reginald Maudling, about the man. He showed Banks a copy of the letter from Maudling, and Banks was reassured. He believed Thorpe and gained the impression that there was nothing in the allegations. Thorpe also told him that if Gleadle was still worried he should contact Michael Barnes, Thorpe's solicitor in Barnstaple. Banks telephoned Gleadle and passed on the message.

In January 1974, Scott's isolated and drugged existence on Exmoor, with just his dog and two horses for company, was disturbed by a series of strange incidents. The oddest was when a helicopter landed in a nearby field and two men came to the house. Scott, terrified, locked the door and hid behind it until the men left. Whether the helicopter incident was real or hallucinatory is impossible to say, but Scott was sufficiently agitated to telephone Tim Keigwin and voice fears for his life. Scott asked Keigwin to visit him and take charge of some documents.

Keigwin discussed the matter with his constituency chairman and they concluded that if Scott felt apprehensive they should listen to him, while at the same time making it clear they would not use his allegations for political purposes. Keigwin, of course, knew them in outline because of his meetings with the Reverend Pennington. The next day Keigwin and a Tiverton solicitor, John Palmer, called on Scott. They expected to hear a blackmail story but instead were flabbergasted as Scott talked non-stop for two hours about his alleged relationship with Thorpe. At the end of his monologue he handed a statement to Keigwin and said that copies of it had been lodged with friends in Germany and France.

As a result of their meeting with Scott, Keigwin and Palmer decided that Thorpe, as leader of the Liberal Party, was a potential blackmail and security risk. They decided to send Scott's statement to the Conservative Central Office, and in the third week of January John Palmer took it personally to the Smith Square headquarters and handed it to the deputy chairman of the party, Lord Frazer, and the director of the Conservative Party Organisation, Sir Richard Webster. It was a short meeting: Palmer outlined the gist of the story and left. Frazer and Webster took the manuscript to Lord Carrington, chairman of the party and Minister of Defence. Carrington is emphatic that he did not read the manuscript, nor did he want it used in the approaching election campaign. 'Don't touch it with a barge-pole,' he warned his colleagues. Carrington did, however, inform the Prime Minister, Edward Heath, that allegations had been made against Thorpe, and told him that he had forbidden them to be used. Heath agreed with Carrington and the matter was dropped.

When the 'state of emergency' General Election was announced on 7 February 1974, Jeremy Thorpe was leading a revitalised and optimistic Liberal Party. Starting with Cyril Smith's success in Rochdale, Liberals had captured three by-election seats. In eight by-elections they had polled more votes than either Labour or Tory candidates. The party had achieved similar success at local council level with its theme of 'community politics'. Thorpe had finally brought the Young Liberals back into the party fold and this had restored the party organisation's confidence.

With a sure instinct, Thorpe presented himself as the leader of the centre, and his party as a creative third force in British politics. In the industrial crisis of February 1974 that position struck many as providing a genuine alternative to the class-war politics of Labour and Tory. The opinion polls reflected this shift in allegiances and Thorpe's personal ratings matched those of Heath and Wilson.

Unlike the other two leaders, however, Thorpe had only the slenderest of majorities in his own constituency. He therefore decided to stay in North Devon for the duration of the campaign but overcame this self-imposed restriction by installing a television link between his Barnstaple head-quarters and the National Liberal Club in Whitehall so that he could hold daily press conferences. But concentrating the media's attention on his own constituency also left him vulnerable to Scott's seedy allegations should Scott surface to make them.

Thorpe was well aware of the threat. His earlier conversation with Lord Banks had alerted him to Scott's mood. This was further underlined when Thorpe met the Reverend Pennington while out canvassing. Pennington had outlined Scott's allegations and Thorpe had denied them. Thorpe may also have heard about Keigwin's interview with Scott, for as soon as the campaign started he instructed his solicitor, Michael Barnes, to warn Keigwin that Thorpe 'would issue a writ if you make any mention of Norman Scott during the next three weeks.' Barnes also showed Keigwin a copy of the Maudling letter which had been used to deflate the internal Liberal Party inquiry. Thorpe had earlier threatened Keigwin with a writ because of remarks he made about Thorpe's role in London and County. Throughout the campaign Barnes turned up at Keigwin's meetings, positioning himself prominently in the front row and taking notes of Keigwin's remarks. Keigwin was bemused and a little angry at this attention. The story inevitably 'leaked' and surfaced in a garbled form in the satirical magazine *Private Eye*, just a week before the election. Thorpe's close friend David Holmes was also particularly concerned about the damage Scott could do to Liberal chances, and was to demonstrate it in a strange way.

Holmes was staying in Barnstaple with Michael Barnes when, at the peak of the campaign, the solicitor told him that he had received a telephone call from a local doctor who said he had a patient with papers which might interest Thorpe. Holmes said that he did not want to bother Thorpe with this information and so he went by himself to see Dr Gleadle at the South Molton Health Centre on 27 February, the eve of polling day. Gleadle told Holmes about Scott's pseudo-psychiatric treatment and said that the only way to rid Scott of his obsession was to give him something useful and productive to do. Gleadle said that as Scott was interested in horses he was trying to raise money so that Scott could pursue this activity. Gleadle did not produce Scott's letters but he did describe them to Holmes, saying that only one mentioned Thorpe. 'I thought Dr Gleadle was acting from the best of motives in trying to rehabilitate Scott,' Holmes said later.

That evening Gleadle drove out to Scott's cottage. By Scott's account he was 'woozy' from taking his sleeping pills and was lying in bed when Gleadle arrived. Gleadle woke him and asked for the Bessell file. Scott gave it him and Gleadle went off saying, 'There' ssomeonewaiting, I'll leave a note on the table. The sky's the limit.'

The next morning Scott found a hastily scribbled message on Health Centre notepaper which read:

G.W. — return photostats
     — return tapes
     — writ against publication
     — *People*—no wish writ.

Scott discovered when he saw Gleadle later that day that the four points were the conditions upon which his file of letters had been purchased. The reference to writs meant that Scott must sue both Gordon Winter and the *Sunday People* if either tried to publish his story. Gleadle told Scott to go to Lloyds Bank in South Molton. There Scott found that he had £1500 in a current account and £1000 on deposit.

The money had come from David Holmes who had paid Gleadle £2500 for the letters earlier that day. He had taken the documents back to Michael Barnes's house in Barnstaple and burnt them in the Aga cooker. 'It was', he said later, 'a most expensive bonfire.' Holmes has always maintained that he operated without consulting Jeremy Thorpe. 'I took the view that it was not in Mr Thorpe's political interest to know what had occurred.' He also said that he was acting in the wider interest of the Liberal Party, which seemed on the brink of a major electoral success.

Thorpe completed his campaign in fine style, exciting press comment by wearing a Russian-style white beaverskin hat instead of the familiar brown trilby. He also caught the newspaper picture editors' attention with his trick of leaping over fences. When the returns were declared at Barnstaple's Queen's Hall his personal triumph was secure. He had increased his majority to 11,082. With Marion at his side, and David Holmes hovering in the background, he thanked his supporters. The only sour note was struck by Tim Keigwin who, apparently ungenerous in defeat, intoned: 'The truth will out and our time will come again.'

The next evening Thorpe led his excited supporters in a torchlight procession through the streets of Barnstaple and

Bideford. As he was giving a television interview in Bideford, a young policeman arrived with a message: 'Would Mr Thorpe please ring the duty officer at Ten Downing Street?'

13. 'One More Heave'

The election result was a disappointment to advocates of firm government but it brought Jeremy Thorpe and his party into closer focus than ever before. For almost a week the Liberals were in a position to dictate on the basic question, 'Who rules Britain?'

As no single party could command an overall majority Ted Heath still remained Prime Minister though with the prospect of almost certain defeat in the House of Commons unless he could secure a firm alliance with the Liberals. The Labour Party might insist that – as the party with most seats – it had the country's mandate, but the voting figures could scarcely be read as a clear-cut endorsement of left-wing policies. The combined Tory and Liberal vote of nearly nineteen million easily outnumbered the eleven million plus cast for Labour.

Ted Heath was, therefore, perfectly within his constitutional rights in exploring the possibilities of a 'Lib-Con' pact though such an exercise would inevitably prompt criticism of him as 'a bad loser'. The exploration began on the Saturday after the election when Thorpe accepted an invitation to Number Ten Downing Street to discuss the shape of the new government. Although the Prime Minister had once been the target of one of Thorpe's finely worked barbs – calling him the 'The plum pudding around which no one has yet succeeded in lighting the brandy' – the Liberal leader responded to Heath's invitation with what seemed, to some of his followers, like unseemly alacrity. With a decoy car stationed outside his Devon cottage, Thorpe left by a back door and ran across a field to where his white

Rover was parked. He then raced off to catch the express from Taunton for an afternoon meeting at Number Ten.

Heath offered him an old-fashioned political deal. After emphasising the similarities between their parties' policies on two central issues – the need for a statutory incomes policy and a firm commitment to the European Community – he offered Thorpe a seat in the cabinet and ministerial appointments for other members of his party. In return the Liberals must pledge support for the Conservative administration in the House of Commons.

Thorpe countered by asking for some form of commitment on reform of the electoral system which he had already publicly described as 'outrageously undemocratic'. The proof of this, in Thorpe's view, was the election result itself. His party's six million votes – the highest total in its history – had been rewarded with a meagre fourteen seats. On the basis of a system of proportional representation (PR) such a vote would have secured between 100 and 150 seats. Thorpe made it clear that no deal was possible without some initiative by the government in this area.

After consulting his cabinet, Heath came back with an assurance that he would be prepared to support the setting up of a Speaker's Conference to consider electoral change. This would ensure parliamentary and public debate on the whole question, and the cabinet would be pledged to support any recommendations the conference might make. It was as far as Heath could go, given the fact that many in his own party were solidly against any tampering with the system of constituency voting. Many Tory politicians held that PR was alien to the British tradition. If it was introduced it could land the country in a permanent three-party stalemate, leading to constant horse-trading between groups inside the major parties. Asking the two major parties to introduce PR was, in the opinion of one shrewd Liberal, like asking them to sit in an electric chair and throw the switch on themselves.

Thorpe, meanwhile, was experiencing criticism from within his own party for treating with the enemy even on

192

a limited basis. Although the prospect of office was immensely attractive to some Liberal MPs it was uncongenial to the rank-and-file who had campaigned so vigorously against the Heath administration. Peter Hain, the former chairman of the Young Liberals and a member of the national council, warned of 'mass resignations from the party' in the event of any collusion with the Tories.

And there was criticism from Thorpe's senior parliamentary colleagues, who were not consulted by him over that crucial weekend following the election and were therefore in no position to advise him one way or the other. 'By meeting and talking with the Conservative Prime Minister, the Liberal leader allowed it to appear that he was considering a deal,' wrote Michael Steed, later party chairman. 'He had not consulted his colleagues beforehand, and the Liberal Party was completely unprepared for any concerted consideration of possible arrangements with another party ... The opportunity presented was badly bungled.' Some of these criticisms were put to Thorpe over a Sunday lunch at his Orme Square home attended by Jo Grimond, Lord Byers and David Steel.

Thorpe was persuaded that while there might be grounds for forming a National government, drawing on all the major parties, a straight 'Lib-Con' pact was not on. On 4 March 1974, five days after the General Election, Heath tendered his resignation to the Queen and Harold Wilson was invited to form a new Labour government.

Although it came to nothing, the episode was encouraging to Jeremy Thorpe personally. While it might have caused anxiety among his activists it did his prestige no harm to be publicly considered as capable of holding senior cabinet rank. (The post Heath had in mind for him, it was later disclosed, was that of Foreign Secretary.) It was also a firm indication that the security services did not consider the suggestion of homosexuality in his past as any disqualification for high office – had they done so, Heath could not have even contemplated a deal with the Liberal leader.

Tim Keigwin, Thorpe's Tory opponent in North Devon,

found the whole process disillusioning. His opinion of the Norman Scott material, which he had forwarded to Central Office for the Prime Minister's attention, was that it must give rise to a suspicion that Thorpe could be susceptible to blackmail. Although Heath had not personally read the material he had been informed of its existence. Keigwin was, therefore, shocked by his leader's apparent readiness to elevate Thorpe to cabinet rank. It reinforced his generally low opinion of Heathite Conservatism and he did not contest another election for the Tory party.

Despite the rapid formation of a new Labour administration it was obvious that another General Election could not be long delayed. Wilson would go to the country again as soon as he saw a chance of coming back with an enlarged majority. In this uncertain political climate none of the parties could afford to relax, and it was the Liberals who were to experience the most acute problems of party discipline. The reason for this lay in the nature of the Liberal vote.

Thorpe's real electoral inheritance in February 1974 had been a huge floating vote, composed primarily of people reacting adversely to old allegiances. They knew what they were against but were less united on the question of what they were for.

A series of studies by Hilde Himmelweit, Professor of Social Psychology at the London School of Economics, neatly exemplified the Liberal dilemma. Her work on social attitudes and voting habits showed that there were basically two kinds of Liberal voters in General Elections: the hardcore party faithful and a much larger group of what might be termed 'temporary Liberals'. The LSE studies indicated that Liberal voters at any one General Election are largely different people from Liberal voters at previous and subsequent elections. The mass of temporary Liberals was composed of voters reacting against their former party on specific issues. Yet on most issues they still tended to have more in common with supporters of their old party than with fellow-Liberal voters.

194

Thorpe's ability as a campaigner, with its emphasis on style as much as content, was an important asset when it came to wooing the disaffected from other parties. On the other hand, the LSE studies suggested that the commitment to a specific Liberal ideology was, for most Liberal voters, only skin deep. If the Liberals were to enjoy continuing electoral success, this was clearly a fundamental weakness.

This weakness was compounded by another historic division within the party: while many of its voters came from the disillusioned right, it tended to draw its activists from the disillusioned left. After the February election, the instinct of many activists was to intensify the party struggle in an attempt to create a stronger identification for the once-only Liberals. It was an instinct that brought them into direct conflict with Thorpe and most of the parliamentary party.

Thorpe's reading of the situation was that the Liberals would have to demonstrate a readiness to act as a national party if they were to secure a national following. Within the party organization the two differences in approach crystallized in a bitter argument around the word 'coalition'. Thorpe's line was that Liberals must declare themselves ready to share in a National government of all the main parties as the country's problems – particularly those of inflation and unemployment – were too grave to be dealt with by either Labour or the Tories, acting alone. In doing so Thorpe was effectively staking a claim for Liberal participation in government in the event of another 'hung' election result. He put it most explicitly in a speech in July 1974 when talking about possibilities after the next election: 'Of course, we should prefer to form a Liberal government. But if the electorate decides that this is not to be, we shall not shrink from the possibility of sharing power.'

For the activists, who included many old-fashioned Liberals as well as the vocal left, such talk by a Liberal leader was anathema. In the run-up to the Liberal Assembly meeting in September, the Young Liberals denounced Thorpe as a 'traitor' and accused him of showing 'utter contempt' for the party by airing his views on coalition. The assembly itself, which was held in Brighton, resulted in a qualified victory for Thorpe. Helped by Christopher Mayhew, a former Labour minister and recent Liberal convert, Thorpe persuaded the delegates that the parliamentary option for Liberal participation in a coalition had to be kept open, after proper consultation with the party. The aim was to break what was called 'the stranglehold of the present class-ridden two-party system' and bring about a complete realignment of political forces in Britain. The debate had opened wounds that might better have remained closed in the approach to another General Election.

Thorpe's other main worry in 1974 was money. After the election the financial pressures on Thorpe were both political and personal. The political problem was the need to settle outstanding election expenses and to start assembling funds for the next encounter. The personal problem was posed by his friend David Holmes who, since the ignominious departure of Peter Bessell, had taken upon himself the task of controlling the threat posed by Norman Scott. Holmes, who had already forked out £2500 for Scott's file before the election, told Thorpe that he urgently needed money, without apparently disclosing what it was for.

Thorpe's solution to these financial problems was ingenious. Inevitably, it involved the good offices of the trusting Jack Hayward. Although Hayward had been badly burned by his experiences with Peter Bessell – to the tune of £35,000 in unrepaid loans and guaranteed overdrafts – he still remained well disposed towards the Liberal Party and its leader. Thorpe did not directly acquaint Hayward with Holmes's problem but constructed a dubious formula for securing the money he required.

On 10 April 1974, he wrote a long letter to Hayward outlining matters of mutual interest. He reported a recent 'friendly talk' with Henry Kissinger at the American Embassy in London where they had discussed the Freeport project which Thorpe was trying to revive. In fact Kissinger

196

had been surprised when Thorpe raised a private commercial matter at the end of what was a formal diplomatic conversation. Kissinger made cluckingly sympathetic noises but did nothing about Thorpe's request for help on the business deal. When Thorpe later visited Washington and again raised the Freeport deal with Kissinger, the Secretary of State was somewhat shocked and once more fobbed him off. In his letter Thorpe also made scathing reference to Peter Bessell – 'He is a bastard. I don't think there are any assets. But I will do whatever I can to minimize the damage to you.' But the guts of the letter concerned the delicate problem of election finance. Thorpe wrote:

To go from 2 million [votes] to 6 million was fantastic. But we have now got (a) to concentrate relentlessly on the seats where we are a good 2nd and (b) try to get up to 9-10 million next time. That would then produce a total break-through.

Your extremely generous contribution of £50,000 made it possible for me to have the closed circuit T.V. which enabled me to sew up N. Devon for good whilst doing a national T.V. campaign; paid for the posters; some of the Press advertising and helped raise the number of candidates. Interestingly out of 517 only 21 polled less than 12% and lost their deposits, compared with 28 lost deposits for the Labour Party!!! We raised a lot more thank God.

However, I am now being asked to pay the bills, and would now be ready and grateful for some help.

Delicately I would like to ask for 2 cheques! My reason is this: each candidate is limited to a total sum for his individual campaign. If he exceeds it by 1 penny he can be unseated! In my case I fought a national *and* a local campaign from Barnstaple. There is therefore an overlap on some expenditure which I would prefer not to have to argue about!

Accordingly Nadir Dinshaw, who is Rupert's Godfather, and who is conveniently resident in Jersey has agreed to settle bills which fall into this ambiguous category. Accordingly it would be immensely helpful if you could send me 2 cheques: one for £40,000 for the Liberal Party General Election Fund and £10,000 payable to Nadir Dinshaw. I can then clear up everything *safely*.

Thorpe omitted to tell Hayward precisely what election bills Nadir Dinshaw would be required to settle. Dinshaw was a wealthy Parsee businessman and Liberal supporter whom Thorpe had met and befriended on a bus at Heathrow Airport five years earlier. In fact, Dinshaw had not agreed to settle any bills direct, but simply to transfer any Hayward money to David Holmes. Dinshaw remembered Thorpe calling him shortly after the election to say: 'Jack Hayward wants to give me £10,000 for my election expenses – will you take it and hand it over to David Holmes?' He also remembered some talk of there being 'unfortunate publicity' about an earlier donation by Hayward. Dinshaw agreed to make the transfer provided there was no publicity.

In May, Hayward transferred £40,000 to the Liberal Party General Election fund and made out a cheque for £10,000 to Nadir Dinshaw. The cheque was drawn on the account of Hayward's company, Protocol Trading Corporation (Exuma) Ltd. Dinshaw promptly instructed his own solicitor to credit it to the ledger account of himself and his wife, and sent the equivalent sum on to David Holmes.

Thorpe's thank you letter to Hayward, dated 14 May, dwelt on past achievements and the glowing prospects for the future. He told Hayward:

It is difficult to tell you with any degree of adequacy just how grateful I – and through me the Liberal Party, have reason to be for your munificent and magnificent help during the election.

Naturally the number of seats was a bitter disappointment: 3 more seats for 4 million more votes! But we are now second in 140 seats, and this now *really* gives us a launching pad next time ...

Our target now is 600 candidates and 9 million

votes. . . . You may have seen that we took over the opposition front bench twice last week. I felt rather at home there!

It was great to see you both at Orme Square. My only regret is that we both and in particular you should have been subjected to a dose of Bessellitis. Damn the man.

Thorpe's public predictions of Liberal success were less extravagant than his private claims to Hayward. By the time the next election campaign came around, in September 1974, he had set his party a target of seven million votes. He went after them with extraordinary zest. The initial phase of Thorpe's campaign consisted of a hovercraft tour of the West Country beaches, where the Liberal leader warned holiday-makers of the economic doom to come under either a Labour or Conservative government. It certainly attracted press attention, though one journalist was moved to observe that the flamboyance of the exercise – the hovercraft cost £300 a day to hire – slightly blunted the message of economic disaster.

The hovercraft eventually came a cropper outside Sidmouth in Devon when a wave damaged the craft's rubber skirt; but it caused no more than a temporary interruption of the campaign. A second tour, this time of Conservative-held marginal seats, was undertaken by helicopter and was inevitably dubbed 'Jeremy Thorpe's Flying Circus'. His speeches dovetailed with a national campaign calling on Liberals to achieve a breakthrough under the slogan 'One More Heave'. Thorpe's plan for the country, which he described as a 'social compact', called for statutory control of incomes, a flexible policy on mortgages and a legislated minimum wage. In all, he visited more than a hundred separate constituencies before polling day on 10 October. It was a prodigious physical effort but the rewards were disappointingly slight.

Instead of the great heave forward, the Liberal achievement was a slight lurch back. The party's total vote was cut by almost a million and its representation in the Commons was reduced by one seat. Thorpe's own majority in North Devon was down by over 4000 votes. A slender Labour majority in the Commons put paid to any fancy notions of a government of national unity with Liberal participation, though Labour's total vote was considerably less than that assembled by all the other parties. In the immediate aftermath of the result Thorpe masked his disappointment by hitting out at Britain's 'obscene' electoral system which made such a result possible. But there was no disguising the fact that the Liberals had failed to attain even their most limited objectives. Thorpe's enemies within the party were naturally inclined to blame 'the coalition talk' that had preceded the election. The Young Liberal newspaper, *Liberator*, ungenerously likened Thorpe's election performance to that of 'a rather battered party hack'.

Thorpe, however, was anything but repentant about having broached the idea of coalition. Indeed, it formed part of a secret plan for extending Liberal influence by persuading key Tory financial backers to promote electoral reform. Thorpe outlined the plan in a long letter to Hayward asking for further funds, dated 28 November 1974. Like many other letters in that year, it began with a ritual indictment of Peter Bessell:

My main reason for writing this long overdue letter is to say that I was *horrified* and shocked to hear of the extent to which that bastard Bessell landed you in the cart. I knew of the £10,000 guarantee [for Bessell's overdraft] and hoped perhaps naïvely that it might not be called in, but the rest is too ghastly for words. I personally feel very much responsible since you would not have met him but for *me*. If I was a rich man I would send you a cheque for the whole damn lot, and try to forget an incident where frankly we were both taken for a ride. Would to God I'd never let him touch the Freeport project and I'd started with Kissinger at the very beginning. The whole thing has sickened me and could have undermined our friendship. It is for me a great blessing that it has

200

not. At least that is a head of damage which he has not inflicted!

In view of all this I feel very reluctant to follow up your generous agreement to help. I will set out the facts and if you think 'enough is enough' then God knows I shall understand.

The political position is this. As you know in Feb. we soared from 2 million to 6 million, and last time – albeit on a smaller turn out – held at 5⅓ million. On a P.R. system that would have given us 116 MPs!! The hopeful thing is that we have (except for Ted [Heath], who is going anyway) convinced some Tories (e.g. Du Cann and Whitelaw) that we are here for good, and may accept (a) that the Labour Party will never and has never polled 50% or more of the votes but (b) under the present electoral system 39% of the vote can and has given one Party a majority. Ludicrously Labour polled 29% of the total electorate – had they all turned out. We now have a group of prominent Tory MPs in favour of electoral reform AND of announcing it well before the next election. Eight of us (e.g. Liberals) are going to see those companies who have been the Tory Party's chief backers *financially* and suggest that they pressurize the Tories to come round in favour of electoral reform by the next GE (a) since it would mean that there would never again be a Socialist majority in its own right and (b) it gives Liberals next time a powerful incentive to return a Tory MP where no Liberal is standing or where his chances are remote. Marks and Spencer are the first converts!

Once we get the system changed then we go into coalition, since we'll have over 100 and possibly 150 MPs. We would never be in this position if we hadn't proved and then held our strength. And for that you deserve a major share of the credit: in 1970 you ensured our survival; in Feb 1974 you helped treble our vote. In October we proved that there was a 3 party system linked to a 2 party electoral system. All of this has to be achieved *before* the Tories recover and start to think they can win without us!! I think we can do it . . .

When I rang you I was £40,000 short and you generously said that you would meet half if I raised half, but to come back rather than spoil the ship. In fact the total needed went up to £42,000, but I raised £25,000. So I am still needing to raise £17,000. With that all election bills can be settled.

If with incredible generosity you felt disposed to close the gap I should be immensely grateful. But if as you say you think you've been Bessellised and that that's that well then I shall understand although will be bloody pushed! . . . Damn the swine. . . .

At that time, Thorpe had reasons for being irritated with Bessell that he was in no position to share with Jack Hayward. Earlier that month a group of workmen had made an embarrassing discovery while carrying out renovations at 41 Pall Mall, which had previously been the address of Bessell's London office. In the course of their work the builders came across a hidden cupboard near one of the ceilings. Inside the cupboard they found a black documents-case containing a cache of letters, accounts and photographs. Much of the correspondence bore House of Commons headings. There was also a large manilla envelope containing photographs of nude men. Some of the documents related to Bessell's own financial and emotional affairs but there were others that concerned Jeremy Thorpe, among them the letter from Norman Josiffe to Thorpe's mother.

The workmen decided to get in touch with the *Sunday Mirror*. After studying the contents of the case, they handed it over to two *Sunday Mirror* reporters who referred directly back to their editor, Robert Edwards. Edwards in turn consulted the chairman of the Mirror Group, Lord Jacobson, who was already familiar with the background, having turned down Gordon Winter's story. Jacobson, in consultation with his legal department, decided that since the letters hinted at blackmail, and had come into the hands of the *Mirror* in dubious circumstances they should be returned to Thorpe, who was a personal friend. Edwards agreed and handed back the letters to Thorpe; they did not, he decided, merit further investigation. The newspaper, however, retained photocopies of the whole file in the safe of its legal manager. The workmen subsequently received a 'gratitude gift' of £200 for thinking of the *Sunday Mirror* first, and Thorpe wrote a thank you letter to Lord Jacobson.

Although Edwards and Jacobson did not appear disposed to mount an investigation on the basis of what had been seen, the episode must have been intensely worrying to Thorpe. At the very least it was a reminder that the consequences of his association with Scott and Bessell were capable of causing embarrassment in the most unexpected ways.

Early in the New Year, Thorpe decided to secure further funds for David Holmes. He telephoned Nadir Dinshaw in Jersey and asked if he would be prepared to channel another £10,000 to Holmes. Dinshaw remembers being more uneasy about this second request, but was assured that the transfer would be entirely confidential. Having obtained Dinshaw's acquiescence, Thorpe wrote a long, chatty letter to Jack Hayward, dated 5 March 1975, which went on to raise the form of his promised contribution:

> You generously agreed to help with the G. Election Fund, and as you will remember the full fury of the Bessell affair having become apparent, I felt somewhat guilty asking you – not least because you had been incredibly generous already: more – you have done more than any one man (with the possible immodest exception of myself!!!) to keep the Liberal Party alive, and see it climb to the 5·6 million mark. I have therefore done all I could to keep down GE expenses, but now the bills are coming in. I asked if you could manage £17,000, since this, coupled with other money raised (£25,000 Weinstock, £25,000 Geoffrey Edwards and others) will enable me just to break even. If you were so disposed a cheque could

be made payable to the Liberal Election Funds but ideally since some expenditure could just conceivably be held by my opponents to be attributable to the North Devon campaign – although the fact is it was almost wholly national expenditure – and since I can be *unseated* if I pay bills which result in me exceeding the permitted total, it would be safest if we could repeat the Feb 74 procedure, and make £10,000 payable to Jeune Fullerton and Dinshaw, La Rocquaise, St Brelades Bay, Jersey, Channel Isles, if possible from an external account. Jeune Fullerton are accountants and Dinshaw is Rupert's God-father. They would then settle bills. The balance can quite safely be paid into the U.K. unless it is easier to do the lot direct to the Channel Islands.

On the same day as he wrote this letter, Thorpe was featured in a gushing interview in the *Daily Express* by Jean Rook, the newspaper's top woman writer. Ms Rook found the Liberal leader greatly revived after the battering he had received in the last election and 'looking more than usual like a super-brilliant monkey with astonishing sex appeal'. But her conclusion was cryptic enough: 'I'll never understand why I didn't – and still couldn't – vote for Jeremy Thorpe.'

14. Running Scared

In the spring of 1975 Norman Scott made a desperate attempt to reach Jeremy Thorpe. He drove out to Higher Chuggaton with the resolve, by his own account, to straighten out the issue over his national insurance card and contributions once and for all. He remembers it taking 'tremendous courage' to drive up to the MP's country cottage; Thorpe's five-year-old son Rupert was playing in the garden at the time.

The front door was opened by Marion Thorpe. Although they had not met before, Scott had seen her attending Liberal functions in the Devon area. Scott remembers that Mrs Thorpe did not express any surprise at seeing Scott but to his request for an interview with her husband she said: 'I don't think he'll see you.'

In a bad state of nerves, Scott found he could not get his car into reverse to back down the drive. At one point he engaged the wrong gear and dented the garage doors. He remembers going back and asking Mrs Thorpe if she would reverse the car out for him. She did so to the accompaniment of Scott's profuse apologies. Marion Thorpe just looked sad.

This strange encounter was the culmination of a strange year for Norman Scott. After accepting the £2500 for his Bessell letters file in February 1974 Scott had gone on a spending spree. He bought a red Honda car and suddenly found himself possessed of 'many friends' and drinking partners. His own consumption of alcohol increased dramatically but it only seemed to exaggerate his fearfulness.

Ever since the mysterious helicopter incident on Exmoor in January 1974 he had felt that he was in some kind of personal danger. The helicopter episode may have been fantasy but the genuine fear that it engendered made him come to regret parting with the Bessell file. The thought occurred to him that without any substantiation of an association with Jeremy Thorpe his story might seem wild enough to have him committed to a mental institution.

He consulted a solicitor and asked him to institute an action against Dr Gleadle for the return of his file (at that time he had no way of knowing that it had been destroyed by David Holmes). Although Scott's money was rapidly running low, a wealthy old friend in London promised him financial help for this venture. Another man who helped Scott with support and advice was the South African-born writer, Ronald Duncan, who lived on a farm near Bideford in North Devon.

Scott had got in touch with Duncan after some remarks of his about Jeremy Thorpe had been headlined in the local press. Duncan had addressed a Conservative lunch meeting in North Cornwall and been asked after the meal what he knew about Thorpe. He replied that he knew very little, but understood that Thorpe's principal virtue was skill in mimicry. This was reported under the headline 'Local Poet Attacks Thorpe'. Shortly afterwards Scott started telephoning him.

Initially, Duncan found Scott a sympathetic character and felt sorry for him. Scott was still living alone on Exmoor and appeared to be taking drugs. He claimed that he had been reduced to eating dog-meat because he could not get a job, and insisted that his troubles were rooted in his association with Thorpe and the fact of having no valid national insurance card. Duncan gave him money and encouraged him to visit his farm from time to time for ordinary companionship.

On one occasion Duncan went with his secretary to see Scott in his cottage and was horrified by the spectacle it presented. The cottage, he remembered, was 'like a chemist's shop' with different drugs littered all over the place. Scott was also drinking heavily at the time.

Through Duncan, Scott became acquainted with a Bideford solicitor, Jeremy Ferguson, who agreed to take on his case against Dr Gleadle for return of his file. Scott furnished Ferguson with a twenty-six page statement outlining his complaint and the two bank paying-in books drawn on Lloyds Bank Ltd, South Molton, one containing a deposit of £1500 and the other a deposit of £1000. On 19 December 1974, Ferguson wrote to solicitors representing Dr Gleadle. Five days later he received a reply stating that their client did not have the papers in question and advising him to contact the Barnstaple solicitors, Brewer and Barnes, for confirmation of this fact.

While representing Scott, Ferguson sought counsel's advice from Neil Butterfield QC, who requested an expert opinion on his client's mental state before venturing an opinion of his own. Scott was then being treated by Douglas Flack, a consultant psychiatrist at the Eve Vale Mental Hospital in Exeter, who also ran an out-patients clinic in Bideford. On 17 January 1975, Ferguson reported a meeting with Dr Flack in a letter to Scott. He thought the psychiatrist could prove helpful in practical as well as medical terms. Ferguson wrote: 'I can tell you that he is not only entirely sympathetic to you and very anxious to help you, but he also feels that he is professionally bound to take certain action concerning Dr Gleadle which may result in your having your file returned without the glare of publicity which would now surround a court case and which might be unhelpful to it.' At that stage Dr Flack thought that 'professional pressure' on Dr Gleadle might be the best method for securing the return of Scott's papers.

On 30 January, Ferguson took Scott over to Exeter for another appointment with Dr Flack at his hospital. On this occasion the psychiatrist formally examined Scott for the benefit of the barrister whose opinion on the case was being sought. Scott was pronounced sane but suffering from an anxiety condition. Flack, who was already concerned about some of the security aspects of the case, also asked Scott's permission to forward details of his complaint to the Medical Defence Union in London. He had been assured that it would be passed on from there to the Treasury solicitors, and that was almost a guarantee of its reaching the ears of the security services. Constitutionally, the First Lord of the Treasury was also the Prime Minister. Scott readily assented to this arrangement.

This was not, as it happens, the security services' sole source of information from the West Country about Scott's situation. Quite independently, Ronald Duncan, Scott's writer friend, had also decided to bring aspects of the story to what he described as 'the authorities' in London. In his view, Scott was not motivated by blackmail but by some obscure but powerful need for vengeance on Jeremy Thorpe. Duncan was not concerned about the sexual allegations but he was alarmed by the evidence of Scott's bank statements. It seemed possible that the money had been paid to protect Thorpe's reputation which made him appear a potential security risk.

It was also at about this time that Detective Chief Superintendent Proven Sharpe, the head of CID for Devon and Cornwall, was drawn into security discussions about the case. Although reticent about the details of his involvement, Sharpe remembers the police being tipped off by 'a public spirited person in North Devon' sometime late in 1974. The man claimed that Scott had written evidence to support his allegations. Many policemen in the West Country knew Scott's story by this stage but the suggestion that he might have written material to back it up was new. According to Sharpe, his informant was most concerned about the security aspect and the potential blackmail threat it raised for Thorpe.

Sharpe took the same view. He had no interest in allegations of homosexuality but he had a duty to concern himself with security questions. He sought advice from the relevant quarter of Whitehall – 'Look, there are people up there whose business is to worry about the security of the state and the vulnerability of men like Thorpe. You'll have to draw your own conclusions.' As a result, he made further inquiries to discover what Scott had. It was not a police investigation, there was no suggestion of criminal activity and nothing was prepared for police files. Sharpe was to do the inquiry himself and report verbally to Whitehall – just as his predecessor, Ranulph Bacon, had done fourteen years before.

Although neither Duncan nor Sharpe can be precise about dates, it seems clear that by the end of January 1975 Norman Scott was the object of very specific interest to the security services. Scott's own personal circumstances, however, became progressively more insecure.

On 4 February, Jeremy Ferguson wrote to Dr Flack about his client: 'I am writing to advise you that Mr Scott tells me that he has been approached by a Foreign Publication and he intends to tell them his story. He seems determined to go through with this course despite the warnings which he has been given and I expect that it will be left to you and me ... to pick up the pieces afterwards.'

The letter was the first indication of a real difference between Scott and his new advisers. Ferguson and Flack felt that Scott's legal and psychological interests were best served by a discreet exploration of his case. Scott, on the other hand, was coming to believe that publicity of almost any kind was in his best interests. The belief was to land him in all kinds of difficulties, but it was not misplaced. Although neither Scott nor his advisers could know it at the time, the first positive steps in a scheme that was to end in a terrifying encounter for Scott had already been taken. In the meantime, Scott was to experience a number of disturbing episodes.

The first of these was his appointment with a representative of a 'Foreign Publication'. Scott had been approached on the telephone by a man called Steiner who said he was a correspondent for the German magazine *Der Spiegel*. He arranged to meet Scott for lunch at 1.30 pm on 4 February at the Imperial Hotel in Barnstaple. Scott arrived at the appointed time, carrying his briefcase with copies of the material he had supplied to his solicitor. He was told by a receptionist that Steiner had called to say he had been delayed on the road but would arrive in time for an early tea. Soon afterwards two men arrived in a car that looked like a Mercedes and sat in the hotel lounge. Although Scott thought that one of them might be Steiner, neither man approached him. One of the men left the room and after a few minutes Scott was called to the phone. He was surprised to find himself talking to Steiner who explained that he had been called urgently to London to do a story on Mrs Margaret Thatcher who had just been elected leader of the Conservative Party. He said they would have to meet at a later date. According to Scott, when he returned to the lounge his briefcase was missing; the two strange men had also disappeared. Scott later learned that *Der Spiegel* did not have a correspondent called Steiner.

Eight days later Scott was beaten up by two assailants after coming out of a public house in Barnstaple. All he remembered noticing of his attackers before he passed out was that they seemed to have London accents and that one of them had called him 'Norman Josiffe', a name he had not used for almost eight years. He was briefly admitted to the casualty department of the North Devon Infirmary where he told his story to a sympathetic social worker.

By now Scott was actually eager to be admitted to a mental hospital, not because he was sick but because he was frightened and wanted sanctuary. Dr Flack was opposed to such an admission, though his reasons were not entirely medical. On 13 February, Scott's psychiatrist wrote to Scott's solicitor: 'I want to avoid admitting him to hospital, because a great deal of group psychotherapy goes on in the wards and there will be no way of preventing him from discussing his problems not only with the nursing staff, but with other patients as well.' Jeremy Ferguson shared Dr Flack's concern about the need to contain Scott's story. On 18 February, Scott's solicitor wrote to Scott's psychiatrist about an encounter with the solicitor to the North Devon area of the county council, 'who was concerned about the approach which had been made to social workers by Mr Scott and about the implications of any further broadcasting of Mr Scott's story.'

Scott's prospects on the legal front did not prove encouraging. The opinion of Neil Butterfield QC as to whether

Scott was entitled to sue for the recovery of the papers held out little hope. On the general outlook, Butterfield commented: 'Every door has been slammed and all the hatches battened down as the establishment, not surprisingly, retreats into close formation to face the threat offered to it.'

The most important door of all slammed when Michael Barnes informed Scott's solicitor that he understood that the papers had all been destroyed.

In March 1975 Scott went 'missing'. He had come to feel that his cottage on Exmoor was much too isolated. He moved about the Barnstaple area sleeping rough on some nights and in the homes of friends. He kept in touch with his solicitor by telephone but kept his movements a secret. On several occasions the mysterious 'Mr Steiner' called a friend of Scott's, who ran a boutique in Barnstaple, with requests for another meeting. The messages were passed on but Scott was too wary to arrange another encounter. It was in this troubled period that Scott tried to get in direct touch with Jeremy Thorpe by driving over to his house at Higher Chuggaton. His other positive move was to write to Gordon Winter in South Africa. Winter had kept photocopies of all Scott's documents and could, if he felt inclined, replenish his file.

Winter responded, in a letter dated 2 April, by inviting Scott to come and visit him in Johannesburg. He wrote in a postscript: 'I'm quite sure that I can break your story from this end. This will make the UK Press very much interested. They will consider you a prize at that time and I'm sure there's some deal you can do with one of them maybe through me if you wish.' Winter, however, was not in a position to return Scott's file immediately as most of the documents were lodged in a safe deposit box in London.

Scott was to claim later, to Jeremy Ferguson among others, that he had actually visited South Africa to arrange publication of his book. He did so partly out of bravado and partly out of a sense that the prospect of publication abroad might assist his cause. In fact, he remained in the Barnstaple area though he did take one trip to London.

Sometime in April he called on the office of Up Against the Law, a radical legal advice group with premises in York Way, behind King's Cross Station. The young woman who interviewed him remembered him as a man literally shaking with fear. On her account it seems that Scott allowed his imagination full rein. He said that he was being pursued by two men with guns, and gave the impression that he carried a weapon himself. The interviewer was fascinated by his story but found it too disjointed to make complete sense at the first hearing. Scott requested advice on his national insurance card and asked how he might secure publicity for his story. The young woman gave him advice on his insurance card and asked him to come back a second time to see if more could be done. He never returned.

In June, Scott falsely claimed that he had lost his social security claims book, and he was issued with another. He cheated the DHSS out of £58.40 by using both books before the ruse was discovered. Scott later claimed that the fraud was deliberately conceived so that he would be charged and then be able to use the privilege of the courtroom to ventilate his grievance. It did not provide any immediate remedy since no charge was made against him until late November.

By early summer his circumstances had marginally improved. Two friends in Barnstaple, Nicky Scoines and his wife Valerie, were able to provide him with more regular lodging in a room over a café they owned in Boutport Street. Scott was also reunited with his papers when Gordon Winter sent photocopies to the address of a friend in London. More than ever, Scott had come to regard his files as the most potent form of protection.

While he was with the Scoines, Scott started receiving mysterious telephone calls. The earliest was from a man with a Cockney accent calling himself Ian Wright who claimed to be the representative of an Italian fashion house. He said the house, which he called 'Pensiero', was eager to acquire Scott's services as a model for a new catalogue of

212

styles. Scott was initially interested but when the man mentioned a possible fee of £400 a week, he was suspicious. It was much too high. He told the Scoines that he thought the caller must be trying to lure him to London.

In August Scott moved to new lodgings over the Market Inn, a public house in the centre of Barnstaple, tucked behind the Pannier Market. Mrs Edna Friendship, the landlady, was a chubby, jolly woman in her sixties who had heard Scott's story and taken pity on him. He was allowed to live rent-free in return for small chores around the pub. The mysterious calls followed him to the new address. The man calling himself Ian Wright persisted with his modelling offer and suggested that they should meet at the Royal Garden Hotel in London. Although Scott needed money he felt too nervous to accept. On one occasion Wright asked Scott to call him back at his London number at a particular time in the evening. It later transpired that the number he had given Scott was that of a call box in Trafalgar Square.

On the evening of 6 September, Scott was arrested while enjoying a night out with Mrs Friendship and her friends at the Chequers night club in Barnstaple. He was taken to Barnstaple police station where two CID officers subjected him to intensive questioning. The reason for his arrest was given as non-payment of a £28 hotel bill which he had run up nine months earlier. Scott found, however, that the officers seemed as much interested in his personal papers as in the details of the alleged offence. Scott remembers one of them saying something like 'You could be locked away for fourteen years.'

Later that night one of the CID men escorted Scott back to his lodgings to pick up his briefcase of documents. Mrs Friendship, who had just returned from the night club, remembers Scott 'shaking and crying' as he was led up to his room. She was given the impression that Scott would be taken to the CID man's home that night. In fact, he spent the night in the female cells at Barnstaple police station. Next day, in a special hearing before a magistrate, he was fined for the hotel bill offence. While he was in custody, one of the CID men told Jeremy Ferguson that his client was talking a lot in public houses and could be in physical danger. Ferguson passed the warning on to Scott, telling him he was in 'very real danger of being badly hurt'. The solicitor also suggested it might be wiser if he left the country for South Africa. Scott wrote to his younger brother in London after the incident: 'Things have been really traumatic. I have just been released from Prison, only because I allowed them to have my briefcase and the book plus copies of the file from "South Africa".' In fact, all Scott's belongings were returned to him on his release.

It is hard to determine the reason for the police tactics in this episode unless it was either to explore the possibility of charging Scott with blackmail or to further Proven Sharpe's security inquiry. It may even have been a combination of both. What does emerge is that the Barnstaple police were openly expressing concern about Scott's safety. Yet Scott was about to enter the most frightening phase of his entire life.

Back at the Market Inn, Scott started receiving a new series of strange telephone calls. One was from a man calling himself Masterson, who said he was a journalist with funds to pay a lot of money for Scott's story. Masterson had a clipped, cultivated voice which sounded reassuring; he also said that Gordon Winter had authorised his approach. After some discussion, Scott agreed to meet Masterson at the Holiday Inn in Bristol later in the week. Subsequently Scott changed his mind after discussing the call with Mrs Friendship, who advised him against keeping the appointment.

On the day after the broken appointment, Masterson angrily rang Scott to complain about his failure to appear. Scott then wrote a letter to Gordon Winter in Johannesburg asking him about Masterson's background and credentials. Winter wrote back: 'I have not authorised any person, particularly not a journalist, to contact you on my behalf.'

Another series of calls came from a man calling himself Peter Keene, whose accent fluctuated uncertainly between Scots and North Country. Mrs Friendship remembered him calling to inquire about a camera that her tenant was offering for sale. She thought this was odd as she was sure that Scott did not possess such a thing.

On the afternoon of Sunday 12 October, Scott was walking through the Pannier Market carrying a bundle of laundry when he was approached by a well-built young man wearing a red rally jacket and dark slacks. He was standing near a yellow Mazda car when he first called out Scott's name and said he wanted a word with him. Scott was instantly nervous but had a vague recollection of the man. He had seen him drinking in the nearby Three Tuns public house about a week earlier; on that occasion the man had been smoking a pipe with a noxious brand of tobacco and Scott had asked him to move downwind.

This time the man introduced himself as Peter Keene. He said that Scott was in great danger and that there was a man coming from Canada to kill him. The man was going to be paid four figures for the job. Keene said he wanted to drive Scott over to Knowstone, a village near South Molton, where someone who wished to protect him was waiting to talk to him. Scott, frightened but intrigued, was reluctant to get into the car. Keene then said: 'At least let me know why I'm being paid to protect you.' Scott said he would show Keene his evidence if he would get in touch with the unknown protector so that they could meet somewhere near.

Scott then took his laundry into the Market Inn, promising to return with his briefcase of documents. Mrs Friendship was working in the bar when he walked in. When told of the encounter she was as suspicious as Scott. She insisted on taking a stroll outside with her dog to look over Mr Keene and take down the number of his car.

A few minutes later Scott re-emerged with his briefcase. Keene said there was no alternative to their driving over to Knowstone if Scott wanted to meet his mystery protector. When Scott resisted this suggestion, Keene became abusive, saying, 'I wish you would fucking well come with me.'

Scott agreed to drink with Keene locally but would not leave the centre of Barnstaple. They then spent most of the

215

afternoon in the lounge of the Imperial Hotel, with Scott going through his documents and Keene taking notes on a sheet of pink paper. Scott remembered Keene saying that he might escape harm himself but 'They'll harm what you love most.' Scott took that to mean his son, Diggory Benjamin. The meeting eventually broke up with Keene promising to get in touch again if the man from Canada arrived, as Keene felt sure he would.

Keene made several further calls to the Market Inn but Scott was too nervous to consent to another meeting. Shortly afterwards Scott moved again to live in a friend's house in Combe Martin near the North Devon coast. The friend was going away for a while and wanted Scott to look after the cats. His departure from the Market Inn was something of a relief to Mrs Friendship. Although she had found Scott 'a model tenant' in most respects, the strain of his acquaintance was beginning to tell. Mrs Friendship's daughter had become concerned about her mother's health because of the panic induced by the weird calls her lodger had been getting. Before moving to Combe Martin, Scott told Mrs Friendship that he would not be on the telephone but in cases of urgency he could be contacted through the Pack of Cards public house.

On the evening of Thursday 23 October, Scott was drinking in the Pack of Cards when he was called to the telephone. The caller was in a coin box and obviously in a hurry. At first he said: 'Hello, this is Andy.' When Scott said he did not know anyone of that name, the caller said quickly: 'It's Peter.' At this point Scott realised it was the man he knew as Peter Keene. He told Scott that the man from Canada had arrived. He said they should meet to discuss what to do as soon as possible.

They finally arranged to meet the next day at 6 pm outside the Delves Hotel in Combe Martin. Scott had recently been given a Great Dane dog, Rinka, as a pet. When he kept the appointment with the man called Peter Keene he took Rinka with him.

216

15. Rinka, R.I.P.

Peter Keene arrived for his appointment with Scott in Combe Martin on the evening of 24 October 1975, armed with a Mauser .25 self-loading pistol. In fact, Keene's real name was Andrew Gino Newton and his real purpose was not to protect Scott from assassination but to try to stop him causing any further trouble. Newton had been hired for that purpose.

The bizarre sequence of events that brought Scott to this edge of danger had begun almost exactly a year earlier in 1974 when David Holmes visited an old friend in South Wales. The friend, John Le Mesurier, was a bluff, glad-handing businessman in his forties who ran a carpet discount firm in Port Talbot. He would consult Holmes on matters of tax and finance.

In Port Talbot they drank together in an establishment called the Carlton Club and it was there that Le Mesurier extended Holmes's circle of acquaintance by introducing to him a slight, red-headed young businessman who had made a lot of money out of distributing fruit machines. George Deakin, still in his mid-thirties, was eager to embellish his local-boy-makes-good image by investing abroad. Le Mesurier thought he would be well advised to discuss the technicalities with his own tax consultant. They made an odd trio, the suave Holmes, the jovial Le Mesurier, and the sharp, watchful Deakin, but the complexities of the exchange control regulations gave them plenty to talk about. They met for drinks a second time and a third.

The drift of their discussions eventually moved to a topic that led to their becoming co-defendants with Jeremy Thorpe at the Old Bailey. They, like Thorpe, were acquitted of conspiracy to murder Norman Scott. Unlike Thorpe, however, they each, in their different ways, were to acknowledge some part in a menacing conspiracy directed against Scott. It is hard to imagine three more strangely assorted conspirators.

George Deakin, 'the king of the one-arm bandits' as he was known in South Wales, came from a much more colourful background than either Holmes or Le Mesurier. He was born in 1940 into a fairground family who toured South Wales for nine months each year, spending the winter in their home town of Brynmawr. Deakin's father and grandmother were 'riding masters' – they owned and operated the big machines such as 'dodgems', 'Noah's ark' and the 'jets'. Deakin left school at fifteen to work for the fair but when he was twenty he saw an opportunity to get in on the slot-machine gambling craze. He bought his first machine on hire purchase, rented it to a working man's club and from the proceeds bought others in the same way. He also converted American machines to take British coins, and by the early 1970s had become the biggest operator of gambling machines in South Wales. His rise in this tough and competitive business brought with it the rewards of the good life. He bought a mock Tudor four-bedroomed house on the outskirts of Port Talbot, acquired a villa in Majorca, and took private flying lessons. He also made a few enemies. He had twice been badly beaten up and his home had been ransacked.

Deakin's career suffered a temporary setback in 1973 when he was convicted of receiving stolen alcohol and lost his gambling licence as a result. He promptly sold his operation and moved into the manufacturing side, building up a new business in Juke boxes, pool tables and pin-ball machines. He later expanded into night clubs in Port Talbot and started a pool hall chain. On paper, at least, his assets made him a millionaire. His main extravagances were clothes and cars. He ran a Mercedes and a 'Rancho' cross-country vehicle, both with personalised number plates.

WAD – the initials of his attractive, blonde wife, Wendy Ann Deakin, a former schoolteacher.

John Le Mesurier was not a successful businessman. A native of Southampton and one of seven brothers, Le Mesurier had served as a regular in the Royal Air Force for six years before going into business as a carpet company representative. A fat, jolly man, he built up a reputation as a good salesman but was ambitious to move into management. In the mid-1960s he moved, with his wife and three children, from the Midlands to Bridgend in South Wales. He started his own carpet business but it did not prosper. The opportunity he hankered after seemed to present itself in 1971 when he became the head of a carpet distribution subsidiary of a large German company. Despite extravagant sales promotion and Le Mesurier's ready conviviality with clients, the venture failed. His last real chance in the carpet business came when he established the Pyle Carpet Discount Centre a few miles from his home at St Brides Major, near Bridgend.

It was through the carpet trade that he had originally struck up an acquaintance with David Holmes. One of Holmes's first business appointments was in a company importing Persian carpets. He later became a director of the Magic Carpet Company and his own company, D.M. Holmes and Associates, had started life as a carpet company before he turned it into a business consultancy. Le Mesurier was inordinately proud of his association with David Holmes and took pleasure in introducing the elegant former deputy treasurer of the Liberal Party to his business acquaintance in South Wales. Holmes's main service to Le Mesurier was to introduce him to a Vernon's pools winner.

As part of his consultancy work Holmes had been asked to advise Terry Gibbs, a South Wales miner, on how to invest his huge £169,000 win. On Holmes's advice Gibbs put a slice of it into Le Mesurier's company. It did not make a great deal of difference; Le Mesurier's carpet centre was to collapse in 1977. But in the last months of 1974 a more hopeful mood prevailed.

George Deakin recalls that it was after their third or

fourth meeting that Le Mesurier casually widened their area of mutual interest by saying that a friend of Holmes had a problem with a blackmailer. The man's activities had already led to a woman committing suicide and the life of a three-year-old child had been threatened. At that time Deakin thought he must be referring to Holmes's wife and child; he did not then know that Holmes was unmarried. When Deakin asked why they didn't go to the police, Holmes had said it was not possible in the situation.

Deakin was asked if he could find somebody who was prepared to frighten the blackmailer off. He said: 'I'll see what I can do.' As the meeting broke up, Deakin remembers Le Mesurier saying that the type of person required would be someone who 'could break arms or legs'.

Holmes subsequently called Deakin on the telephone to discuss some tax and investment matters and obliquely raised the problem of the blackmailer again. Deakin remembers his saying something like: 'Any joy in finding somebody?'

Deakin did not have much to report. Thus far he had only discussed the problem with one other person, a man called David Miller who ran a printing shop, Zeno Editions, in The Parade, Cardiff. The two men had been friends for some years and Miller did printing work for Deakin's firm. Miller had told Deakin that he had a friend who was good for 'a laugh and a giggle' and who would do almost anything for money. He did not, however, mention the friend's name at that stage.

The friend Miller had in mind was Andrew Newton. They had both been students at the Chiswick Polytechnic many years earlier and had kept in touch ever since. They shared an enthusiasm for rugby football and Newton would often come to South Wales to watch the international matches with his friend at Cardiff Arms Park.

At first glance Newton's qualifications as a professional 'heavy' were not impressive. He was twenty eight years old and had never been in serious trouble with the law. His

220

background was intriguing but not of the kind that normally produces hardened criminals.

He was born in Chiswick in October 1946, the son of a Polish-Canadian airman called Niewadomski and his wife, Maria Bernardi, a woman of Italian descent. Three years later Mr Niewadomski moved out to start a new life on his own in Toronto where he ran a laundry and dry-cleaning business. His wife stayed on in Chiswick, changed her name to Newton and kept her son by renting out rooms in the house. Andrew left school at sixteen and worked as a salesman for a while before deciding to further his education at Chiswick Polytechnic.

At the polytechnic, Andrew conceived a desire to become a pilot and went on for further courses at the flying school in Hamble and then to the Kidlington Flying College at Oxford. He obtained a commercial pilot's licence when aged twenty four. His first flying job was with Air London and in 1972 he landed a more remunerative post with British Island Airways, based on Squires Gate Airport in Blackpool. He went to BIA as a second officer and by the end of 1974 had been promoted senior first officer. He was under consideration for promotion to captain.

As flying careers go, Newton's rise had not been meteoric but it had been capable and consistent. With reasonable progress he could expect to achieve a lucrative job with one of the big international airlines by his early thirties. His immediate boss at the BIA regarded him as 'a good pilot' with the potential to go further. Newton's career was certainly not of the kind that someone would normally consider putting at risk by a reckless act of criminality.

Off the tarmac, however, Newton was not a conventional person. In his case an adolescent taste for practical jokes had endured into the late twenties. His reputation as a wag and a bit of a lad was one he valued above all others, though it earned him the nickname 'chicken-brain'. He liked to show off for the benefit of his friends – particularly his girlfriends, who were numerous – and generally enliven the proceedings. It was not always easy to sustain such an image even on a junior pilot officer's pay of almost £6000 a year.

The opportunity to supplement this income came on 26 February 1975, when Newton accompanied his old friend Dave Miller to the Showmen's Dinner at the Savoy Hotel in Blackpool. Among the diners was Miller's other friend, George Deakin.

The Showmen's Dinner, though organised for charity, was one of those events that seem almost calculated to bring out the worst in people. The admission fee was £15 a head and each guest was provided with a bottle of spirits, either whisky or brandy. Among the entertainments was a mock 'auction' of topless women for charitable purposes. At one stage Newton almost got into a fight, when a boyfriend of one of the women took exception to his efforts to place meringues on strategic parts of her anatomy. Newton's favoured tipple that night was brandy straight out of the bottle.

In this heady atmosphere, it is unsurprising that memories of any business transactions that took place should be confused and contradictory. Miller did, however, remember introducing Newton to Deakin with the words: 'This is the bloke I said would do anything for a laugh.' He then plunged off for another round of drinks leaving them both together.

Newton remembers boasting to Deakin about his prowess as a hard man, and sums of money ranging from £5000 to £15,000 being discussed. Deakin's recollection is less specific. He only remembers Newton asking the fee for a 'frightening job' and his own reply as being: 'I don't expect they would want you to do it for nothing.'

After the incident with the topless lady, a legless Newton was driven back to his flat in Romney Road, St Anne's, by Deakin. Once there Newton was comprehensively sick over his bed and left in the care of two patient girlfriends. Deakin went off to join Miller for further revels in Blackpool.

According to Deakin, Newton rang him in Port Talbot a few days later to ask for further details of the 'frightening job'. Deakin remembers being irritated with Newton

222

because he had tried to 'chat up' his wife Wendy in an earlier call when he was not at home. He also remembers referring Newton to David Holmes for further details, and giving him Holmes's telephone number in Manchester.

Newton confirms that it was Deakin who put him in touch with David Holmes though he says it was not in quite the same way as described by the Welshman. After Newton made contact with Holmes, Deakin dropped out of the picture.

Meanwhile, John Le Mesurier was also active in a practical way. He was under the impression that Norman Scott had threatened to kidnap David Holmes's godson, Rupert Thorpe, after being refused more money. He also thought that the death of Thorpe's first wife, Caroline, was in some way a consequence of Scott's activities. Le Mesurier was to say later that he was responsible for convincing Holmes that Scott would only be silenced by 'having the life frightened out of him'. Le Mesurier saw his own motives and those of David Holmes as being dictated by 'what any red-blooded Englishman would do for a friend.'

Among Le Mesurier's more red-blooded activities in early 1975 was organising the theft of Scott's briefcase and arranging his subsequent assault by two men. As neither event had the effect of silencing Scott, it became clear that sterner measures were required. Newton was deemed to be the man to carry them out, though his efforts in this direction began on a note of low farce.

Newton's basic 'kit' for the enterprise was a folder of photographs of Scott in a variety of modelling poses. The photographs had two telephone numbers and a street name, like 'Hillview', written on them. In the spring of 1975 Newton further equipped himself with an area map of Dunstable in Bedfordshire and went looking for Scott. He thought he would get £10,000 for his troubles.

Once in Dunstable, he tried the two telephone numbers that were inscribed on the Scott photographs and drew a blank. The local telephone directories were no help; neither was the electoral roll. Newton then checked back with one of his 'controllers' and found that he would have had more luck in Barnstaple in Devon.

Newton's first attempts to contact Scott in Barnstaple were made by telephone. He adopted the name Ian Wright and a hustling style to try and interest Scott in a modelling commission for the Italian Pensiero Group, which he had just invented. At one point he thought that he had persuaded Scott to come to London and stay at the Royal Garden Hotel in Kensington, where terms could be discussed.

When Scott failed to put in an appearance, Newton asked for further instructions, and was told he would be furnished with another idea. Soon afterwards Newton received a call in Blackpool and was told that it had been arranged for Scott to be at the Holiday Inn in Bristol on a day that coincided with his next rest period. Scott would be there expecting to be interviewed by a Reuter's reporter going by the name of 'Matheson'. Someone had arranged the interview with Scott himself by posing as the reporter on the telephone. Newton drove down to Bristol on the day of the appointment. Once again, Scott did not appear.

Newton then decided to make personal contact with Scott in Barnstaple himself. Prior to his arrival, in a hired yellow Mazda car, Newton spoke to both Scott and Mrs Friendship on the Market Inn telephone using the alias Peter Keene. When he first met Scott, in the Pannier Market on the afternoon of 12 October, Newton's main object was to get Scott's confidence. The fiction about the Canadian 'hit' man and his own cover story of being paid to protect Scott by a certain person were directed to this end. When Scott tumbled out his story and showed him his documents in the lounge of the Imperial Hotel, it was Newton's first clear insight into the background of the whole affair.

Newton's next move was to get a gun. He looked up an old schoolfriend in Chiswick who he knew collected antique firearms. After telling the friend that he needed a weapon to frighten somebody who was blackmailing him, Newton found himself in possession of a 1910 model Mauser, still in reasonable working condition though the self-loading

224

mechanism had a tendency to jam. He also borrowed a clip of ammunition.

Newton was between flights at Glasgow Airport when he called Scott at the Pack of Cards in Combe Martin on 23 October. In his haste, he almost gave his identity away by mentioning his real first name but he recovered and set up what was to be his final meeting with Scott the next evening. He drove down to Combe Martin in a girlfriend's car, a blue Ford Escort. When they met at six o'clock outside the Delves Hotel, Newton was disconcerted by the size of Scott's Great Dane, Rinka. He later described it to a friend as being 'like a donkey'. Scott insisted that he would not go anywhere without the dog.

Scott agreed to accompany Newton (Keene) on a drive to Porlock, a small town on the North Devon coast some 25 miles to the east. Newton said he had business there with a young woman whom he wanted to recruit for a private investigation he was carrying out. They could talk on the way. As they drove along they discussed the threat posed by the 'hit' man from Canada. By now Scott was almost at ease in Newton's company.

Newton dropped Scott and his dog outside the Castle Hotel in Porlock, saying he would return at eight o'clock. When he did not come back on time, Scott began to get nervous. At around 8.20 pm he came out of the hotel with Rinka, thinking he had better look for a taxi to get home. He saw Newton sitting in his car parked across the road. Newton flashed his headlights.

'I'm sorry,' said Scott, 'I understood you were going to come in and pick me up.'

'Oh no,' said Newton, 'I can't be seen with you.'

Once Scott and his dog were back in the car Newton drove up Porlock Hill in the direction of Combe Martin. As they came over the top of the hill on to the flatter ground of the moors, Newton's driving became more erratic. As the car veered from side to side of the narrow road, Scott said: 'You must be very tired.'

'I'm knackered,' said Newton.

Scott suggested that he might like to spend the night at his place in Combe Martin and offered to take over the driving.

'Oh, well, yes, in a minute,' Newton replied, 'that will be all right.'

Soon afterwards Newton stopped the car on a rise on the right hand side of the road at a remote spot on the Porlock side of Lynton. It was already dark and pouring with rain. Scott said to him: 'If you just move over, it'll stop Rinka jumping out and jumping back in and making the car all wet.'

Scott then got out of the car and ran, head down in the pelting rain, around the front of the vehicle to take over the driver's seat. As he came round through the headlights he found the driver's door was already open with Newton standing beside it, silhouetted in the light from the interior of the car. Rinka, excited by the chance of exercise, was already bounding around beside him. Scott tried to grab the dog's lead to calm her down and said: 'I'm sorry. I meant just move over and then she wouldn't get out.'

'Oh no,' said Newton, 'This is it.'

He then shot Rinka through the head. As the dog crumpled against the car Scott was at first too dazed to appreciate what had happened. The noise of the wind and driving rain had muffled the gun's explosion. It was only as he tried to revive Rinka that it began to dawn on him what had taken place. 'You can't involve Rinka,' Scott shouted. 'You can't involve the dog.'

Scott felt something hard behind the back of his head and heard the voice of Newton saying: 'It's your turn now.' When Scott looked round he saw Newton illuminated in the headlights of the car with his arms extended in front of him like a marksman. Although Scott could not distinguish the outline of the gun, he felt sure that the man he knew as Peter Keene was about to kill him. In fact, it seems that Newton had no intention of killing Scott but felt that the nature of his assignment compelled him to go through with an apparently lethal charade.

226

For some seconds Scott just froze, but there was no second shot. Newton began to wave the gun up and down in apparent exasperation, saying, 'Fuck it. Fuck it. Fuck it.' It seemed as if the mechanism had jammed.

Scott began to run across the moor in the direction of the Bristol Channel. He had only gone a few paces when he realised that he was a clear target in the lights of South Wales from across the water. Feeling that flight was useless, Scott decided to go back to Rinka. Newton levelled the gun again but the only sound was of another 'Oh. Fuck it.'

Newton suddenly jumped back into the car, shouting, 'I'll get you.' He slewed the car around and drove off at high speed back towards Porlock. Scott, sobbing hysterically, knelt beside the dead Rinka. He then tried to give the dog the kiss of life.

When he saw the headlights of a car coming across the moor from Lynton, he ran out into the centre of the road to flag it down. The four occupants of the car included an off-duty AA scout, Edward Lethaby.

While Lethaby was attending to the terrified Scott, his wife noticed another car coming rapidly towards them from the direction of Porlock. It approached to within 300 yards, then abruptly turned in the road and went back in the opposite direction. As a result of what Scott told him, Edward Lethaby contacted the police.

16. The Three Musketeers

Few policemen in the West Country were unaware by this stage of Norman Scott, his allegations, and the man against whom he was making them. When the duty CID officer at Bridgwater police station learned that Scott had been involved in a shooting incident on the moors, he knew at once that it would have to be handled from the top. He made two immediate calls, one to Devon and Cornwall police, the neighbouring police authority whose territory bordered the Porlock moors, the other to the Somerset and Avon headquarters at Bristol.

The second call was significant. It meant that from the outset senior police officers were involved in handling an incident which would normally have been a job for local detectives. Detective Chief Superintendent Michael Challes, who was in over-all charge of crime investigation in the area, was reached at his home in Taunton and told that there seemed to be more to the shooting than just the death of a dog. Challes in turn warned Detective Chief Superintendent Proven Sharpe, head of Devon and Cornwall CID, who was woken up just after 1 am. His immediate reaction was that Scott had probably shot the dog himself in an attempt to create more publicity.

Next morning Challes and Sharpe divided responsibilities. Challes and the Somerset police would pursue the shot dog case; Sharpe would furnish background material on Scott, and keep himself available for follow-up inquiries in Devon. They decided to maintain a press blackout since no one quite knew whether to believe Scott's account, and discretion seemed the most advisable policy.

That weekend Mrs Edna Friendship walked into Barnstaple police station and handed over the registration number of the suspicious yellow Mazda car that she had seen in the Pannier Market when Scott first met 'Peter Keene' on 12 October. The vehicle belonged to a car hire firm in Blackpool. Newton's anonymity lasted just forty eight hours. He was traced by Braund and a colleague, Detective Sergeant Peter Hinde, but they decided not to arrest him immediately. Instead they tailed him in the hope that he would lead them to the gun.

Newton had already disposed of it. On the night of the shooting he had arrived at the printing premises in Cardiff of his friend Dave Miller and had let himself in. Miller returned just after midnight to find him sitting upstairs at a table stripping down a large Mauser pistol. When Miller asked him what he had been up to, Newton replied enigmatically that he had been 'doing a service for the community'. He asked Miller for emery cloth and oil, and began filing down the firing pin of the pistol which, he said, would not retract properly. As he worked, he told Miller what had happened that night on the moors. He complained bitterly that he had been working for 'a bunch of amateurs'. Everything had gone wrong: the man he had been after, Norman Scott, had brought a dog and he had had to shoot it. Now the car seat was covered in blood. Looking over Newton's shoulder, Miller saw a matchbox full of bullets.

Next morning Newton cleaned up his car and tried a couple of practice shots with the pistol which now seemed to be working. He then put it in a paper bag and concealed it, unknown to Miller, in a cavity above his office door. He told Miller he was thinking of going on a holiday to the Far East, and asked him if he would like to come too. As a pilot, Newton was entitled to concessionary tickets for himself and his family, and he thought he would be able to stretch a point and include his girlfriend, Eleanor Rooney, as well as Miller himself – which was against the rules.

Sometime later Newton called Miller from London. The trip, he said, was on, and Miller should come up to London.

He asked him if he would mind bringing the paper bag he would find above the office door, and Miller, unenthusiastically, agreed. On 31 October 1975 all three of them left Heathrow Airport bound for Karachi, after a more than usually thorough search by customs officials which disclosed Newton's illicit ticket deal, but not the piece of hardware which the police had told them they might expect to find.

On 18 November, Newton and Miller were detained at the airport when they flew back from their holiday, and questioned about their concessionary tickets. Miller was allowed to go, but Newton was held overnight in the detention centre. Next day he was questioned by two detectives who seemed interested in more than just the ticket deal.

'You know why you are here, I think you know something about it already,' said Detective Inspector Braund. 'Let's go back to the 12th October. Did you hire a yellow Mazda in Blackpool?'

'Yes,' replied Newton. 'Oh, that's what it's all about . . I'd better explain something now.'

Newton's 'explanations' were to be considerably modified as time went on. His first instinct was to protect himself and his backers. He realised that there was still a good chance of collecting at least some of the money he had been promised, provided he kept the police off the right trail. He therefore began to put together an account of the shooting which cast Scott in the role of blackmailer, and himself as the victim of blackmail. He would admit to shooting the dog, but would deny everything else.

The bones of the story had been assembled in his mind by the time he arrived at Bridgwater police station, and after another long interview he felt confident enough to begin making a statement. He explained that Scott had been blackmailing him over a photograph he had obtained which showed Newton in the nude in a compromising pose. Scott had obtained the photograph after Newton had written replying to an advertisement in a 'contact magazine' catering for people on the look-out for sexual partners. Newton had enclosed his photograph, and had been amazed when, instead of hearing from a 'lady of leisure' as he had hoped, a strange young man called Norman Scott had turned up at his Blackpool flat demanding money and threatening to reveal the photograph to Newton's employers. Newton had given in to the threat and agreed to pay up. The amounts, he said, were not exorbitant – £4 a month – but after a time he had decided to put an end to the matter by driving down to Barnstaple and trying to frighten Scott off.

Their first meeting had been a frustrating one, said Newton. All Scott wanted to talk about was Jeremy Thorpe and the Liberal Party and how badly he had been treated by them. In the end he had given up and gone back to Blackpool.

At this point in his statement, Newton broke off and asked the police casually what he was likely to be charged with. He was told that it looked like being possession of a firearm with intent to endanger life.

Newton hesitated, then he said: 'I might as well tell you all of what happened. I did try to fire the gun later. I shot the dog, but it jammed . . . I pointed it towards him but not directly at him. I wanted to frighten him but the gun wouldn't go off.'

This version now ended with Newton struggling to release a bullet jammed in the firing mechanism of his Mauser pistol as Scott tried to revive his dying dog. The police seemed reasonably satisfied with it, though they could not quite understand why a man would travel twice all the way from Blackpool just for a miserable £4 a month. On 20 November Newton was charged. The gun, together with two pieces of pink paper, were retrieved by police from a shed in the garden of Newton's mother's house in Chiswick, and Newton was released on bail.

His first move was to make contact with David Holmes. He drove to Dave Miller's home in Cardiff on 26 November and told him that he had arranged to meet Holmes that evening in London. He was apparently a little nervous at the reception he would get following his arrest as he scribbled down the details of his rendezvous with Holmes on the back of a sugar packet. He told Miller to pass it on to the police if anything happened to him. Then he set off for London.

Over the next few weeks Holmes and Newton were to meet on several occasions as they discussed Newton's forthcoming appearance in court. They met at Paddington Station in London, where they talked to each other on the telephone from adjoining call boxes; at a Pancake House in Chelsea; at Victoria Station in Manchester and Euston Station in London; and in the gloomy privacy of a church in Bolton, Lancashire, where on one occasion they thought they were being watched by a man with a camera and fled to the relative security of a nearby public house. In the course of these meetings Newton was promised £5000 and paid £400 on account. There was an atmosphere of mutual suspicion between the two men as they discussed the matter. Holmes, neat, precise, meticulous in dress and manner, must have found it a frustrating experience to deal with the brash and garrulous Newton – described succinctly by a schoolfriend as 'a screwball'. Hard to pin down at the best of times, Newton tended to shoot from the hip in any conversation and to turn truculent if challenged. He was mistrustful of Holmes and refused to allow him to keep a copy of the statement he had prepared for his lawyers.

Holmes told him that he would be going to America and would get a statement from someone which would be extremely helpful to him in court.

By this time some of the ramifications of the dog-shooting incident had begun to surface in public. The very first story about it had appeared in the local *West Somerset Free Press* whose headline became a collector's item: 'The Great Dane Death Mystery: Dog-in-a-Fog Case Baffles Police'. Despite this enticing line Fleet Street had been slow to follow up the story, but after questions in the House of Commons newsmen gradually gathered from the police that there was more to it than met the eye. In a report for the DPP in early January, Detective Chief Superintendent Proven Sharpe noted: 'In spite of the blanks so far presented, one does have the feeling that given time the truth will one day present an even more bizarre situation than that so far experienced.'

Newsmen were soon hot on the trail of Andrew Newton, helped by Dave Miller who was the first of many to detect that there might be richer rewards to be gained from selling information rather than sitting on it. To Newton's fury, he handed out pictures of his friend and guided reporters towards Blackpool.

There Newton called a hasty press conference and gave a circumspect account of the background to the case. Since most of what he said was *sub judice* in view of the forthcoming proceedings, little could be printed, but he whetted the appetite of the press by dropping statements like: 'I think it is wrong for Mr Thorpe to be dragged through the mud by men of straw ... I have never met Thorpe or Wilson, and Scott is a petty vindictive man ...'

For Thorpe himself, the main concern in all this was the opportunity Newton's case offered for Norman Scott to go public with his allegations. The case had been set down for hearing in March, and the battle would then move into the public arena where he would need some heavyweight legal advice. He turned, therefore, to Lord Goodman, the most famous solicitor in the country and a man whose advice in matters political as well as legal had been sought by the rich and famous up to and including the Prime Minister himself. His reputation was that of a fixer, working behind the scenes to ease deadlocks and provide a solution to problems which had defeated lesser men. His friendship with newspaper editors and proprietors meant that his advice was listened to with respect even though this advice tended more towards the withholding of information than its dissemination.

The nature of Goodman's advice to Thorpe remains secret, but one can only conclude that he had nothing to do with the events that followed since they were so contrary to legal ethics that a lawyer of Goodman's standing would never have condoned them.

In mid-January 1976 David Holmes went to America. His mission was to persuade Peter Bessell to write a letter which would help to establish Scott as an inveterate blackmailer (this was what Holmes had hinted at to Newton). Holmes had telephoned Bessell in California and informed him that he would like to see him. Bessell was delighted to hear again from his old colleague and asked after Thorpe.

On 19 January, Holmes, accompanied by a friend called Gerald Hagan, arrived at San Diego airport and was met by Bessell. After dropping Hagan at the Hotel Coronado in San Diego, Bessell drove Holmes along the coast road to Oceanside where Bessell now lived in a modest bungalow with Diane Kelly. On the way Holmes explained that the problem he wanted to discuss was Norman Scott.

Bessell professed himself amazed. Surely, he said, that was all in the past. The last time he had been actively involved in dealing with Scott had been in 1971, and although Thorpe had mentioned to him sometime later that the Scott question had still not been resolved, he had forgotten all about it. Holmes, however, told him that not only was Scott still a problem, the threat was probably more serious than ever before. An airline pilot called Newton had been blackmailed by Scott over a nude photograph and in the course of an argument between the two of them, Newton had shot Scott's dog. The case was due to come up in court, and Scott was likely to use it as an occasion for talking in public about his relationship with Thorpe.

Bessell found the story faintly absurd. He said it was puzzling to learn that Scott had turned to blackmail since it sounded out of character; whatever his faults, that was not one of them. Holmes replied vaguely that Scott had 'deteriorated' since Bessell had last known him. Anyway, he went on, the threat to Thorpe was sufficient that Holmes now wanted Bessell to write a letter. In it Bessell would state that he had once been blackmailed by Scott. This letter would be shown, in strictest confidence, to Scott's solicitors, and Scott would be warned that if he mentioned Thorpe's name in court, an affidavit would be signed by Bessell which, coupled with Newton's evidence, would be enough to have him convicted and sent to prison. This threat would be sufficient, Holmes thought, to deter Scott from mentioning Thorpe's name.

Bessell, who was no stranger to the art of composing misleading letters, did not immediately reject the proposal. But he pointed out one serious objection. Even if Scott had ever blackmailed him – which he had not – it could only have been over the relationship with Thorpe.

Holmes argued that Scott might easily have found out something about Bessell's business, or possibly about a woman, which would have given him grounds for a blackmail threat. Bessell quickly rejected the business angle, but he conceded that he might once have been open to blackmail over his extra-marital affairs. He wanted to know what would happen if Scott's solicitor called his bluff and demanded that he appear in court to back up his claim. The last thing he wanted was an appearance in a British court – his plans for financial recovery would hardly benefit from that. Here Holmes was able to offer reassurance. He had checked personally with lawyers, and there was no risk of Bessell being forced to come to Britain to give evidence. He added that neither he nor his friends would think of asking him to do anything that might harm his career. To lend emphasis to the point, Holmes took out of his bag a book, A.J. Sylvester's *Life with Lloyd George*. Thorpe had inscribed it: 'For Peter from Jeremy with affection from one Liberal to another Liberal about a third Liberal. Vive les trois Mousquetiers!' Holmes suggested that Chapter 9 might be instructive in the circumstances, and so it turned out to be. It described Lloyd George's fears that a scandal about his private secretary, Frances Stephenson, might cost him his seat, and recounted the plans which Lloyd George was contemplating to prevent it getting out.

Still Bessell hesitated. Then Holmes revealed that he had once paid several thousand pounds for a collection of letters which Scott had in his possession, and Bessell began to grasp the seriousness of the matter. If Scott had been paid large sums of money for his material, then he must realise how greatly his evidence was feared. It was this revelation, according to Bessell, which finally persuaded him to write the letter. He sat down and began typing. The final copy was addressed to Thorpe's Barnstaple solicitor, Michael Barnes. It began: 'I am writing to you so as to put on record my connection with Norman Scott.' Having given a qualified account of his early connection with Scott, he continued:

> [Scott] then came to see me and threatened to expose the fact that I was having a relationship with my private secretary. Naturally this alarmed me since an exposure of this kind would have been disturbing to my wife and children and damaging in my political career. Furthermore, at that time I was leaving for a business trip to America. I submitted to his demand in part, gave him a few pounds, and promised to see him again on my return. Of course this was the wrong thing to do, but under the pressure of the moment I took the wrong course [...]
>
> A year or two later he contacted me again and made new threats. I refused to be intimidated [...] This was my last contact with Scott. Although I have always felt some sympathy for him since he is clearly mentally sick, I have no doubt that he is also vicious. He does not hesitate to turn on those who, like myself, genuinely tried to help him.

Bessell seems to have had some misgivings about this damaging letter almost as soon as he had written it. As he turned it over in his mind, he became convinced that the letter would land him in serious trouble. On the way back to pick up Holmes's friend and then drive to the airport, he told Holmes that the letter would have to be withdrawn. Holmes appeared to accept that this was inevitable. The letter was in his case, he said, and he would get it out at the airport. They drove on to the hotel, picked up Hagan, then continued to the airport where Bessell dropped off both men with their luggage before parking the car. This took longer than he expected, however, and when he returned to the

236

terminal there was no sign of Holmes or Hagan. By the time he reached the departure gates the plane had finished boarding.

Bessell was left to reflect on the mistake he had made. 'In retrospect,' he says, 'I recognise that I was wholly wrong and irresponsible to write the letter to Barnes. I was destined to pay for it.'

Holmes's mission was at best a stop-gap. By late January 1976 yet another hole had appeared in the dyke of Thorpe's defences: in Barnstaple Michael Barnes, his solicitor, learned that Scott was due to appear in court accused of defrauding the Department of Health and Social Security of the £58.40 he had falsely claimed by holding on to two books. The case was set down for 29 January.

Despite the strain that this latest threat imposed, Thorpe continued to present a cool and resolute facade to friends, colleagues and the public. Once again, his ability to conceal the inner conflicts of his life from the outside world seemed actually to grow as the crisis deepened. Those who knew nothing of what was happening in the background recall him and his wife Marion during the early part of this year as an ideal couple at dinner parties. His wit and natural appetite for gossip seemed undiminished, though some people thought they noticed a harsh edge to his manner which had not been there before (one hostess recalls a conversation which ended suddenly when Thorpe launched a bitter attack on someone he suspected of being hostile to Marion). But at the same time there are others who recall small and spontaneous acts of generosity by him which were remarkable considering the tensions which preoccupied him. He had always been good, for instance, in remembering other peoples' anniversaries, and births, deaths or illnesses among his friends were marked by affectionate messages.

In public, however, he sometimes appeared to be over-playing his hand. He entered the debate about the Soviet influence in Africa by claiming to have sensational evidence that the Kremlin had bribed an African leader to recognise the new Cuban-backed regime in Angola, but never produced the proof; he injected a melodramatic note into the grey issue of devolved government in Britain by comparing it in potential to the bloody conflict in Ulster.

At the same time he was preparing the ground for Scott's appearance in court as a witness at Newton's trial. The Liberal Party now had a new chief whip – Cyril Smith, the MP for Rochdale, probably the most conspicuous member of parliament on account of his astonishing girth. At 27 stone he was a notable contribution to the weight of Liberal representation in the House of Commons where his reputation as a blunt no-nonsense Northerner concealed a sharp political mind. It was important for Thorpe to have him on his side since as chief whip he would be on the receiving end of any press inquiries involving the Liberal Party.

Early in January, Thorpe warned him about the impending appearance in court of a man called Norman Scott. The case involved a pilot, Andrew Newton, who had shot Scott's dog, but in the course of the court proceedings Scott was going to allege that he had had a homosexual affair with Thorpe. Smith's initial reaction was one of disbelief. He doubted whether the press would listen to the ravings of a malicious lunatic – which is how Thorpe portrayed Scott.

However, over the next few days, Smith made it his business to find out more. He learned about the 1971 inquiry from David Steel and Emlyn Hooson who told him about the payments which Peter Bessell had made to Scott. He then went back to Thorpe for more detail. Thorpe told him that Scott had a history of psychiatric trouble and suggested that it might be helpful if Smith were to go and see Roy Jenkins, the Home Secretary, and pass on to him details of the treatment Scott had received. This might well be useful to the police in Devon who were making their own inquiries.

Smith seems to have seen no harm in this and made an appointment to see Jenkins whom he visited along with David Steel.

'Roy, a man of the highest possible integrity, said he would draw the attention of the police to Scott's background,' wrote Smith later in his autobiography, 'but he could not interfere further. The visit to the Home Secretary was in no way an attempted cover-up, but a move prompted by genuine concern to ensure that the police had all the facts available.'

On 29 January, the dyke began to crumble under the impact of two blows which struck with devastating coincidence: the first was a report, issued by the Department of Trade, on the London and County affair. It exposed the machinations that lay behind the collapse, and though Thorpe was acquitted of any malpractice, the fact that he had lent his name to such a dubious operation was, in the words of the Department of Trade inspectors, 'a cautionary tale for any leading politician'. As the report said: 'Unless [a director] is properly informed of the affairs of the company he joins, he cannot make his own judgement on the propriety of its transactions.'

Thorpe had escaped relatively lightly from the affair. But within hours of the report being issued, another story was being filed from Barnstaple in Devon. It read: 'A man describing himself as an author, Mr Norman Scott, claimed today in court in Barnstaple, North Devon, that he was being ''hounded by people'' because he had once had a sexual relationship with the Liberal leader, Jeremy Thorpe.'

The political reporters of the London evening papers got to Cyril Smith first. 'Would Mr Thorpe be making any statement?' he was asked. Smith was caught off guard. He had been ready for the London and County report, but no one had told him anything about this one.

'Why?' he asked. 'What's been said?'

Once the implications had sunk in, he set off to look for Thorpe – but his office was empty.

Thorpe was in fact visiting Lord Goodman and seeking his advice on what to say. That evening two separate statements were issued by the leader of the Liberal Party. The first, on the London and County affair, was the most eloquent. Thorpe admitted an error of judgement, and added: 'I placed total reliance and faith in quarters where it is now, alas, all too clear that confidence was wholly misplaced.'

The second was miserly by comparison. 'It is well over twelve years since I last saw or spoke to Mr Scott,' it read. 'There is no truth in Mr Scott's allegations.'

Having issued it, Thorpe returned to his house in Orme Square, locked the door and gave instructions that anyone telephoning should be told that he was not at home.

The full onslaught of a press hungry for information fell on the luckless Smith, and he in turn began to entertain the first serious doubts about his leader. By leaving him out in the cold, Thorpe had risked the support of a valuable ally. Pursued by reporters, Smith pressed Thorpe the next day to tell him more and was informed, in confidence, that there was a letter, written by Peter Bessell, which proved that Scott was a common blackmailer who had extorted money from Bessell. This explained the payments Bessell had made to him. What is more, said Thorpe, Bessell was prepared if necessary to hand over an affidavit to that effect. Smith was heartily relieved – that did indeed seem to explain a lot. Perhaps he could see the letter? Thorpe, however, was unable to produce it. It was, he claimed, in the hands of the police in Devon. Surely, said Smith, there had been a covering letter? Yes, said Thorpe, but he had thrown it away. Smith's doubts returned.

That weekend, Smith travelled to the West Country for a Liberal gathering, pursued by reporters. His hotel in Totnes was staked out; photographers patrolled the corridors; newsmen joined him at his table for breakfast. Finally, an exasperated Smith decided to force Thorpe's hand and he deliberately 'leaked' the existence of the Bessell letter and his offer to swear an affidavit to the effect that Scott had blackmailed him. Thus David Holmes's solemn undertaking to Bessell – that on no condition would the existence of his letter be made public – had been broken.

Attention now swung inexorably in the direction of the man Bessell. The trouble was, nobody seemed certain exactly which direction that should be. Some newspapers speculated that he might be in South America. Venezuela, for some reason, seemed a likely bet.

On 1 February Bessell received a telephone call from Holmes who told him about the double blow which Thorpe had suffered that week. Because Scott had jumped the gun, he said, Bessell's letter would not now be needed; indeed he would destroy it himself and Bessell could consider the whole episode over. There had, unfortunately, been some references in the press to retainers paid by Bessell years earlier, but that was all.

Bessell's relief lasted just twelve hours. At three in the morning of 2 February, a call came through to Oceanside from his London solicitor, Charles Negus-Fancy, who told him what had really been dominating the columns of British newspapers. Amongst a welter of revelations, it appeared that Cyril Smith had seen a letter which proved that Scott was a blackmailer, and which was signed by Peter Bessell. Everyone was asking for an explanation, and Negus-Fancy was taking the brunt of it. What, he demanded, was the truth of the matter?

Bessell was appalled. Surely, he said, Smith must have broken some deep confidence of Thorpe's, and had exaggerated what he had been told. Bessell needed time to think. Could Negus-Fancy hold off the press until the following day when he would issue a statement? It began to dawn on him just how serious the matter had become. His impression was confirmed by two telephone calls later that day, the first from Michael Whitmarsh, a BBC reporter in the West Country whose father was Bessell's accountant, and the second from the *Daily Mail*. Both revealed more about the extent of press coverage, and the *Mail*'s editor persuaded Bessell to give an interview.

For the first time in ten years of protecting Thorpe, Bessell now began to distance himself from his friend. He denied to the *Mail* that Scott had ever blackmailed him, and said that he knew nothing about an affidavit. At the same time, however, he continued to maintain that no third party had been involved in his transactions with Scott and insisted that the payments had been made as acts of charity. Next day the *Mail* carried its dramatic story under a front-page headline: 'My Part in the Thorpe Affair'. The effect in the Thorpe camp was instantaneous. Thorpe rang Bessell in California that evening, and two long and agonised conversations followed. In the course of them, Bessell pointed out how badly let down he felt over the use that had been made of his letter. Thorpe assured him that he was as shocked as Bessell had been, and that by talking to the press Smith had broken his word. Bessell informed Thorpe that he had been advised by his solicitor to withdraw the letter and he intended to do just that. Thorpe became urgent at this point. He asked Bessell if he himself could contact Negus-Fancy and help to coordinate the story that Bessell intended to issue.

'Peter, I am begging for time,' he said. 'That's all. Give me time.'

In the face of this plea, Bessell relented. He said he did not want to make Thorpe's life more difficult, and if he wanted he could certainly work out with Negus-Fancy a statement which would reconcile their two attitudes. But he warned him that he had already issued a flat denial of the blackmail story to the *Mail*.

'Oh well,' said Thorpe, 'I'm going to have to sue somebody sooner or later. It might as well be the *Mail*.'

The conversation then took an intriguing turn as Bessell pressed Thorpe for an explanation of what Holmes had been up to. Much was to be made of this exchange by prosecuting counsel at the Old Bailey during Thorpe's trial, but for the time being Bessell was convinced by it that Thorpe still desperately needed his help, which he was willing to give.

Over the next few days the newspapers, swamped by a series of bewildering disclosures, concentrated on locating the mysterious Dr Gleadle who had apparently paid £2500 for the Scott letters. They found some difficulty in taking the story further. Not only did they have a silent and all-denying Thorpe, they had to make up their minds about Scott himself. By all accounts he was an unattractive fellow with a chip on his shoulder and the kind of obsession which experienced journalists recognise and try to avoid. His wife was contacted and she described him as a liar with a fixation about Thorpe. Was it really possible, reporters and editors wondered, to rely on the story of a man like that, faced with the public reputation of a politician of Thorpe's standing?

Unknown to the press, Thorpe had, by early February, acquired a powerful new ally – the Prime Minister. Harold Wilson's intervention in the Thorpe case was to have a sensational impact, so it is worth pointing out that his initial gesture was made not off his own bat, but in response to a *cri-de-coeur* from his celebrated political secretary, Lady Falkender.

The extent of Lady Falkender's power at Number Ten Downing Street is still a matter for debate, but it was summed up persuasively by Joe Haines, who worked alongside her for seven years as press secretary to the Prime Minister. In his book *The Politics of Power*, he wrote:

> That Lady Falkender's influence with Harold Wilson was powerful – indeed, all-pervasive – is undeniable, however much it may be denied. No one who worked in his office, in Downing Street or in Opposition, for more than a few minutes could be unaware of it. Every typist and every civil servant knew of it and could testify to it. Many of them went in dread of her; the fact of her power was like a baleful cloud hung permanently over their heads ... Any future historian's appraisal of Harold Wilson's role as Prime Minister and leader of the Opposition will be incomplete unless he comprehends the full extent of her sway.

It is only fair to say that Lady Falkender herself – formerly Marcia Williams, from Northamptonshire – has consistently maintained that her influence over Wilson has been exaggerated. 'He was, and remains, his own man,' she says; it is certainly the case that once he had taken an interest in the

243

Thorpe cause he needed little convincing that it was one worth championing. But it was Lady Falkender who first took it up and she who supported his conviction that there was more to the whole affair than met the eye.

On 30 January, the day after the news of Scott's appearance in court had broken, Marcia Falkender walked into Wilson's office in the House of Commons and told him: 'Harold – you've got to save Jeremy!' She was convinced that the Scott allegations were untrue and that the campaign against him was being maliciously encouraged. She was personally fond of Jeremy Thorpe, enjoyed his company and felt a natural sympathy for anyone who found himself the target of attacks in the press, which she regarded as biased and right-wing.

Wilson had promised to do what he could, and over the next few days gave it considerable attention. On 3 February he came to Thorpe's office and, in the presence of Cyril Smith, asked if he could meet him later that afternoon 'behind the Speaker's Chair', a reference to the Prime Minister's private office in the House of Commons.

That day a new Speaker – George Thomas – was being installed, and during a break in the cermony Thorpe got up from his place in the chamber, where he had been sitting beside Cyril Smith, and walked over to Wilson's office. When he returned about twenty minutes later, the following conversation, according to Smith, took place:

'Have you seen the PM, then?' asked Smith.

'Yes,' replied Thorpe.

'Well?'

'Well, what?'

'Well – what happened?'

'We were talking on Privy Council terms.'

'Come on – is it good or bad?'

'It's good – it will be pushed on to the South Africans.'

'What the hell does that mean?'

'The Prime Minister thinks that there are South African influences at work.'

17. 'Tell 'em Nothing'

There is no doubt that the Prime Minister and Lady Falkender were convinced in early 1976 that outside agencies were involved in a general smear campaign against politicians – particularly left-wing politicians – and that they themselves had been targets of this campaign. There had been numerous burglaries at Wilson's homes, both in London and the country, and over the years a series of unexplained incidents had aroused Lady Falkender's suspicions that South African agents might be involved.

What Wilson had suggested in his conversation behind the Chair was that the Scott allegations against Thorpe might have been encouraged and exploited by agents of South Africa in order to discredit the Liberal Party which had been a consistent critic of South Africa's racial policies. By exposing allegations about Thorpe's relationship with Scott they could suggest that the leader of the Liberal Party was a man who led a life of double standards, and thus undermine his status. The smear would damage the party as a whole and might even tarnish the fabric of political leadership in Britain, rather as the Watergate scandal in America threatened at one point to undermine the Presidency as a whole.

This presumption by the Prime Minister began one of the most celebrated and misleading episodes in the whole Thorpe saga. There were only two South African aspects which bore any kind of scrutiny. On 31 January, the role of Gordon Winter in trying to market the Scott story had been revealed by the *Daily Mirror*, part of the newspaper group which had originally turned it down. Under the headline 'Thorpe Hunter', Winter's background was described and the newspaper said that he was 'believed to have had contact with the South African security services'. Winter, however, had by now returned to South Africa and had abandoned his efforts to sell the story.

The second South African clue – though there is no evidence that Wilson was aware of it at the time he first approached Thorpe – was a strange interview which Peter Hain, the chairman of the Young Liberals, had had on 3 February with a man called Kenneth Wyatt who had become involved in some fairly dubious international deals. In the course of his conversation with Hain he claimed to have uncovered evidence of a coordinated South African campaign to discredit various public figures in Britain. One of these was Hain himself, who had in 1975 been accused of taking part in a London bank robbery. His arrest was a case of mistaken identity, but he was to spend an unpleasant few months before he was finally able to establish his innocence. Wyatt claimed that the actual robber had been a 'plant' by the South Africans who had recruited a man bearing a striking resemblance to Hain so as to implicate him.

The trouble was that Wyatt's evidence was at its best second-hand and he lacked any convincing documentation. The man who had this evidence, he claimed, was a Lebanese 'operator' named Fouad – 'Flash Fred' – Kamil, a former employee of the Anglo-American Corporation of South Africa for which he had worked in an undercover role to recover stolen diamonds. Kamil was engaged in trying to extract £1 million in compensation from the company and had managed to get hold of files from their offices which revealed the existence of the campaign in Britain.

Hain said that this was all very interesting but he needed more proof. Wyatt promised he would do his best by contacting Kamil who was in Barcelona. But two weeks later Wyatt was arrested. One part of his story at least was true: he was charged with involvement in a conspiracy against Anglo-American. Hain was sufficiently disturbed to report his conversation to Thorpe.

None of this, however, had reached the ears of Mr Wilson when he first made his approach to the Liberal leader, though later it was to provide powerful support for his suspicions. In the meantime he merely outlined his theory to Thorpe, and said that he had asked the security services to report back with all they could find out about the South African dimension.

Next day – 4 February – Thorpe faced his fellow-Liberals at one of the parliamentary party's weekly meetings. It was the first time he had been asked to explain what he knew about Norman Scott to the whole party, and, as always when under pressure in public, he acquitted himself well. It was Emlyn Hooson who began by putting to him, one by one, the allegations made against him. Thorpe began tensely, but as he got into his stride his conviction of his own innocence seemed to grow and by the end of the meeting most of the MPs in the room had been won round to his side. It was, in a sense, a repeat performance of his devastating counter-attack in 1968 when he had vindicated his handling of the leadership. On this occasion he found unexpected support in a document handed round at the meeting by Emlyn Hooson who stressed that the key to the whole affair lay in the hands of Peter Bessell and until he had been interviewed face to face no real conclusion could be reached.

'It would be an appalling injustice and a condemnation of our democratic society', wrote Hooson, 'if Jeremy were to resign merely because the party is embarrassed by allegations which were untrue. The parliamentary party at least have a broader back than to tolerate that situation. On the other hand, if there is a sound basis of truth in the allegations, Jeremy Thorpe owes it to the party, which he has led so well and so ably, not to lumber us with the stark choice between apparent disloyalty and engagement in a kind of cover-up, which I do not believe the party would indulge in, in any event.'

At a dinner following the meeting, Hooson proposed a

toast to Thorpe: 'I will drink to your health, Jeremy,' he said, 'but I'm afraid I fear for your future.'

Four days later, Thorpe faced another, less testing inquiry – this time from the police. Detective Chief Superintendent Sharpe, who had been given the responsibility of investigating Scott's background following the dog-shooting, had consulted the Director of Public Prosecutions, Sir Norman Skelhorn, who had agreed that he should question Scott. Sharpe also considered that Thorpe should be interviewed and on 8 February one of his officers took a statement. Thorpe told him that he was in the process of preparing a comprehensive account of 'Mr Norman Josiffe, otherwise Norman Scott', and would be giving it later to the police, 'subject to the advice of my legal advisers'. In the meantime he would confine himself to specific questions, which related to the role of his solicitor, Michael Barnes; the payment of £2500 for Scott's letters; and the dog-shooting episode on the moors. He replied to the first two in detail, explaining what he knew of the part played by Dr Gleadle, but denying any direct knowledge of the affair, and on the third, said: 'I have never met the accused, Mr Newton, I have never seen him or had any contact with him direct or indirect. In respect of this incident I again know no more than I have read in the press.'

Sharpe was never to receive Thorpe's promised 'comprehensive account'. Thorpe explained to him, when he telephoned to inquire about it, that his legal adviser, Lord Goodman, was ill. Thereafter, events overtook it.

As the month wore on, the press itself was floundering in a mass of rumours. Bessell, having begun by talking freely, now began to be more circumspect. His prepared statement had included the sentence: 'Since I understand that it is possible I might be required to give evidence in these matters I have concluded that it would be unwise to make a detailed comment.' This was hardly true – Bessell had absolutely no intention just now of returning to Britain – but it gave him an excuse to be more selective in his press contacts. He wrote to Michael Barnes in Barnstaple with-

248

drawing his 'blackmail' letter, but did not publicise the fact. And he wrote to Emlyn Hooson that there was nothing he could add to the information they had obtained in 1971.

Thorpe's growing confidence was reflected in a letter he wrote on 19 February to Bessell in California. Headed 'In Confidence. Personal', it read:

My dear Peter,

I tried telephoning but wisely you are off the hook. I think we are emerging from the Tunnel and I owe you an explanation and hope to be allowed to give a piece of advice.

Your letter was shown to *no one* (that is including Cyril Smith). However, his Loyalty was critical and I did *paraphrase* the broad outlines of your letter. *Phase I*, Cyril having panicked, *wrongly* referred to its existence, and *wrongly* described its contents (e.g. submitted your London solicitor/affidavit available etc. etc). This was disastrous & quite unauthorised by me. (He's opened his mouth too often.) *Phase II* you were caught off the hop by the Press + denied almost *everything* in the letter. I don't blame you but it didn't enhance anybody's credibility. *Phase III* you put out your statement confirming the broad outline + *Phase IV* to my horror you *now* tell Barnes that you want to withdraw the letter in view of the adverse publicity. What I want you to consider is a) the letter is already with the police b) They are not likely to publish + nor is anyone else. No more publicity is likely. c) the only result of withdrawal is to suggest, (i) that your letter was a fabrication – *which it wasn't* (ii) that there may be some other explanation for those payments *which frankly there isn't* (iii) that we are lying like troopers *which we are not.*

The Police I gather don't know whether to believe the dog man (Newton) or Scott. Scott has some ridiculous theory that Marion, self and/or the Government hired Newton! Newton according to the D. Mirror crime reporter had been living with Scott homosexually; went straight and was then blackmailed by Scott. Who do they believe? There is nothing to compell you to come to Britain to give evidence against Scott, particularly if you are not prepared to allege blackmail. But if they think that Scott at least tried to pressurise you as he did then it appears consistent with Newton's experience.

In view of the denials and counter-denials it is not impossible that the Police may want to interview you. my advice is a) Your letter is correct b) You wanted to withdraw since the undertaking of confidentiality was breached c) Scott *is* a Lunatic d) Whatever interpretation may be placed on the letters you do not wish to prefer a charge of blackmail against Scott – partly because your health would not permit travelling to Britain, + partly because Scott has tried to wreck enough lives without having a go at yours.

All the above is vital if justice is to be done. The Press are still being bloody + trying to destroy me. Harold on the other hand is being quite superb.

The Police asked me what my view was + I said I thought it looked as if Scott had tried to pressurise you but you had slapped him down. Am I right? Alas I think the Press would have hounded you in *any event* since 3 papers had copies of your letters + had had them for several years [. . .] All this is conjecture but I think reasonable.

The whole story has been a nightmare, but I am damned if that bloody Lunatic is going to destroy the Party. So far I've had 700 letters in support. Good news: Pauline [Bessell's wife who lived with the Thorpes in London] has got a good job with Esso and sets off on Sunday. My love + apologies to Diane. Stand firm and we shall win through. You need say nothing more. Your

letter is enough. Bless you. Take care of yourself +
remember Ll. G! [Lloyd George]

                    Ever your affectionately.

                    Jeremy

Your letter was superb to Emlyn
None of us have anything to hide.

Thorpe's letter was open to more than one interpretation.
It could be read as confirming Thorpe's insistent belief that
Bessell's blackmail letter was *not* a complete fabrication.
But as a record of events it was misleading: there was, of
course, another explanation for Bessell's payments. The
'superb letter' to Emlyn is a reference to Bessell's dismissive
response to Hooson.

Bessell's reply to Thorpe showed that for the time being
at least Thorpe could count on his help. He explained that
he had *had* to withdraw the 'blackmail' letter, but had told
Barnes the solicitor that his reasons for doing so were that
its contents had been made public by Smith, had been
hurriedly written, and had contained serious inaccuracies.
'All this was correct and factual and if you consider carefully
the reasons I gave, they are *not at all* unhelpful,' he wrote.

He went on: 'It is hard to believe that the Police can be
so credulous as to believe anything Scott says. But if they
are prepared to waste one second of their time on his
allegation that H.M.G., you and Marion conspired to shoot
his dog, then I would think the tax-payers are entitled to
ask why they haven't got something better to do.' He
emphasised that there was no question of his helping the
police, and said that he hoped, in return for his help, Thorpe
would try and protect what remained of his good name.

'My credibility has taken a further blow as a result of the
last few weeks. But it is simply self-destructive to try to
shatter the remnants. Cannot you see that it is imperative
that I am believed. Alas, too often, innocent people are
destroyed by their persecutors. *The fact of your innocence
does not, of itself, guarantee your survival* ... Nixon did

not fall because some idiots broke into the Watergate Hotel.
He didn't (in my view) fall entirely because of the cover
up. He fell because at the end he trusted no one, not even
his friends and betrayed even those who were seeking to
help him.

'Jeremy you are no Nixon! You are no betrayer of friends
– but under great pressure (as I know from bitter experience)
the dangers are enormous.'

The letter contained an implicit warning: Thorpe could
rely on his support so long as Bessell could depend on his.
Within two months Thorpe was to ignore that warning,
with disastrous results. For the time being, however, the
letter gave him some much-needed help. Another source of
moral support to Thorpe at this time was his wife Marion,
who began to show her own resilience in the face of outside
pressures. She echoed Thorpe's iron will to survive politically and joined him in the battle, adding in his defence an
unexpected passion of her own. She found it hard to conceal,
however, her distaste for some of those on whom Thorpe
relied for help, and Peter Bessell in particular found himself
being treated with icy contempt.

By now Thorpe felt that he had some powerful allies on
his side. Peter Hain, who visited him at this time in his
office at the House of Commons, was told: 'I have the three
most powerful pillars of the state on my side – Harold
Wilson, Lord Goodman and MI5.' (It was a phrase he clearly
relished. He repeated it later to Cyril Smith.) Hain asked
Thorpe if he could really trust 'the blokes in MI5' and
Thorpe replied that of course he could, since Wilson himself
was the over-all head of the service.

In the course of that meeting Hain told Thorpe about his
strange encounter with Kenneth Wyatt, and the story he
had heard about the South African campaign against the
Liberal Party. Thorpe reacted with considerable interest and
asked Hain if he would put it all down in an *aide-memoire*.
On 24 February Hain set out the details of Wyatt's story.
This document was to acquire great importance in the minds
of those who were convinced about the South African

connection, but Hain himself expressed deliberate caution about his source.

'I doubt whether the Liberal dimension is true in all its various details,' he wrote. 'But my own feeling – based partly on instinct – is that Wyatt's account has some substance to the extent that there is a generalised attempt at discrediting the Liberal Party.' Thorpe's reaction on reading it was immediate: 'The Prime Minister will want to see this,' he told Hain and, picking up the phone, he asked to be put through to Harold Wilson.

A meeting was arranged in Wilson's room at the House of Commons, attended by Wilson, Thorpe and his wife Marion. The memo was read and a long discussion followed that continued until the early hours of the morning.

A few days later, on Friday 5 March, Thorpe was travelling back from Liverpool where he had been helping the Liberals wind up in a by-election campaign in the Wirral. His contribution, as usual, had been well received though it was plain that the party was going to do badly. In London that afternoon the legal firm of D.J. Freeman, solicitors for David Holmes, issued a statement on behalf of their client. In it Holmes, in the face of intense press speculation, admitted that it had been he who paid £2500 for Norman Scott's letters. They had turned out to be worthless, he said, and he had subsequently burnt them, but his original intention in buying them had been to protect the Liberal Party on the eve of a General Election. The payments, said his solicitors, had been made 'entirely on his own initiative, and in particular without the knowledge of Mr Thorpe'.

It was no off-the-cuff statement, for as Holmes was later to reveal in a telephone call to Peter Bessell, it had been seen by no less a figure than Harold Wilson himself. Holmes said that Wilson had twice vetted the statement, and that his solicitor, David Freeman, had represented Wilson in the past. He would have asked Lord Goodman to help with it, but since he was acting for Thorpe there might have been a conflict of interests.

The story that it was Holmes – Thorpe's best man,

godfather to his child and a former deputy treasurer of the Liberal Party – who had paid the £2500 broke as Thorpe was still on his train from the North. A party aide was dispatched to meet him and hurry him out of a side entrance at Euston Station to avoid the waiting press. Thorpe was tense as they drove to Orme Square. He had known nothing about the payments, he told the aide. Once they arrived he made three telephone calls. The first two were to Harold Wilson and Lord Goodman. Gesturing to his aide to leave the room, Thorpe made the third call, in private, to David Holmes himself. 'David, how could you . . .' was his opening remark. A statement that Thorpe had known nothing about the payments was issued that night.

Holmes's admission created a sensation in the newspapers which naturally christened him 'The Godfather'. Within the Liberal Party itself the impact was immediate. Those who had committed themselves publicly to Thorpe's defence now began to have acute doubts. Senior members began to suggest that the time had perhaps come for Thorpe to step down 'until all this can be sorted out'.

On Sunday 7 March, Thorpe telephoned Cyril Smith who was being besieged by press men in his Rochdale home. He informed him that he had spoken to the Liberal Party's president, and it had been agreed that Thorpe would resign at the party assembly in September, then immediately seek re-election under new rules which would give the rank-and-file of the party a chance to vote.

Smith was left speechless. As chief whip he was entitled to feel that he at least should have been consulted over a decision which would fundamentally alter the constitution of the party. But it was too late to protest. Thorpe had issued the news himself and it would be on television that night.

Smith now began discussing with his family the possibility that he would have to resign as chief whip. In the course of the evening, however, he was taken suddenly ill and rushed to hospital where he was again surrounded by eager reporters. Finally he agreed to talk to one of them from his hospital bed.

'There are things going on I know nothing about,' he said. 'I am being made almost to carry the can for something that's nothing to do with me.'

Thorpe saw the interview in an early newspaper edition and called Smith at the hospital at 1 am. A portable telephone was wheeled by an angry nurse down the public ward where Smith was sleeping.

'Is it true you are going to resign?' demanded Thorpe.

'No,' replied Smith drowsily, 'but I'm thinking about it.'

'Well, we'll ask Alan Beith [a junior Liberal MP] to stand in for you while you are ill. You can have the job back as soon as you are fit – if you want it.'

Two weeks later a sick, and bitter, Smith tendered his resignation. It was accepted.

Another man who, for different reasons, had been shocked by the news that it was David Holmes who had been the letter-buyer, was Nadir Dinshaw, yet another godfather. It was Dinshaw who had agreed to act as a conduit, in Jersey, for Hayward's £20,000 payment to Thorpe. He had always been concerned about the arrangement but he had trusted Thorpe implicitly. Now he began to be seriously worried. What, he wondered, if some of that money had gone towards the purchase of those letters?

He remembered that receipt of the first £10,000 had been acknowledged by Holmes on 31 May 1974. Dinshaw had paid it directly into Holmes's bank account where it served to pay off an overdraft.

Holmes had asked Dinshaw for a different arrangement for the second £10,000. In early 1975 he requested payments in small amounts of cash to be made as and when he wanted them. Dinshaw began to make the payments *before* he got the second Hayward cheque. Over the next year he met Holmes on several occasions, each time giving him sums of about £500 or £600 in cash. After a time he began to grow concerned about the absence of any compensating cheque from Hayward. But Hayward duly paid up, and on 27 November 1975 a second cheque for £10,000 was paid into Dinshaw's bank account in St Brelade, Jersey. The cash payments to Holmes continued, and by March 1976 Dinshaw calculated that he had paid out £7500 exactly.

The publicity about Holmes that month prompted Dinshaw to seek advice. He went to see his friend Dr Edward Carpenter, the Dean of Westminster, and told him the whole story. Carpenter's advice was to return the balance to Hayward, but Dinshaw pointed out that since he had received the money as a trustee at Thorpe's request, he thought he should hold on to the £2500 balance until the fuss had died down, then pay it off as quickly as possible to Holmes. He also consulted David Steel, the former chief whip, who was surprised to hear about the arrangement. The final payments to Holmes were made in October 1976. The timing of these payments was to figure prominently in Thorpe's trial at the Old Bailey three years later.

The Holmes admission had in the meantime prompted the Prime Minister to step publicly into the affair. Although Wilson's soundings with MI5 had failed to elicit any concrete proof of a South African involvement, he felt justified in drawing public attention to it. On Tuesday 9 March he met his advisers in his office at the House of Commons to discuss the answers he would be giving to the written questions which are submitted twice a week by MPs to the Prime Minister. The usual practice was to go through the answers which had been prepared and see what political points might be made in the course of delivering them. On this occasion, Wilson seemed reluctant to discuss the answer to one particular question which was down on the order paper. It was from the Labour MP James Wellbeloved, and it asked Wilson 'whether at his next meeting with Dr Waldheim, the United Nations Secretary-General, he would raise with him the activities of South African agents in the internal affairs of democratic countries, including Britain.' None of Wilson's advisers were allowed to see the answer Wilson proposed to give, and he went so far as to shield the red file containing it so that curious eyes could not glimpse the contents.

Norman Scott, a fine horseman, riding to hounds.

February 13·1961

My dear Norman,

Since my letters normally go to the House, yours arrived all by itself at my Breakfast Table at the Reform, & gave me Tremendous pleasure.

I cannot tell you just how happy I am to feel that you are really settling down, and feeling that Life has something to offer.

This is really wonderful, & you can always feel that whatever happens Tommy & Mary and I are right behind you. The next Thing is to solve your financial problems and this James Walters & I are on to. The really important point is that you are now a member of a family doing a useful job of work ~ with Tish ~ which you enjoy. Hooray!! Faced with all that no more bloody clinics.

I think you can now take the Ann Gray incident as over & done with. Enclosed another [vv!! I suggest you keep them all — just in case — but will you send back the Photo? Thank the guy but say you are fixed up.

Bunnies can (+ will) go to France. In haste.

Yours affectionately

Jeremy

I miss you.

Thorpe with Prime Minister Harold Wilson and the premier's political secretary, Lady Falkender, on the occasion of a Variety Club tribute to Dame Vera Lynn in the Savoy, July 1975. Wilson and Falkender subsequently became convinced that Thorpe was the victim of a smear campaign by South African racists.

Legal advisers: in defending himself, Thorpe retained some of Britain's top legal brains, among them Lord Goodman (left) and Sir David Napley (right).

Charged with conspiracy to murder: John le Mesurier (above, left), David Holmes (above, right) and George Deakin (below, left).

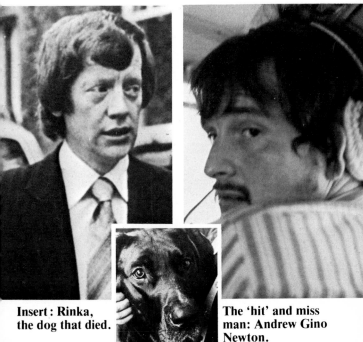

Insert: Rinka, the dog that died.

The 'hit' and miss man: Andrew Gino Newton.

David Steel MP (Liberal)

Richard Wainwright MP (Liberal)

Emlyn Hooson MP (Liberal)

Sue Scott, Norman's wife

Reginald Maudling MP (Conservative)

David Ennals MP (Labour)

George Thomas MP (Labour)

Sir Frank Soskice MP (Labour)

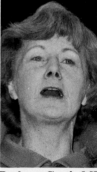

Barbara Castle MP (Labour)

**Lord Beaumont
(Liberal)**

**Lord Byers
(Liberal)**

**Cyril Smith MP
(Liberal)**

Jack Hayward

Henry Kissinger

Nadir Dinshaw

Gerald Caplan

George de Chabris

Gordon Winter

Jeremy Thorpe campaigning in Barnstaple.

Following the discussion, he went to the chamber of the House and stood up to deal with the questions. James Wellbeloved now added, as he was entitled to, a 'supplementary' to his main question: 'Can you say if you have received any evidence of South African agents in the framing of leading Liberal Party members?'

Mr Wilson replied: 'I have no doubt at all there is a strong South African participation in recent activities relating to the leader of the Liberal Party.' It was, he said, privately masterminded and 'based on massive resources of business money and private agents of various kinds and various qualities.' But he concluded: 'I have seen no evidence at all that the South African government or its agencies have any connection with these unsavoury activities.'

John Pardoe, the Liberal MP who was sitting next to Thorpe, asked Wilson what action he proposed to take. Wilson replied merely that he hoped that fellow-members of the House would be 'revolted' that such things were going on in a democratic country. Outside the chamber Joe Haines, Wilson's press secretary, was surrounded by members of the press 'lobby', all asking him what evidence the Prime Minister had for his allegations.

'Now what do I say?' he asked Wilson, as soon as he had returned.

'Tell 'em nothing,' said Wilson jovially.

'I can't tell them nothing,' protested Haines.

'If they ask, just say there's nothing to say,' insisted Wilson.

Glumly the Prime Minister's press secretary passed on the message, to the outrage of the waiting newsmen.

The onus was now on the press to do the digging and reveal the secret enemy within. But there was a strange lack of leads. The Wyatt/Kamil axis used up a great deal of journalistic time but led nowhere. Gordon Winter was closely questioned, but proved unsatisfactory. As he himself pointed out: 'Why should the South Africans want to get rid of Mr Thorpe, a moderate, and replace him with someone possibly more radical?' Most editors found it hard to take the story seriously and in the end it was not a diversion which did much to help Thorpe. As Robert Carvel of the London *Evening Standard* wrote: 'Jeremy Thorpe had still to struggle to keep afloat even with the lifebelt kindly tossed to him by the Prime Minister.' Press scepticism was shared by some of the policemen most involved in the case. Detective Chief Superintendent Proven Sharpe's March report to the DPP's office commented that there was 'some doubt as to whether the truth of this incredible affair has so far been discovered.'

Thorpe's elegant house in Orme Square was besieged by television cameramen and the press, but he was persistently refusing to answer any questions. On the Friday following Wilson's statement in the Commons, however, the editor of the *Sunday Times*, Harold Evans, got through to Thorpe on the telephone to press for an interview and was told he could come round ('Use the more private tradesmen's entrance at the back'), though Thorpe said he was not yet ready to talk. Evans went armed with a long series of questions from the newspaper's Insight team which was preparing an article. Marion Thorpe was strained, furious about the press, especially the television men encamped in vans outside, but Thorpe affected high spirits as he settled down in his study overlooking the press siege.

He had been told by Lord Goodman, he said, to say nothing. He had prepared a long statement, which he flicked through as he spoke. Evans naturally pressed him to release it. Eventually Thorpe agreed to go back to Goodman about releasing the statement and began to respond to Evans's questions. To the inquiry about whether there had been any correspondence between himself and Scott, Thorpe replied: 'There might have been one or two purely formal letters, but that was all.' He vehemently denied any homosexual relationship at any time with Scott.

'You know how it is,' said Thorpe. 'Politicians are often the subject of malicious rumours. There is a woman called Joan who is in a mental hospital at the moment who claims that I married her and I am also said to be the father of three children by another woman . . .'

After the interview, Evans passed Thorpe's detailed replies to the Insight team. He later received an abbreviated version of Thorpe's statement which the newspaper ran on Sunday 14 March under the front-page headline: 'The Lies of Norman Scott, by Jeremy Thorpe'. It read:

When Norman Scott made his outburst in court I issued a brief statement that I had not seen him for 12 years and that the allegations were baseless. I would have hoped that that assurance would have sufficed, but I am advised that a further refutation in the most categorical and unqualified terms is necessary.

Mr Scott has made the following allegations against me:

(a) the existence of a homosexual relationship with me;

(b) that I stole his National Insurance card;

(c) that the Liberal Party, Lord Byers and others have made him from time to time subventions to keep him quiet;

(d) that, in the incident of the shot dog, my wife or I had hired a gunman at a five figure sum to kill the dog, or Scott, or both, towards the cost of which the Government had contributed;

(e) that the identity of the gunman was variously, my helicopter pilot, or a Liberal worker in the Devon and Cornwall region.

(f) In addition, it is alleged that I was acquainted with or involved in a correspondence between Scott and Bessell and that I knew of, or was involved in, the purchase of the Bessell letters from Scott for a sum of £2500.

All these allegations are totally false.

Although this was not evident to the newspaper at the time, the manner in which some of the allegations were exaggerated made it easy for Thorpe to parade them and

259

simply deny them. On the same day the *Sunday Times* published its Insight investigation' headed by a quotation from *Henry IV, Part Two*:

> Open your ears; for which of you will stop
> The vent of hearing when loud Rumour speaks?

The article was favourable to Thorpe. Where he had made statements that could be checked they were found to be corroborated. For instance there was the curious affair of the Cartier's cuff links. Scott had been reported as saying that Thorpe had given him an expensive pair of sapphire cuff links from Cartier's. Ask Cartier's, said Thorpe. Cartier's, who keep close records, duly confirmed to the Insight team that there was no record of any purchase of cuff links or anything else by Thorpe. Thorpe conceded he did have some sapphire cuff links, but said they had been stolen and a man was later jailed for the theft. When the *Sunday Times* on the Saturday before publication asked Scott to explain in more detail about the cuff links, he said that Thorpe had not bought them specifically for him but had given them to him one day. When he was asked to show the cuff links he said: 'I sold them some years ago when I was broke.'

The article was also influenced, not surprisingly, by the view of its senior executive editor, Bruce Page, who felt that Peter Bessell, as well as Scott, was not a man who could be given credibility. He formed the opinion that Thorpe had been the subject of a vicious smear campaign. Scott was portrayed as an inveterate liar and Bessell as a gullible dupe who had exposed himself to blackmail. But though the article had some substance, it was flawed by misjudgement about the relationships.

Thorpe was delighted with the Insight article but it was not in the end helpful to him. Peter Bessell, reading it next week in Oceanside, was hurt and then furious with the knowledge that some of the information it contained could only have come from Thorpe. His decision to withdraw his help from Thorpe, he now maintains, dated from his reading of the Insight article. An angry correspondence with the newspaper threatened legal action, but Bessell was in no position to proceed with it.

Two days later, the Newton trial opened in Exeter Crown Court. Newton arrived affecting a jaunty nonchalance which was surprising in view of the experiences he had undergone during the four months he had been out on bail. He had gone to America (the police had generously allowed him his passport) and had stayed in New York to attend a flying school. On leaving his motel on 9 February he was struck by the trailer of a dairy truck and knocked unconscious. He was taken to the Brunswick Hospital in Queens and treated for concussion and shock. Newton later found it convenient to allege that this was a clear attempt to eliminate him and that the truck driver had made three runs at him. But an account of the incident from the local FBI shows that it fell somewhat short of a murder bid. There was a witness who said that the driver had been unaware that his trailer had struck Newton, and when the driver was traced Newton said that he had no desire to press charges. 'Due to above mentioned facts', concluded the FBI report, 'this incident should be changed from a Hit & Run to a Motor Vehicle Accident . . .'

When he returned to Britain, Newton found he had lost his flying job. But by the time the trial opened he had developed a cocksure demeanour with which he managed to irritate both judge and counsel throughout the proceedings.

The opening day of the case, on 16 March 1976, was attended by reporters from all over the world, but two 'splash' stories drove it from the front page: Harold Wilson announced that he was resigning as Prime Minister, and Buckingham Palace issued a statement that Princess Margaret and Lord Snowdon were separating. Much has been made of the coincidence of these three events, and elaborate theories have been woven around it. But without strong evidence to the contrary, they remain mere coincidences.

It was clear that the Newton trial was to be no ordinary

one, and there was some apprehension that names uncon-
nected with the case might be brought up in the course of
proceedings. Unusually, the Attorney-General spoke to the
leading prosecuting counsel before the case began. Although
Newton was the defendant at Exeter Crown Court, most
interest focussed on the prosecution witness, Norman Scott.
He did not let his onlookers down. The name 'Thorpe' was
soon established and referred to, despite efforts to make Scott
stick to the point. He was taken through his story, then
cross-examined by Patrick Back QC, who began to find, as
other barristers in future proceedings would discover, that
Scott was a difficult witness to deal with. Though nervous
to begin with, and sometimes reduced to tears, he was
capable of giving as good as he got.

When Back referred to him absent-mindedly as 'Scott',
he snapped back: '*Mister* Scott', and elicited an apology.

'Has anybody ever told you that you are an incorrigible
liar?' asked Back.

'Yes,' said Scott sharply, 'Mr Thorpe, on Sunday' – a
reference to Thorpe's statement in the *Sunday Times*.

At another point Scott said, with unconscious pathos: 'I
wasn't very good with people, but with animals I know I'm
all right.'

He refused to corroborate a word of Newton's blackmail
story, but mention of money led him inexorably into a
description of his relationship with Jeremy Thorpe, and
when Back assumed a look of weary resignation, he ordered:
'I would like you to look at me, and listen.' Reporters in
court took brisk notes as Scott detailed his charges, protected
by courtroom privilege.

Newton's evidence just about held together, though no
one seemed greatly convinced by it. His account was col-
oured by a sub-Damon Runyon kind of language which
included terms like 'frozen custard' to describe a frightened
man, and 'tranquillising' as a word for shooting. On the
central point of whether or not he had tried to fire his gun
a second time, he was adamant. He had pointed the gun
away from Scott and then pulled the trigger – but nothing

had happened. 'I tried to unjam the gun . . .' he said. 'I could see there was a spent cartridge inside which was jamming it.'

By the time his cross-examination by Lewis Hawser QC was nearing its end, much of the jauntiness had gone. His manufactured explanation grew frayed at the edges and he had to plead a fading memory to get out of trouble, especially when his differing explanations were alluded to.

'Why is it necessary for lawyers to link up documents?' he asked plaintively.

A girlfriend of Newton's who was supposed to have met Scott in Blackpool almost fell down on her evidence when she was asked to identify him. She looked round the courtroom in some desperation, but just as the silence grew embarrassing, Scott suddenly stood up.

'That's the end of that experiment,' commented the judge.

Two pieces of pink paper containing notes which Newton had scribbled in the course of his first long interview with Scott were exhibits in court but not read out. They contained the names of various Liberals and a reference to a member of the Royal Family which had nothing to do with the case but which Scott had mentioned in the course of one of his wilder allegations. Newton had studiously noted it down. The court was told that police inquiries had revealed no link whatsoever between Newton and any member of the Liberal Party or any people 'mentioned by this man Scott'.

On Friday 19 March the jury was sent out only to return shortly to ask more about the 'jamming' of the gun. Newton suddenly interrupted and told the jury that if they wanted to know more about it there was a man in court who could help them, and he pointed to his old schoolfriend, Dave Miller, who was sitting in the public gallery. The interruption was ignored, the jury retired, and finally came back with a unanimous verdict of 'guilty'. Newton was sentenced to two years. He was lucky – the maximum was twenty years. Newton had nurtured the belief that he would get off with a suspended sentence. In one of his confident moments, he had bought himself a ticket to fly out of Exeter Airport to freedom.

Another man who came badly out of the trial was Norman Scott. The press picked up counsel's description of him as 'a spiteful blackmailer, eaten with hatred', and Thorpe was praised for standing up to him. Thorpe himself announced that he intended to sue the satirical magazine *Private Eye* which had hinted that there was more to the case than had so far emerged.

But April 1976 was the last 'good' month Thorpe was to know for some time to come. Unknown to him the short fuse which was to lead to his resignation had been lit and was being assiduously fanned from California. From as early as February, Bessell had been in touch, by letter and telephone, with Richard Wainwright, the Liberal MP for Colne Valley, who had remained in the background during the public controversy but who was increasingly convinced that Thorpe should resign for the good of the party. Wainwright had first telephoned Bessell from the offices in York of Bessell's former friend and business partner, Richard Rowntree.

Over the succeeding weeks Wainwright learnt Bessell's full story of his role in the Scott affair and began to lobby within the party for Thorpe's resignation. He met with initial resistance since most Liberal MPs were united in their hostility to a critical press. By March it was about 50-50.

The tapes of Bessell's calls were kept in Rowntree's safe, since Wainwright had been alarmed to find that a file he had kept on the Scott affair had mysteriously disappeared from his office in the House of Commons that February. The tapes were played to one other MP – Russell Johnston, the MP for Inverness – but their contents were summarised to interested parties.

Following the *Sunday Times* article of 14 March, Bessell began to throw his weight actively behind a campaign to get rid of Thorpe. He took to his typewriter and prepared a lengthy statement explaining his own conduct and rebutting the allegations made against him in the *Sunday Times*. He then wrote several letters of great length to Richard Rowntree in which he stated his view that Thorpe was now 'a sick and frightened man' who should be persuaded to resign as soon as possible. 'Those of us who worked for the success of his candidature in 1967', he wrote solemnly, '... did not give Jeremy a licence to use the party for his own ends.' Everyone should realise that they were dealing with someone who was ill. 'Jeremy is ill because for over 20 years he has been haunted by the spectre of revelation.'

Tactics were discussed by Rowntree, Wainwright and Lord Chitnis, former head of the party organisation. They decided that one of them should go to New York to get first-hand evidence from Bessell.

But events were to overtake them.

On 1 May, Scott issued a summons against the new Commissioner at Scotland Yard, Robert Mark, to force him to surrender the two letters taken from him by police in 1962. Thorpe's solicitors promptly applied for them as well.

While Mark was deliberating, the *Daily Mail* exploded another bomb. It ran an exclusive interview on 6 May with Bessell under the damning headline, 'I Told Lies to Protect Thorpe'. The story told of David Holmes's clandestine trip to see Bessell and his revelation that the real reason for paying Scott in the late 1960s had been to prevent him making his allegations public.

Harold Evans of the *Sunday Times* heard about the *Mail* story the day before it was published and was eager to find out the response Thorpe would be making. Thorpe was on his way to the annual dinner at the Royal Academy – a sparkling occasion of the kind he much enjoyed where white tie and tailcoats were still *de rigeur* – when Evans reached him and persuaded him to stop off at the RAC Club. They spoke before Thorpe had been confronted with Bessell's story, and Thorpe's immediate response disturbed Evans in the light of what Thorpe said to reporters later in the evening. Evans recounted his suspicions in a memo dictated the following morning for the information of reporters on the story:

I said two things [to Thorpe]: one, I would like him to see Bruce Page to discuss a serious development in the affair. He said he would. I then said I wanted to put to him a charge that was almost certainly going to be made in Thursday's *Mail* by Mr Bessell. His immediate response was 'Yes, they know about the meeting – they've found out about the meeting'. This is a reference to the meeting between Holmes and Bessell and, dictating this on Thursday morning, I see that Thorpe maintains [in the *Daily Mail*] he did not know of any visit by Holmes to Bessell. But that is not the way it came to me last night. It creates a serious doubt in my mind about the honesty of Jeremy Thorpe and what he said to me.

I then said to him that the allegation was much more serious than a meeting – though his response to that was suspicious enough – and that it was to the effect that Bessell had written his letter in response to a request from Holmes which had been transmitted to Bessell with or without knowledge of Jeremy Thorpe. I said that if that was so, would he please tell me now and get all the facts out in the clear. He said 'No, no, of course it's not true, I would not lie to you.'

I then put it to him more hardly and said that surely it was something that Bessell could not imagine. Could Holmes have done this without his knowledge? His immediate response was that he must 'phone Holmes. Holmes, he said, was in London, and I got the impression he had been in touch with Holmes all day and that Holmes had been in touch part of the day with Bessell. Again it struck me as odd that a man going about his Party business should be in such incessant contact with one of the denied parties to a cover up . . . He had been in London all day trying to evade reporters apparently.

When Thorpe finished his call, I asked him again: is the allegation by Bessell true in part or fully true? He said it was not true at all and that Holmes had described it as absurd and laughed at it. I must say I thought the idea of a man laughing at allegations as serious as that was most unconvincing. I said again that we would want to talk to Mr Thorpe in some detail about what had happened and he agreed. His last remark was that Bessell was a judas.

Thorpe meanwhile was faced with a difficult decision. Scotland Yard's legal advisers told Commissioner Robert Mark that the Thorpe letters to Scott belonged to Scott. Thorpe owned the copyright in the wording, but the Commissioner would have to yield up the originals to Scott. Scotland Yard was under pressure to avoid or delay this delivery, but on Friday 7 May, the Yard told Goodman they were going to return the letters to Scott without a court hearing and probably sometime the following week. Goodman asked for and secured copies for his client and Thorpe, in consultation with Goodman, now made the fateful decision to publish them. They knew that Scott would not hesitate to reveal the contents of the letters once he had the originals as documentation. Any action to suppress their publication, would look as though there was something serious to hide and they reached the view that the letters, though awkward, were perhaps not as bad as more lurid speculations surrounding them.

Thorpe and Goodman chose to offer the letters to the *Sunday Times*. By this time the paper was taking a more jaundiced view of Thorpe's story and negotiations leading up to publication of the letters took place in an atmosphere of some strain. On 7 May, two days after his encounter with Thorpe at the RAC Club, Evans was attending a press awards lunch when he received a call from Lord Goodman asking him to call at his office as soon as possible. He arrived there to find Thorpe and Robin Salinger, Thorpes financial adviser. Evans could have two Thorpe-Scott letters for publication provided, said Goodman delicately, the letters were not presented in a blatantly hostile way. Thorpe was glum and took little part in the discussions beyond asking occasionally and embarrassingly for assurance that the letters were completely harmless. Salinger suggested that perhaps not all of each letter need be reproduced: some parts might be misunderstood. Evans, with Goodman's support, resisted; it was all or nothing, though he agreed he would not present the letters in a hostile way. Thorpe agreed to give explanations of a number of references in the letter, but when Evans asked him to explain 'Bunnies can and will go to France' he said he could not remember after all this time. The letters were published in full on the Sunday – they were the main news story – with another long article inside the newspaper which included Thorpe's explanations.

Meanwhile, Bruce Page, following Evans's request to Thorpe, had been given an interview. Page had put to Thorpe the allegation that Thorpe had once had 'homosexual tendencies'. Thorpe did not deny the suggestion and Page took his silence to be an admission. He wrote a passage to that effect into the inside article which pieced together new information and revealed, among other things, the purpose of Holmes's trip to California. Evans, despite his suspicions about Thorpe, felt that the reference to Thorpe's earlier homosexual tendencies could not be published. The lawyers said that Thorpe's silence did not in itself amount to a useful admission in a libel case that might follow. Evans was prepared to take that legal chance and said so. But he was also concerned whether the paragraph threatened to breach the undertaking he had given in their private meeting to Thorpe and Goodman. The undertaking was justified, he felt, by the nature of the scoop – and the letters themselves told their own story. Page was unhappy about the decision; he thought that at this stage Thorpe's homosexual tendencies were central to the affair and he regarded Thorpe's silence as significant. However, the publication of the letters promptly destroyed Thorpe's last lingering hopes of surviving as leader of the Liberal Party

On the eve of publication, Richard Wainwright took part in a radio discussion of the latest situation. He asked Thorpe over the air when he was going to issue a writ for defamation against Scott. It was a logical question, but Thorpe claims that Wainwright's 'defection' was the last straw which forced him towards resignation. Next day, the *Sunday Times* appeared carrying the letters. If Thorpe had hoped that they would somehow dispel suspicion, he was mistaken. At every breakfast table that Sunday the questions were about 'Bunnies' and the meaning of that final postscript. By next day an enterprising manufacturer had started selling T-shirts in London's Oxford Street, bearing the slogan: 'Bunnies can and *will* go to France'.

That weekend Thorpe went to stay with Clement Freud, the Liberal MP for Ely and one of the last Liberals in the parliamentary party to remain loyal. Freud gently suggested that the time really had come for him to step down, and finally Thorpe agreed. Freud telephoned David Steel, who was acting chief whip in the absence of Alan Beith, and told him the news. Steel immediately took the train down from his Scottish home to London, and arrived on Monday 10 May. He and Thorpe met at Freud's London home, and Thorpe tendered his resignation as leader, just two months after Steel had first asked him for it. They discussed a draft resignation letter which Thorpe had already drawn up, and it was typed out. Later that day it went out on the wires. It was a bitter letter:

My dear David,

In the absence of Alan Beith, I am writing to you in your capacity as acting Chief Whip. You will recall that the Parliamentary Liberal Party having passed a unanimous vote of confidence in the leadership subsequently agreed that the Party would hold a Leadership election in the autumn. This was a course which I myself had suggested to the President. Until such time it was clearly agreed that we act as a united party.

Since then two things have happened: first, sections of the press have turned a series of accusations into a sustained witchhunt and there is no indication that this will not continue; second, a parliamentary colleague has now taken to the air publicly to challenge my credibility.

Although other parliamentary colleagues have come to my support, and agree that nothing has changed since our decision to hold an autumn election, I am convinced that a fixed determination to destroy the Leader could itself result in the destruction of the Party.

I have always felt that the fortunes of the Party are far more important than any individual and accordingly I want to advise you that I am herewith resigning the leadership.

You will appreciate the sadness with which I do this, but I feel I owe the decision to my family, my constituents, and the many loyal Liberals who deserve better of us than the continued spectacle of a Party wrangling with itself with more concern for personality than policy.

You will know that from the very beginning I have strenuously denied the so-called Scott allegations and I categorically repeat those denials today. But I am convinced that the campaign of denigration which has already endured for over three months, should be drawn by me as an individual and not directed at Liberals collectively through their leader. No man can effectively lead a Party if the greater part of his time has to be devoted to answering allegations as they arise and countering continuing plots and intrigues.

To Liberals all over the country, whose loyalty and understanding has been quite superb and a source of great strength to my wife and to me, I ask that they use this period to redouble their efforts to build up the Party and to recreate the unity upon which alone we can build on our substantial and dedicated Liberal support.

Perhaps you would make this decision known to my colleagues and be responsible for making it known to my fellow Liberals in the country.

Yours affectionately,

Jeremy

Norman Scott, approached for a comment, said he 'personally felt very sorry for Jeremy'. His lawyers announced they would be proceeding shortly against Thorpe with an action for libel and slander.

18. The Big Fat Spider

Sir Harold Wilson's belief that there were foreign influences at work in Britain seeking to undermine the institutions of the country had not waned in the weeks following his resignation as Prime Minister.

Indeed, as he contemplated the ups and downs of his premiership he became increasingly convinced that there had been hostile elements within his own security services, as well as South African interference in British politics. Now, however, he lacked the facilities to investigate further. Of his Downing Street staff, only Lady Falkender and Lord Murray remained. He therefore decided to enlist the aid of the press.

His decision to do so was not destined to help the interests of Jeremy Thorpe. It is one of the supreme ironies of this story that in encouraging two BBC reporters to investigate a South African involvement in the Thorpe case, Wilson actually speeded the disclosure of matters which would form the basis of the prosecution case against Jeremy Thorpe.

Wilson had already tried unsuccessfully to interest two Fleet Street newspapers in his South African theory when, in early May, an inquiry reached his private office from Barrie Penrose, a freelance reporter for the BBC who had been following up the unproductive 'Flash Fred' Kamil story. Wilson responded by inviting Penrose to come and see him.

On 12 May 1976, Penrose and a colleague, Roger Courtiour, who had also been working on the story found themselves seated in the upstairs drawing room of Wilson's home in Lord North Street. They listened in some awe as the former Prime Minister, standing jacketless, a glass of sherry beside him and a large cigar between his fingers, described in Churchillian rhetoric a speech he had made that afternoon to the parliamentary press gallery.

'I said, frankly, that democracy as we know it is in grave danger,' he said. 'Anti-democratic agencies in South Africa and elsewhere put all our democratic futures at risk ... I think you as journalists should investigate the forces that are threatening democratic societies like Britain. I think you will find an investigation rewarding. I will help you, although for the time being I cannot speak too openly.'

For the next ninety minutes Wilson explained his concern about the South Africans and sections of the British security services. He said he was suspicious of the role of Gordon Winter who was now back in South Africa, and he believed that the South Africans had attempted to smear Jeremy Thorpe. He disclosed that he had met the heads of MI5 and MI6 to discuss his fear that a small, right-wing group of secret service men had encouraged slanderous stories about the existence of a 'communist cell' at Ten Downing Street under his premiership. He was worried about the burglaries which had taken place at his houses and offices, and disclosed that he had once entrusted the publisher Lord Weidenfeld to undertake a secret mission to Senator Hubert Humphrey in America to see if the CIA had any involvement.

He explained, in conspiratorial terms, what his role would be in advising Penrose and Courtiour in their task: 'I see myself as the big fat spider in the corner of the room. Sometimes I speak when I'm asleep. You should both listen. Occasionally when we meet I might tell you to go to the Charing Cross Road and kick a blind man standing on the corner. That blind man may tell you something, lead you somewhere.'

He took them downstairs and showed them a large pine cupboard. 'Looks like a man's wardrobe or an ordinary cupboard, doesn't it?' he said. Then, with a dramatic flourish, he seized the handle and pulled back the door. 'There should be no problems now that I've had this monster put in,' he said, and stood back to admire a new seven-foot-tall

Chubb safe. 'When you've had as many robberies as we have, you'll begin to understand.'

The first clue that Wilson gave the reporters concerned Norman Scott's social security file which, he said, had gone missing. He recommended that they see Barbara Castle, who had been Secretary of State for the Department of Health and Social Security in Wilson's cabinet. It turned out to be an unsatisfactory lead. Although Mrs Castle seemed embarrassed by their questions, this was probably only because one of her aides, Jack Straw, had examined the file and produced a political digest from it. Lady Falkender had gone through it later and had drawn up a list of the 'clues' about Scott's past which it had furnished. The file itself would, of course, have been revealing, since it would have charted the uncertain history of Scott's attempts to get a new insurance card and the efforts of others at various stages to help him. But it would not have helped establish the South African link.

Back at the BBC, Penrose and Courtiour's meeting had produced scepticism. Senior editors informed the director general, Sir Charles Curran, who went to see Wilson as well. Curran was at first suspicious, as he told BBC reporter Tom Mangold:

'Clearly you have to ask with any politician, Harold Wilson or any other, what is the motive? ... Now, I knew nothing to suggest that Harold Wilson had any improper motive in concerning himself with this inquiry. On the other hand, I knew that he had made a very serious statement ... about South African involvement in British political affairs. Now if, as seemed to be the case, he was saying that he was willing to help us go into the background of that charge, that seemed to me to be an extremely important inquiry for the BBC to undertake, both on the grounds of domestic politics and international relationships.'

Curran had reported back to his board of governors who had approved the proposal that Penrose and Courtiour should continue to work with Wilson. Meanwhile Wilson himself, in various public pronouncements, continued his attacks on

South African agencies – much to the annoyance of South African politicians.

He was challenged publicly and privately to produce evidence to substantiate his allegations, but was also supported. One Downing Street hand commented: 'With Wilson there's rarely smoke without some fire.'

The most obvious conflagration, however, arose from two newspaper stories, both sensational, being shot down in flames.

The first, in the *Guardian* of 15 May, claimed to have uncovered links between a South African diplomat and an attempt to discredit British MPs. The story was based on the activities of Andre Thorne, a nineteen-year-old homosexual, who was later convicted of blackmail. The story caused a political row, but was only to be a seven-day wonder. On the Sunday following its appearance, both the *Sunday People* and the *News of the World* disclosed that Andre Thorne had admitted he had lied.

The second story did not even last a week. It concerned a self-styled 'Colonel' Frederick Cheeseman who had contacted David Steel's parliamentary office claiming to have been an intelligence agent who had seen files on Liberal politicians at the headquarters of BOSS, the South African secret service, in Pretoria. The news of Cheeseman's approach leaked out and Penrose and Courtiour, in a race against other papers, got an exclusive interview with him. They seemed to have confirmation of Cheeseman's claims from South African sources but when the BBC broke the story it did not take long for newspapers to discover that the Colonel was not a reliable source. He had been a sergeant in the U.S. air force but was now broke, living on the dole, and had convictions for fraud.

Following this chastening experience, Penrose and Courtiour improved their working equipment. They already had a small BBC-issued Nagra tape recorder which allowed them to tape every interview they had – unknown to the other person. Now they invested in a specially 'bugged' briefcase.

It meant that they kept an unshakeable record of events when the going got rough – as it was to do.

As their inquiries into the background of the Thorpe affair continued, there was growing disquiet in the BBC executive hierarchy. The investigation seemed to be leading in a rather different direction from the one that had been planned. Norman Scott, Peter Bessell, national insurance cards, shot dogs – all this was miles away from a South African connection. As Sir Charles Curran put it: 'I was concerned that the story that was coming out was not the story that I had commissioned. I had been interested in the South African allegation. I was much less interested in revelations about Jeremy Thorpe because ... Jeremy Thorpe had lost the leadership of the Party. The political status of Jeremy Thorpe was finished.'

Penrose and Courtiour's foot-in-the-door techniques had also begun to upset some important people. David Ennals, the Social Services Minister who had helped Peter Bessell with the Scott problem back in 1969, demanded a personal meeting with Sir Charles Curran to ask why he had been approached for an interview, and insisted that a senior reporter should be assigned to the task. Lord Goodman wrote several stiff letters complaining about the filming of Norman Scott in Devon. He wanted the BBC to stop harrassing his client.

Finally the BBC decided that they must put these over-eager young reporters on a tighter rein. Penrose and Courtiour were informed that if they wished to continue with the BBC they would have to sign new, restrictive contracts. They took legal advice and rejected the offer, accusing the BBC of trying to suppress a story that was too hot for them. Curran rejects the idea: 'That is bunk and they were told so ... The story seemed to be turning into a kind of semi-criminal investigation and I thought that for the BBC to be financing air trips for two people to California and South Africa on what was going to be a police investigation anyway seemed to me to be an unjustified use of public money. I was not interested in pushing Jeremy Thorpe further down the hole . . . ' This was despite the fact that the BBC contract was for an investigation into Thorpe as well.

The result of this argument was the BBC's loss and Secker and Warburg's gain – a few days later Penrose and Courtiour signed a contract with the publishers and continued the investigation, quickly earning themselves the collective title 'Pencourt' in the style of the *Washington Post* reporters Woodward and Bernstein, dubbed 'Woodstein', who had uncovered the Watergate scandal. Indeed, Pencourt seemed to believe that they were investigating a British Watergate and some of their conspiracy theories were on the wild side.

It was not just the BBC which was becoming disillusioned about the direction of the Pencourt inquiry. Harold Wilson, their original mentor, who had given the reporters many hours of wide-ranging interviews, was increasingly concerned by what they were turning up. He decided to limit his own contacts with Pencourt, though Lady Falkender continued to see them for long periods at a time. At one stage, apparently, Wilson suspected that Penrose and Courtiour might themselves have been subverted by South Africans, but soon it became clear that they were simply on a rapidly diverging track, however helpful they had originally wanted to be. Since they were now looking into a matter that might lead to criminal charges, Wilson was advised by the omnipresent Lord Goodman not to see them again.

One name which Pencourt, the police and other journalists had come across and which, in the rumour-fed atmosphere of the time seemed well worth investigating, was that of George de Chabris, a Canadian who had helped Thorpe in various fundraising ventures, but whose chequered past made him an object of grave suspicion.

He had written to Thorpe some years earlier offering his services as a fundraiser and had been enthusiastically taken up. He set up the '100' Committee designed to raise £1000 each from 100 wealthy individuals. Lunches were held and on these occasions de Chabris would flourish a rather dog-eared cheque for £2000 in order to stimulate donations. Despite this performance de Chabris only managed to raise a total of £2400 for party funds. Thorpe had introduced him to the Liberal Party treasurer, Philip Watkins, and in the summer of 1976 Watkins and others had suggested that he might be the man to take over and revive the ailing National Liberal Club, once one of London's grandest clubs, was now losing nearly £1000 a week.

Thorpe endorsed de Chabris with an exuberant enthusiasm. Introducing him at a dinner in his honour, Thorpe announced that 'throughout history there have been entire families who have devoted themselves to the cause of Liberalism; the Gladstones, the Lloyd Georges, the Asquiths, and now the de Chabris.'

Once again, Thorpe's judgement of people seems to have let him down. Far from being the millionaire he pretended to be, de Chabris had a dismal business record and was in the process of being sued for £700,000 as a result of the collapse of a Cayman Island registered property company which he ran. More surprisingly, he was not called George de Chabris at all, but had been born George Marks. Among the other names he had used during his business career was George Marks Levy, the Duke de Vatan, Baron de Mornay, and His Serene Highness Prince de Chabris. The liquidator who had wound up his property company had accused him of gross negligence, breach of trust and improper favours.

None of this, of course, was known to Thorpe at the time, but no inquiry into de Chabris's background was undertaken by the Liberals before they placed the National Liberal Club, with its valuable collection of books, paintings and furniture, into his care. Philip Watkins, Thorpe's old Oxford colleague and chairman of the Liberal Party's finance and administration board, vouched for de Chabris's financial standing to the club trustees. Watkins was at that time handling accountancy work for de Chabris and had been briefly a director of one of his companies.

De Chabris officially took over the club on 2 July 1976.

His tenure was brief – it lasted until 24 March 1977 – but it was packed with incident.

He started by giving the club an indemnity for £10,000. He was allowed total control, and set about reorganising the accounts and business policy. A few months later Philip Watkins moved his accountancy practice into an office in the club, and the Liberal Party Organisation was persuaded to take offices when their own lease ran out. Other revenue was raised by renting bedrooms to tourist organisations and relaxing the rules for membership. It still remained a members' club, but income increased – to the delight of the trustees.

With the club committee's approval, all the income and expenditure was handled through one account, that of de Chabris's own company, Charlton Park Holdings, to which Watkins acted as accountant. This account was to lead to considerable criticism of de Chabris's management for he also used it to pay his own personal bills for his house at Charlton Park, as well as for his children's school fees and so on.

De Chabris wanted to secure the lease of the building from the Crown Commissioners who owned it, but to do so he had to carry out £400,000 worth of repairs. Although he did put in new carpets, he did not touch the major repairs and the Crown Commissioners decided not to grant him the lease. Their private financial investigations had disclosed that he was 'a man of straw'.

To help run the club, Michael Woods, a former special constable, was brought in as manager. One of Woods's tasks was to take care of an increasingly visible problem within the club – homosexuality among the young male waiters and kitchen staff. Woods, though, was hardly suited for such a job. He had convictions for indecent assault against young boys. During his stewardship of the club several allegations of violence and homosexuality were made against him. He was dismissed then rehired, but left the country in 1977 for Saudi Arabia.

In October 1976 an article in *The Times* revealed the

279

truth about de Chabris's financial background – but no action was taken. Over the next few months, de Chabris used about £60,000 of the £100,000 income during that time for his own purposes. He paid for furniture from Harrods, paid his gardener and the Charlton Park bills. He bought a Lancia sports car for his daughter and sold off the club's wine stock to Christies, taking one of the resulting cheques for himself. He sold to the club a painting for £10,000 – at least ten times its actual value. He lived rent free at the club, as did members of his family.

Eventually the complaints about his conduct caused such disquiet that de Chabris was asked to leave. On the day of his departure he cleared out the Charlton Park Holdings bank account of £19,000 and also scooped up the day's cash takings at the club – approximately £800.

The events had caused such a split among members and trustees that eventually police looking into the Scott case were contacted. They decided that the allegations surrounding the National Liberal Club, while worth examining, did not form part of the main investigation, and handed the file over for a separate Scotland Yard inquiry. Watkins's attitude was that de Chabris was entitled to between £30,000 to £40,000 of the £60,000 he had drawn because de Chabris had to meet his own expenses and drew no other remuneration. However, after de Chabris had left, Watkins and the club's trustees considered suing him for the balance. A compromise was reached when de Chabris agreed to repay £25,000 on an instalment basis.

Meanwhile, in April 1977, Andrew Newton was released from Preston Prison. His spell inside had not been without incident. Among his visitors had been several journalists, but the most enterprising had been Barrie Penrose who had forged a letter from Newton and sent it to David Holmes to see what response it would elicit.

The letter had precipitated some panic. Le Mesurier had contacted Newton's friend, David Miller, in an effort to authenticate the letter and had assured him that as soon as

Newton was released he would get his money. The arrangements were up to Miller.

Three weeks after leaving Preston Prison, Newton met Le Mesurier and Miller on a quiet piece of moorland in mid-Glamorgan. As the three men talked, another car roared past them with a photographer hanging out of the window taking shots of the meeting. Startled, Le Mesurier jumped quickly into his own car and drove off. The photographer, it emerged, had been laid on by a detective agency hired by Miller to record the scene for posterity and win him a large fee from any newspaper willing to offer enough.

In spite of this interruption, Newton got his money from Le Mesurier, this time in private, and counted out his £5000 on the journey back to London.

He did not regard this as by any means the final pay-off. During his time in prison he had realised from newspaper interest in the affair that if he told the right story it might be worth even more than the sum he had already earned. Like David Miller, who had begun tape-recording every conversation, Newton did his best to assemble evidence which would make his story more marketable. Between them they built up a small library of tapes, most of them inconclusive as direct evidence, though they would be mulled over at length in the course of the subsequent Old Bailey trial.

The tapes did record, however, that David Holmes was concerned to help Newton now he was out, by finding him a job abroad, possibly in Rhodesia as a pilot with the Rhodesian air force. It was Le Mesurier who was to pay for his ticket.

Newton wanted to effect a sale before he left. Several journalists were on his trail, but in the end it was the London *Evening News* which won the race. They did not, however, pay the asking price.

Newton had held a series of meetings with reporter Stuart Kuttner of the *Evening News*, in the course of which he had held out the prospect of naming some impressive names for which he expected some impressive sums of money. He appeared none too sure about the going rate for his kind of story, but quickly formed the impression that if he could produce evidence that big names were involved, his chances would be vastly improved. He was worried, however, about going back to jail again.

Kuttner decided to talk to the Director of Public Prosecutions, Sir Thomas ('Tony') Hetherington, to see whether Newton might get immunity from prosecution if there was a criminal charge. He got the impression that were charges to be brought Newton might indeed be more valuable as a witness than in the dock.

Newton, however, was still insisting on large sums of money for his information; he thought that he was worth £75,000, plus another £25,000 if he was sent back to prison. Kuttner suggested a more realistic figure would be around £40,000.

Newton retorted: 'You're dreaming at that figure. I think you'd better wake up right now.'

Newton then managed to tape-record a telephone conversation with David Holmes, and armed with this piece of evidence, told Kuttner that now even £150,000 would not secure his story. Kuttner and the *Evening News* decided, therefore, to run it anyway.

They got it cheap. In the end the most they paid was £3000 for the privilege of listening to the tape of the Newton-Holmes conversation – which was to be a matter of some dispute at the subsequent trial of Jeremy Thorpe.

19. The Ditto Man

The story which the *Evening News* got from Newton broke on 19 October 1977 in unequivocal headlines. It made the fantastic claim: 'I WAS HIRED TO KILL SCOTT. *Exclusive*: Gunman tells of incredible plot – a murder contract for £5000.' Underneath, on the front page, Stuart Kuttner and Joanna Patyna's story revealed that Detective Chief Superintendent Challes would now be undertaking a new inquiry at the behest of the Director of Public Prosecutions, Tony Hetherington.

A brief statement from Thorpe announced: 'I know nothing about an alleged plot, but welcome any inquiries the police may make.'

Reporters on rival newspapers, desperate to trace Newton and talk to him themselves, were out of luck. Four days earlier he had booked himself on to a flight to Johannesburg in South Africa, from where he had flown to Salisbury, Rhodesia. He had been assured by David Holmes that there would be a good job available for him in Rhodesia, and that it would help towards his ambition of piloting longhaul jets. All he had to do was to make contact with General Peter Walls, head of the Rhodesian armed forces, who would be ready to help.

Unfortunately for Newton, when he tried to get through to Walls's office it appeared that the General knew nothing at all about him. Instead, the Rhodesian security police, suspicious of this strange young man with his unlikely story, arrested him, held him in prison for two days, then put him on a flight back to Britain.

On his return he was detained for questioning by Challes who took a long statement from him on 28 October before allowing him to go. When Newton left he took with him his tape recordings, and a copy of his statement.

Newton's claims were quickly followed by press accounts from an increasingly garrulous Peter Bessell, all of which intensified the pressure on Thorpe to begin some explaining himself. There were calls on him to resign his seat – though not from North Devon Liberals who remained loyal. The growth of public interest was evidently causing Thorpe concern. He had already paid a visit to the offices of Penguin Books, who were considering a book about the whole affair examining the South African links, and had tried without success to secure a copy of the manuscript. His ubiquitous friend Robin Salinger had also been in touch with the book's authors and had encouraged them to emphasise the involvement of South African agents. Salinger offered to finance their researches in that area. In the end, however, Penguin decided that the evidence to back up the book was not strong enough, and it was dropped. In October Thorpe paid a call on another publisher, Tom Rosenthal of Secker and Warburg, who was assembling *The Pencourt File*. Aware of the legal difficulties, Seckers were working in conditions of strictest secrecy. Again, Thorpe asked to see a manuscript, and again he was turned down. Rosenthal listened to his arguments but said that any decision to publish would be his alone.

On 27 October Thorpe gave in to pressure and called a news conference. A list of journalists, carefully vetted by Thorpe's loyal supporter, Clement Freud MP, was drawn up, and invitations sent out. A last-minute switch of venue to the Victorian gloom of the National Liberal Club meant that Thorpe escaped many of the waiting photographers, but inside the atmosphere was brittle. Thorpe, his wife Marion, Freud, and a lawyer from Lord Goodman's office, faced eighty two reporters, most of them armed with a list of lethal questions. He began to read a long prepared statement which he had worked out with his lawyers beforehand. 'I must stress', he said, 'that anyone expecting sensational revelations is likely to be disappointed ... not a scrap of evidence has been produced to implicate me in any alleged plot to murder Norman Scott.'

He then placed on the record his own account of the relationship with Norman Scott: 'He is neither the only nor the first person I have tried to help,' he said, 'but a close and even affectionate friendship developed from this sympathy. However no sexual activity of any kind took place.'

He admitted that he had asked Bessell to help out with the Scott problem, but denied that he had been party to a cover-up. Holmes's purchase of the Scott letters, he said, was made without his knowledge: 'Had I known of these negotiations I would have stopped them at once.'

When it came to discussing the intervention of Sir Harold Wilson and the South African involvement, he was more cautious: 'I had no reason to disbelieve this, coming from so authoritative a source. I did not myself promote this belief, and it is fair to say that Sir Harold himself has now expressed his doubts.'

Then, in an aside intended for the ears of Peter Bessell, and which went down badly when transmitted to Oceanside, he said: 'As far as Mr Bessell is concerned, it is my considered opinion that if he had credible evidence to offer, he should have gone to the police rather than the press.'

The statement covered ground by now familiar to most of Thorpe's audience, and ended on a defiant note:

'It would be insane', he said, 'to pretend that the re-emergence of this story has not placed an almost intolerable strain on my wife, my family, and on me. Only their steadfast loyalty and the support of many friends known and unknown from all over the country has strengthened my resolve and determination to meet this challenge.

'Consequently I have no intention of resigning, nor have I received a single request to do so from my constituency association.'

He put a hand on his wife's shoulder, took a long drink from a glass of water, then sat down to wait for the real engagement. It was not long in coming. There were a few preliminary questions, then Keith Graves, a BBC reporter, got to his feet and asked: 'The whole of this hinges on your private life. It is necessary to ask you if you have ever had a homosexual relationship.'

The question was not heard at the back of the room, and there was a confused uproar as people asked what had been said. Then Marion Thorpe made her first, and last, public intervention on her husband's behalf. 'Go on – stand up,' she snapped angrily at Graves. 'Stand up and say that again.' The reporter obliged.

'Would you comment on rumours that you have had a homosexual relationship?' he said.

The question was never answered. Thorpe's lawyer stood up and pronounced: 'I cannot allow him to answer that question. I do not propose to say why. If you do not know why it is improper and indecent to put such a question to a public man, you ought not to be here.'

'I thought this press conference had been called to clear the air,' complained Graves, 'and that is the major allegation.'

'That is not the major allegation,' replied Thorpe. 'The major allegation is that there was a Liberal hired to murder a man.'

'Because he was having a homosexual relationship with you,' insisted another journalist.

'It may be that our priorities are different,' retorted Thorpe. 'It has been alleged that a man was hired to murder somebody. That is a very very serious crime.'

Though Thorpe had been clearly nervous at the start of the proceedings, by now he was icily calm – more so than either his wife, his lawyer, or indeed many of his questioners. When, after seventy minutes, Freud indicated that the session was over, Thorpe thanked his audience for the courtesy of their questions, then left quickly by the back stairs.

In the weeks that followed, more began to emerge about what newspapers called 'the South Wales connection'. The names of Newton, Deakin, Miller and Le Mesurier became familiar as tapes and photographs circulated around Fleet

Street and large sums of money changed hands. Miller and Newton were assiduous in marketing their information, though not always in clarifying it. One Sunday newspaper ran what must qualify as the most baffling news picture ever to have dominated a front page – the snatched photograph of Newton's pay-off had suffered badly from the circumstances in which it was taken and had come out almost entirely blurred.

George Deakin, advised by his solicitor, now took the initiative and told the police that he wished to volunteer a statement, which he gave them on 18 November. He claimed that his only involvement in the affair had been to put David Holmes in touch with Andrew Newton by passing on Holmes's telephone number. Deakin's willingness to talk was in marked contrast to others whom detectives were to approach in the following months.

Detective Chief Superintendent Challes and his Number Two, Detective Superintendent David Greenough, decided that their inquiries should take in Peter Bessell, and on 12 December they flew to California. It was no coincidence that the journalists Barrie Penrose and Roger Courtiour were on the same flight, since they had acted as intermediaries between Bessell and the police. Much would be made of this association in the course of Thorpe's trial, and in particular of the unusual arrangement whereby the two reporters sat in on the week-long series of interviews which the detectives held with Bessell. The fact is, however, that Challes had not been certain about Bessell's willingness to help and Penrose and Courtiour were invaluable in setting up the meeting.

The interviews took place in one of Bessell's Oceanside bungalows, and at times were more like a monologue as Bessell read long passages from the 60,000-word *aide-memoire* he had prepared towards the end of 1976. It was this *aide-memoire* which was to provide a large and controversial part of the prosecution case.

Bessell raised one matter which weighed heavily on his mind. If the police wanted him as a witness, he said, he would have to return to Britain where he still owed substantial sums of money. There were a number of creditors who would be delighted to see him back on British soil where they would be able to serve their writs. He wondered whether there was anything Challes could do to help. Challes replied stiffly that in civil matters he was unable to be of assistance.

The question of Bessell's willingness to return and give evidence exercised others as well. Over the next few months, as the police sifted through the evidence and interviewed witness after witness, Jeremy Thorpe decided to take some action himself.

In March 1978 Jack Hayward received a call in the Bahamas from Thorpe's secretary, who said that Thorpe was extremely anxious for a meeting. He would be prepared to fly out to Freeport, she said, but if Mr Hayward was intending to visit Britain perhaps they could meet there. Hayward was in fact coming to London, and on 4 April Thorpe called on him at the offices of his solicitors. The conversation was soon steered round to Peter Bessell whom Thorpe referred to simply as 'the rat'. He said that Bessell was threatening some kind of trouble by coming to Britain, and he wondered if Hayward could dissuade him. Since Bessell still owed Hayward £35,000, it might be possible, suggested Thorpe, for Hayward to contact him, warn him against coming to Britain, and threaten him with a writ for bankruptcy if he did. Hayward found it hard to take the suggestion seriously. That was not the way he did business, he said, and he had no intention of issuing a writ. In fact he later rang Bessell and told him so.

It was not until a month later that Hayward began to grasp what might have been the purpose of the visit when he was contacted by Challes and asked about the £20,000 payment he had made to Dinshaw. Hayward rang Thorpe and asked him to remind him of the details of the arrangement. He asked him why the police were involved, and Thorpe said: 'Dinshaw has presumably panicked.'

Nadir Dinshaw had not panicked but he had told the full story of the £20,000 transaction to the police. This was in spite of an extraordinary warning he had received from Thorpe. Four months earlier Thorpe had been in touch with him and had raised the subject of the money. Over lunch in a London restaurant, Thorpe had asked him to pretend to the police that the money had been part of a business deal between him and Hayward, and to deny that any of it had gone to David Holmes. Dinshaw was deeply shocked. He said he could not conceivably mislead the police if they were to ask him about the money.

On 13 April – nine days after Thorpe's meeting with Hayward – Dinshaw, who was staying at the Chesterfield Hotel in Mayfair, received another call from Thorpe, who suggested that they might take a drive together round St James's Park. Thorpe appeared to Dinshaw to be in some distress. He said that there were people anxious to destroy him, and that his political career might be finished unless Dinshaw could help.

'What does your career matter, you have to clear yourself of any possible charges,' said Dinshaw.

'I'm not worried about that,' said Thorpe abstractedly.

'If I was in your place I would be,' replied Dinshaw.

The following Tuesday Dinshaw received another call in which Thorpe told him that he was under no obligation to tell the police more than he was asked. In particular the second £10,000 was one of which he himself had only 'the vaguest recollection'.

Dinshaw, by this stage extremely upset himself, repeated that he would have to tell the truth.

'It will be curtains for me,' said Thorpe. 'And you will be asked to move on.'

Dinshaw took this to mean that his status as a resident of Jersey might be threatened if he gave evidence. 'I thought it was a very crude threat,' he recalled later, ' . . . a threatening remark which I didn't take all that seriously because it was such a foolish one.' A few days later, Dinshaw made a full statement to the police.

Challes had by now made his first formal approaches to the men who would eventually take their place in the dock at the Old Bailey. On 4 April David Holmes, accompanied by a solicitor, was interviewed at length at Bristol's central police station. His response to questions was guarded, with heavy reliance on the phrase 'no comment' which was occasionally supplemented by 'no comment on that' or 'no comment on that at all'.

He was, however, talkative compared to Le Mesurier whom Challes interviewed two days later. Le Mesurier, on the advice of his solicitor, chose the bleak formula, 'nothing to say' to record his position, and chalked up some kind of record by repeating it 105 times in the course of a five-hour interview.

On 10 May Holmes was again interviewed. The 'no comments' had multiplied, and, indeed, were now extended to cover questions to which he had previously given answers. He was warned that inquiries were continuing.

A month later, on 3 June, Jeremy Thorpe himself was interviewed in the presence of his new solicitor, Sir David Napley, a distinguished lawyer and former president of the Law Society. Thorpe handed over a five-page statement, which thus became the fifth – and most detailed – explanation of his role in the affair. His relationship with Scott was explored at greater length than before, though the sexual element was again denied. He pointed out the absurdity of suggestions that he had been involved in any plot to murder, and expressed his rejection of allegations that he had contributed to Newton's payment. He accepted that he had received the two Hayward payments, but said that they had been made personally to him, and instead of being paid into Liberal Party accounts had been held as 'an iron reserve' against any future shortages of funds. This explanation was to be examined closely by the prosecution at the Old Bailey, and was commented on by the judge. But in the meantime, Thorpe felt that this should be his last word on the subject. His statement ended:

'Having regard to the unusual way in which these current

allegations have emerged, there is a real danger that if specific details relating to matters which can be proved are made known at the present time, they may, in the course of the investigation, become known to, or be deduced by, those minded to further the allegations with consequent readjustment of their version.

'In these circumstances I have been advised that, whilst it is right and proper that I should re-express the denials which are contained in this statement, it is neither incumbent on me nor desirable to add anything further.'

When Challes began asking him specific questions Thorpe asked if he could respond to them by merely using the word 'ditto' to indicate that he was repeating the sense of that last paragraph. A bizarre session then ensued with Challes doggedly plodding through his case, putting allegations to Thorpe, while Thorpe simply answered, 'ditto'.

On 4 July the police delivered their file on the case to the Director of Public Prosecutions, Tony Hetherington, for his consideration.

The role of the DPP is to decide whether there is sufficient evidence to proceed with a prosecution in any criminal case referred to his office by the police. Any case which raises unusual problems, or where the question of 'public interest' is involved, is generally discussed with the office of the Attorney-General of the day, who is a political appointee.

The Thorpe case, if it were brought, was clearly going to be political dynamite. Not only did it involve a Privy Councillor and former leader of the Liberal Party, it touched on the role of senior ministers, lawyers and the police. Any decision to proceed had to be taken from the very top. Hetherington therefore consulted the Labour government's Attorney-General, Sam Silkin, before making up his mind.

Clearly it was not an easy decision. On 16 July it was revealed that Hetherington had asked the police to carry out further investigations to gather their evidence.

Sam Silkin was later to say that he had left the final decision entirely up to Hetherington. Since he, Silkin, was a politician, he felt that he should stay uninvolved. But, as

291

the events of the next fortnight showed, the Attorney-General's office was still closely interested in the affair right up to the eve of a final decision to go ahead with charges.

In that period the *Sunday Times*, which had pursued its investigations and had already spelled out the implications of 'the South Wales connection', pieced together the progress of the £20,000 payment from Hayward. On 22 July the newspaper sent a letter by hand to Thorpe asking him for an explanation of the way in which the money had been passed from Dinshaw.

Thorpe's lawyers replied with a stern warning: 'As you well know,' wrote Sir David Napley, 'there has been proceeding for some while a police inquiry and a report has been made to the Director of Public Prosecutions. While there is doubtless a place, under proper circumstances for what has become known as investigatory journalism, this hardly seems appropriate at this stage of the inquiries.' Napley referred the newspaper to the Director of Public Prosecutions.

It was, however, the Attorney-General's office who replied to a request for information from the *Sunday Times*. The laws of contempt lay down that where criminal charges are 'imminent', any comment on a case in a newspaper may be judged a contempt of court rendering the editor liable to imprisonment. On the eve of publication of the *Sunday Times*'s story, the Attorney-General's chief legal adviser phoned the office and told a senior executive on the paper that charges were to be brought 'within a matter of days' against Thorpe, Holmes, Le Mesurier and Deakin. The story was dropped, and that Sunday the paper ran a bare announcement of the imminence of the charges though without the detailed article which had been prepared. That same weekend David Steel, the Liberal leader, was also told that charges would now be made 'shortly'.

Challes applied for arrest warrants for Thorpe, Deakin, Le Mesurier and Holmes from a Justice of the Peace on 2 August, and two days later all four men, at his request, presented themselves at Minehead police station. The charge they faced was conspiracy to murder. Thorpe was charged in addition with 'incitement to murder'. He was the only one to make any reply. When cautioned and charged by Challes, he announced: 'I hear what you say. I am totally innocent of this charge, and will vigorously challenge it.' Later that day all four appeared briefly at West Somerset Magistrates Court and were remanded on bail.

It had always been David Steel's impression that if charges were brought, Thorpe would resign as a member of parliament. In fact Thorpe had not given a specific undertaking to his leader – he had merely said he would not stand again. It soon became clear that he had changed his mind

Amidst a rash of advice to the contrary, he accepted the invitation of his local party to continue as their MP and to stand again at the next election. As the annual party conference in September approached, senior officials asked him to save the party embarrassment and stay away. Most thought he would do that, but Thorpe was having none of it. It became clear that he considered he had as much right to attend as the next man, and in a gesture of defiance he walked into the conference hall in the middle of a debate. It was Steel who saved the day by escorting him to his seat amidst an embarrassed mixture of applause and silence. While several platform delegates examined their shoes, Thorpe appeared not only unaffected by the discomfort he was causing, but actually to be relishing it. Inevitably it was the party which suffered – next day's headlines were dominated by Thorpe's appearance while the debate itself was forgotten.

Behind the scenes at the conference, some Liberals had begun to raise again the question of Liberal Party finances during the Thorpe era. An inquiry was set up at the request of Jack Hayward to find out where his donations had gone.

The inquiry, headed by Michael Steed, the party's president, was not to report until much later, but some matters were quickly established.

Two sums amounting to £49,000, donated by Hayward, had gone to an account at Lloyd's Bank in Finsbury Circus:

£40,000 had been paid into the Liberal Party General Election fund and a further £9000 sent to the direct aid committee. The Finsbury Circus accounts were run separately and exclusively by Thorpe. David Steel had been a founding co-signatory but he had little involvement after that. The Liberal Party inquiry into these funds received a four-page explanation from Thorpe about Hayward's £49,000. The inquiry decided that the money had been legitimately spent on election work.

A sum of £25,000 donated by Arnold Weinstock of GEC had been paid into the Liberal Party organisation's fund and had been properly accounted for.

Another figure of £25,000 donated to Thorpe by a retired arms salesman, Geoffrey Edwards (who had first donated money to the Liberals in 1970), did not show up on the party accounts. It was believed to have been returned by Thorpe to Edwards's estate following his death in early 1978.

Of the £20,000 donated by Hayward and paid through Nadir Dinshaw in Jersey there was no trace. Its fate was to be a major plank in the prosecution case at the Old Bailey trial. Thorpe was to offer to repay £20,000 to Hayward before the committal proceedings but Hayward demurred. That sum was eventually paid over after Thorpe's acquittal.

By the time the committal proceedings, twice postponed, were finally fixed, for 20 November, Peter Bessell, whose evidence would be crucial, had been granted immunity from prosecution in return for his undertaking to come to Britain. Helped by his father-in-law, he managed to reassure his remaining creditors, and could arrive in safety. Newton, too, had been informed by the Director of Public Prosecutions that as a Crown witness he would be immune.

The focus of attention now shifted to the small Somerset town of Minehead where the local magistrate would have to decide whether there was sufficient evidence – to use the legal jargon – on which 'a reasonably minded jury, properly directed, might convict'

294

Under the Criminal Justice Act of 1967, a defendant in a criminal case may agree to be committed to trial merely on the formal tendering of written statements from witnesses. Otherwise the prosecution is required to lay out its full case and produce its witnesses so that the defence can see what they have to answer and can cross-examine the witnesses. If, as a result of this procedure, the case is revealed as a weak one, the magistrates can throw it out before it goes any further. The advantage for the legal system is that it weeds out cases where there is insufficient evidence to justify proceeding, and for defending counsel it reveals the strength of the Crown case without disclosing the defence.

Another important change introduced by the 1967 Act was the limiting of any public reporting of the committal stage, so as not to prejudice in advance a prospective juror if the case went to trial. This restriction can only be lifted at the specific request of a defendant.

The committal proceedings against Thorpe and his co-defendants took place in Minehead, a summer tourist resort, because it was the nearest magistrates court to the spot, six miles away from Porlock hill, where the shooting of Scott's dog had taken place. The small courtroom was not designed to cope with the invasion which built up over the weekend of 18 and 19 November. Only 37 seats had been designated for the press, and there were 140 applications for them. But the local hotels, restaurants and pubs enjoyed an unexpected winter boom as this horde of hard-drinking visitors settled in for what was expected to be a three-week hearing.

On Monday morning there was a long queue outside the prosaic 1930s building as the first of the defendants drove into the courtroom car-park under the gaze of the television cameras. Few of the journalists there believed that there would be anything substantial to file to their waiting offices apart from the 'courtroom sketches' which are all a British reporter is allowed to record while reporting restrictions are in operation.

At 10.17 am the three local magistrates, facing a packed courtroom, called for proceedings to begin, and the charges were read out. Then the clerk of the court announced that the defendants might apply for restrictions to be lifted if they wished. Otherwise they would stay in force.

Suddenly Gareth Williams QC, counsel for Deakin, got to his feet and said quietly: 'I wish to apply for reporting restrictions to be lifted. My client, George Deakin, welcomes the fullest scrutiny.'

The atmosphere in the public gallery changed dramatically – it required just one defendant to break ranks and ask for publicity for the magistrates to comply. Reporters from agencies and the evening papers raced for the doors to phone their offices. Front pages were cleared and journalists skilled in shorthand were put on trains to replace the 'colour' writers and the masters of the courtroom sketch.

The decision to ask for restrictions to be lifted had been taken finally only that morning by Deakin's defence team of Gareth Williams QC, defending counsel, and Barrie Stephens, Deakin's solicitor. They had calculated that there would be a distinct advantage in seeking to demonstrate that their client had, from the moment he requested an interview with the police, done nothing to shun public appraisal of his case.

It was less welcome to the other defendants. Jeremy Thorpe, sitting alone on the front bench below the press, which he occupied somewhat in the manner of a seasoned MP in his place at the House of Commons, listened grimly as Peter Taylor QC, for the prosecution, began to outline the case which would now be spelt out in relentless detail in next morning's papers.

'In 1959 Jeremy Thorpe became an MP,' were his opening words. 'In the early 1960s he had a homosexual relationship with Norman Scott . . .

The story which was to be spun out, explored and unravelled over the next four weeks, was as outlandish as any that the British public, addicted as they are to courtroom drama, had been regaled with in many a year. And the prosecution witnesses contributed in different ways to the bizarre mixture of high politics and low life.

296

Peter Bessell, his face lined and tanned, spelt out his evidence in a deep firm voice with the precision of a politician delivering an election address to a hostile audience. Cross-examined by Sir David Napley, a firm believer in the theory that a solicitor should be able to handle committal proceedings in court just as skilfully as a barrister, Bessell showed himself to be a composed and self-confident witness. He was quite capable, if necessary, of correcting Napley sharply if he thought he was wrong, and several times produced supplementary evidence which appeared to catch Napley off-guard. At the same time he was ready to concede his own fallibility, and Napley's strategy was to reveal weaknesses in his story rather than to challenge him head on. Napley concentrated on Bessell's conflicting testimony in the past, on a lucrative contract he had signed with the *Sunday Telegraph*, and on the wide-ranging immunity he had been given. All these were to be more ruthlessly examined in subsequent proceedings at the Old Bailey.

The next two witnesses, Jack Hayward and Nadir Dinshaw, gave their evidence in a straightforward manner, and it was clear that the defence did not intend to challenge it in substance, only to question the prosecution's interpretation of it. But the appearance of Andrew Newton was a different matter. He arrived outside the court wearing a balaclava as an uncomfortable and unconvincing disguise, and delivered his evidence in a rambling style which did little to enhance his credibility. His poor memory and even poorer wisecracking were quickly exploited by Gareth Williams, Deakin's eloquent and quick-witted counsel. Newton was clearly going to pose problems for the prosecution.

Norman Scott, on the other hand, was surprisingly self assured as a witness. Although in moments of stress he was apt to raise his voice in anger, and at times seemed close to tears, any attempt to browbeat him revealed an unexpected steeliness. Napley decided to treat him gently: 'It is not my intention or desire to be in any way unkind to you,' he said. But he incurred Scott's wrath on several occasions, particularly when Napley refused to believe that there had ever been a homosexual relationship between him and Thorpe.

This led to an absurd exchange in which Scott announced that he knew of certain physical characteristics on Thorpe's body which he could only have been aware of if he had seen him naked. They were some warts or nodules under one arm, he said, and a curvature of the spine. The description was so vague that it was laughed out of court – partly, perhaps, through sheer embarrassment.

The line of Napley's questioning showed that the defence would seek to undermine Scott's testimony by exposing his weakness and irrationality.

The main witnesses were succeeded by police evidence and by the tapes, read out by lawyers – who took different roles in speaking the parts – with evident enjoyment. Then came the defence submissions, which would be crucial if the magistrates were to decide there was no case to answer.

For Deakin, Gareth Williams suggested that his client had been 'plucked from obscurity on the evidence of a single creature – Newton.' And Newton, he said, was 'made and shaped by his own greed and self-delusion, finished and polished by the financial rewards he seeks . . . he has been paid, paid and paid again.'

Napley, on behalf of Thorpe, made it quite clear where he thought the prosecution's weakness lay: 'I contend that in terms of direct evidence, the case for the prosecution stands or falls on the evidence of Mr Bessell,' he said. The Hayward money, to which Taylor had devoted much time, was 'the last desperate act of the prosecution', and Scott's evidence had 'as much to do with the case as the flowers that bloom in the spring.' All three of the main witnesses had admitted they had been inveterate liars, and Bessell in particular aroused his scorn. 'In my submission,' said Napley, 'when you looked at his demeanour, mendacity was oozing out of every pore of his body.'

John Mathew QC, for Holmes, said there was insufficient evidence against his client for a conspiracy to murder – as opposed to a conspiracy to do anything else. 'The quality of the evidence, given against a background of intrigue, rumour and self-interest probably without parallel, has been shown to be the most corrupt and tainted ever to be placed before a court of criminal jurisdiction.'

On Le Mesurier's behalf it was submitted in the briefest terms that there was no evidence he knew of a conspiracy *before* it took place. 'Knowledge after the conspiracy ceased is not sufficient to make a person a party to a conspiracy,' said his counsel.

Peter Taylor summed up the prosecution case succinctly: 'There was one conspiracy', he said, 'and one conspiracy only, and it came into existence after a number of attempts by Thorpe over a number of years to persuade someone to join him, someone who finally did, to kill Scott.'

The case for the Crown, he said, was that 'Thorpe, from 1968-9 on, was urging there should be agreement to kill Scott, but nobody agreed with him until some time when Holmes did agree.' He conceded the importance of Bessell and argued prophetically: 'Unless Bessell can be regarded as a witness wholly discredited, there is a case.'

Following the last submissions, the three magistrates withdrew and considered their decision overnight. Next morning, on 13 December, it was given: 'We find there is a *prima facie* case in respect of each of the four of you. There is also a *prima facie* case in respect of you, Thorpe, of inciting Holmes to murder Norman Scott ... you will all be committed to stand trial.'

For those who had been covering the proceedings, the past four weeks had provided heady stuff. But, as one journalist said: 'That was the out-of-town run. Just wait for the West End premiere.' The notices had been spectacular, and had led to outspoken attacks on the whole function of the committal proceedings and its public airing of evidence in advance of the trial. It was, however, Sir David Napley himself who argued in favour of full publicity by quoting Edmund Burke: 'Where mystery begins, justice ends.'

With that, the circus headed for town.

20. The Trial: Prosecution

'I think you know how much I love North Devon, and the people who live within its borders.' The words' had been proclaimed twenty years earlier to a wildly enthusiastic crowd in the Pannier Market, Barnstaple, by the young Jeremy Thorpe, as he celebrated his first election victory. Now, in April 1979, facing the grimmest crisis of his life, Thorpe decided to draw again on the special relationship he had built up over the years between himself and his constituents, and stand again as Liberal candidate for North Devon.

The General Election of 1979 had been called by Labour's Prime Minister, James Callaghan, for 3 May – right in the middle of the period set down for Thorpe's Old Bailey trial. Most of Thorpe's party colleagues had urged him, either publicly or privately, to stand down and allow another candidate to fight the seat, on the grounds that Thorpe would only divert attention from the party's national campaign; most commentators assumed that it would be out of the question for a man to fight an election campaign with such serious charges hanging over his head.

But they reckoned without Thorpe's obstinate confidence. By now he was isolated from the party leadership whom he regarded as hostile, and contemputuous of the press whom he blamed for his misfortunes. He turned instead to his faithful constituency association, and they unhesitatingly adopted him as their candidate. 'We all support Mr Thorpe,' said an official proudly.

A 'Jeremy Thorpe Defence Fund' was set up by members of Thorpe's former club, the Reform in Pall Mall. One of the fund's chief sponsors was former Liberal Party president,

Lord Lloyd of Kilgerran. The fundraising work was later taken over by Lord Avebury – the former Liberal MP, Eric Lubbock – who also stood as Thorpe's bail surety. He collected over £30,000 for Thorpe's defence, including a cheque for £5000 from food and publishing magnate Sir James Goldsmith.

On 4 April, Thorpe applied for, and was granted, leave to have his trial postponed for eight days until 8 May, and began preparing for the campaign. 'I am grateful and very proud to have been asked to stand again,' he announced. 'This will be my eighth election, and I am delighted to be back in the fray. The adrenalin really starts pumping. My wife is also delighted.'

Soon, however, it became clear that something was going wrong. As the campaign got under way, reporters noted that Thorpe's magic rapport with the locals seemed to be crumbling. His style was the same – there was much plunging into crowds, embracing familiar figures, chatting over the garden gate. But there was also a quality of embarrassment which had never been there before. Prospective voters seemed to be avoiding the glad hand as it was proffered, and the unspoken subject of Thorpe's impending trial became an intrusion between the candidate and his people.

More important, the great national surge towards Margaret Thatcher and the Conservatives was eating into the Liberal vote. Tony Speller, the Tory candidate who had cut Thorpe's majority back to less than 7000 in 1974, pointed out that there had been a ten-per-cent change in the electorate since the last election, and that most of the newcomers were city commuters who were natural Tory voters. A host of fringe candidates, attracted by the publicity, and standing for such specialised causes as the Dog-Lovers' Party and the Democratic Monarchist Public Safety White Resident Party, threatened to draw away a few hundred vital votes. The Liberals would have been hard-pressed to hold the seat under normal circumstances. As it was, the task began to look impossible.

Liberal headquarters in London withheld support from

Thorpe. The most David Steel would do was send down a tape-recorded message. Only John Pardoe, from the nearby constituency of North Cornwall, himself facing a knife-edge battle, came over to speak on Thorpe's behalf.

Towards the end of the campaign, Thorpe began to look and behave like a beaten man. He had lost his taste for the fight. Increasingly it was his wife Marion, generally a reluctant campaigner, who had to encourage him up unwelcoming garden paths and down deserted village streets. At one point the couple found themselves addressing a 'crowd' consisting of three people – two of them reporters. Thorpe put a brave face on it. 'Don't believe the Tories,' he said, 'they always say they are going to win by 1000 votes. I have seen off four Conservative, and eight Labour candidates.'

But by now the Conservatives were beginning to talk of a 5000 majority. On election night in the Queen's Hall, Barnstaple – four days after Thorpe's fiftieth birthday and five days before his trial – the candidates lined up in front of the television cameras to hear the result. The audience pressing forward from the floor, as well as the millions watching on television, were shocked by Thorpe's appearance. His face had assumed a waxen look. Gaunt and unsmiling, he stared fixedly ahead as the teller read out the figures.

They were worse than he had ever dreamt. The Tories had demolished his majority of nearly 7000 and turned it into a crushing Conservative lead of 8473.

Thorpe's supporters in the crowd let out a low moan of disbelief, then turned on reporters with angry shouts of 'scum'. Tony Speller's victory speech was drowned by defiant cries of 'We want Jeremy', but Thorpe himself left the hall quickly, his face set and unflinching. 'The gap was much wider than I thought,' was as much as he could bring himself to say.

Next day he held a small press conference at his North Devon house. But he refused to talk about the trial, or to contemplate his political future. He said he would have to analyse the figures in order to explain why the result had gone the way it had. But those questioning him knew that no amount of explanation would compensate for the fact that North Devon's love affair with Jeremy Thorpe was over, and in the struggle ahead he would no longer be able to rely on the comfort of that support.

The events leading up to the trial were also stressful for Norman Scott, who had established himself in a rambling cottage on the edge of Dartmoor near the village of Chagford. Although his relations with the villagers were generally good, his most intimate relationship with Hilary Arthur, the mother of his three-year-old daughter Bryony, was deteriorating. Mrs Arthur had moved out to protect their daughter from the effects of the publicity surrounding the whole case.

The trial opened a little late on the morning of Tuesday 8 May at the Old Bailey where cameramen and crowds jostled round the one swing door which allows entry to lawyers, public and defendants alike. Over the following weeks regulars outside the court, waiting for a glimpse of the four accused as they arrived and left each day, settled into a friendly routine behind wire barriers, swapping predictions about the verdict and following the course of the case with an attention that was never to be relaxed. Not until Wimbledon did the focus of public interest switch.

Court Number One is a high-domed room in the old part of the building. For a courtroom which has seen some of the great criminal trials of the century its scale is modest. The judge, flanked by his clerk, looks down from his leather-backed chair on to a small and crowded well, where barristers and their juniors face the jury over a double row of pressmen. High above and behind the lawyers sit the public on steeply ranged benches which offer the best view of witnesses and defendants alike. Only the dock itself is unusual. Raised to the judge's level, it faces him across the well of the court, surrounded on three sides by thick panes of glass surmounted by decorative bronze knobs. There are two ways in and out:

through a glass door to the public part of the court – or down a steep stairway to the cells beneath.

As in most major trials, the proceedings began with an anti-climax. Selection of a jury (three women, nine men) and lengthy legal submissions took up all the first day and half the next. The drama of the day lay in the contemplation of Jeremy Thorpe himself, his face still bearing the rigid look it had assumed in public ever since election night. He sat on the left-hand side of the dock nearest the press, in one of the four high-backed chairs provided for the defendants, protected from draughts by a velvet-collared overcoat, his back supported by small red cushions. Although it was clear that his weak spine was causing him acute discomfort, he rarely shifted his position, in contrast to the plump figure of John Le Mesurier next to him who fidgeted often, calling for frequent glasses of water from an attendant. George Deakin, whose choice of suits at Minehead had ranged from a light blue to a virulent salmon pink which had clashed with his orange hair, had opted for something more sober this time, and listened pale and expressionless as the court settled down. David Holmes seemed languid by comparison. Always immaculately dressed and groomed, he affected an attitude of casual interest only, as he sat, propped on one elbow at the far end of the dock, occasionally leaning forward to look down at his defence team directly below him.

The charges were read out: Thorpe, Holmes, Deakin and Le Mesurier were charged with conspiring together and with others between 1 October 1968 and 1 November 1977 to murder Norman Scott. Thorpe in addition was accused of unlawfully inciting Holmes between 1 January and 31 March 1969 to murder Norman Scott. All pleaded not guilty.

The judge handed out his first warning of the case: anyone interfering with the jury would be punished – 'better bring a toothbrush if you're going to do that,' he announced. Mr Justice Cantley, sixty eight, with fifteen years judicial experience behind him, had once presided over a famous IRA trial and had been threatened with terrorist reprisals after imposing stiff sentences. But his reputation at the Bar was not that of a stern or overbearing judge, and his interventions in the Thorpe trial showed that he favoured the lighter touch. He combined occasional severity with a testy humour which delighted the press but frequently irritated the lawyers in court whose submissions and cross-examination would occasionally be interrupted by a damaging judicial aside. Kindly and solicitous towards the jury, he did not mince words when it came to the prosecution's witnesses, and his summing-up was to be a matter of controversy.

By the time the case had got properly under way on the second day, it was the solid presence of counsel for the prosecution which dominated the court. Peter Taylor QC combined the build and rugged looks of a second-row forward with a remarkable clarity of speech and exposition – 'the very best type of Roman Senator', wrote one journalist admiringly. A Northumberland man who had just celebrated his forty-ninth birthday, Taylor was familiar with cases involving public figures – his most celebrated prosecution had been against the architect John Poulson on charges of corruption. He quickly won judicial approval for the economy and directness with which he outlined his case – 'Don't worry, Mr Taylor, it's all been very interesting,' said the judge when he apologised for taking too much time. As each prosecution witness appeared, he led him patiently through his evidence, pausing occasionally to turn away from the judge and jury and face the body of the court as if to allow the implications of what had just been said to sink in around him.

As he questioned the main prosecution witnesses over the next few weeks, Taylor was aiming to prove four things: first, the existence of a homosexual relationship between Thorpe and Scott; secondly, Thorpe's determination to keep Scott quiet once the affair had ended; thirdly, his attempt to incite David Holmes to kill Scott when the threat of exposure increased; and finally, the birth of a conspiracy to murder Scott when all else had failed. Witnesses such as

Jack Hayward, Nadir Dinshaw and Michael Challes, would fill important gaps, but Taylor's case would stand or fall on the performances of Norman Scott, Peter Bessell and Andrew Newton.

Although the thrust of the prosecution had already been heard at Minehead, Taylor's opening words still sent a ripple of anticipation around the room. 'Twenty years ago, in 1959,' he began, 'Mr Jeremy Thorpe was elected MP for Devon North. During the early 1960s he had a homosexual relationship with Norman Scott. From then on, Mr Scott was a continuing danger to his reputation and career . . . the higher Mr Thorpe climbed the political ladder, the greater was the threat to his ambitions from Scott.'

Taylor stressed that Thorpe himself had always denied a homosexual relationship with Scott, but the prosecution, he said, would rely on more than Scott's words alone to prove it had taken place. Having outlined the full extent of the prosecution case he went on to examine the events in detail.

The affair had begun, he said, on the night of Wednesday 8 November 1961 when Thorpe had driven Scott with his dog, Mrs Tish, from the House of Commons where they had met, first to some friends in Dulwich, South London, then to his mother's house in Surrey where he had introduced Scott as a member of a TV camera team with whom he was travelling abroad the next day. Scott (then still called Norman Josiffe) had signed the visitor's book, at Thorpe's instigation, with a false name.

The story was taken up by Scott himself, giving evidence later, on the ninth day of the trial. He told the court that he thought the name had been something like Peter Johnson of Colchester, and he remembered having to ask Thorpe in some confusion which county Colchester was in. The visitor's book was produced in court, and the entry seemed to have been altered subsequently though the original entry could not be made out.

'That night,' said Taylor, 'Mr Thorpe visited Josiffe's room on more than one occasion. The first time he brought and left with Josiffe a book entitled *Giovanni's Room*. It is a novel describing a relationship between two men. Later Mr Thorpe returned to the bedroom, sat on the bed and talked to him.'

'He was wearing a dressing-gown and pyjamas,' Scott told the court. 'He just began talking to me about how I looked so ill, that things would be all right ... he said I looked like a frightened rabbit. He decided, I suppose, from then on he thought I was his frightened rabbit and he just hugged me and called me "poor bunny" ... he got into bed with me. He was hugging me.'

Thorpe, he said, then left the room and came back with a towel and a tube of vaseline which he put on his penis. He laid the towel on the bed and made love to him, with Scott the passive partner.

'I just bit the pillow,' said Scott. 'I tried not to scream because I was frightened of waking Mrs Thorpe.'

Afterwards, Thorpe got up, patted Scott's thigh, and left. 'I just lay there with my dog,' said Scott. 'She was by the bed. I picked her up, brought her into my bed with me, and just lay crying.'

Next morning Thorpe returned to his room and asked him how he liked his breakfast eggs done.

The affair continued, said Taylor, in London and the West Country. Thorpe made love to Scott in the flat Scott had found in Draycott Place; he took him four or five times to his mother's house – once when she was not there; they would meet in the Reform Club or in a Chelsea restaurant to have dinner; or Scott would come to the House of Commons to listen to debates. At Christmas 1961 they travelled together down to the West Country, where Scott stayed with Thorpe's friends the Colliers. On Christmas or Boxing Day they all had lunch together at Broomhills Hotel where Thorpe was staying, and after lunch, while the Colliers walked in the garden, Thorpe made love to Scott in a green-tiled bathroom.

'I think at that stage I loved him,' testified Scott. 'But I was very troubled about the sexuality. I think I loved him.

He was being very kind in one way, in that he was showing me some sort of caring.'

Gradually, however, the strain in their relationship began to show. One day when they were driving together in Thorpe's Sunbeam car, they had an argument. 'He tried to kiss me', Scott told the court, 'and I said I couldn't stand it and I said I would show him up in public. He said I couldn't hurt him because a friend of his was a man called Norman Skelhorn, the Director of Public Prosecutions' (Skelhorn did not in fact become DPP until 1964). Thorpe told Scott he was being 'very suburban' by threatening to show him up in public. On another occasion as they quarrelled in the car, Thorpe started driving 'like a maniac' and threatened to end it all.

Taylor read out the famous 'Bunnies' letter, with its postscript 'I miss you', and told the court that its tone was entirely consistent with Scott's account of the relationship. As he took Scott through his evidence he asked him about the 'Ann Gray incident' mentioned in the letter, and questioned him about the occasion on which a policeman had come to interview Scott in Thorpe's office near the House of Commons following the disappearance of Ann Gray's sheepskin coat.

> SCOTT: Jeremy and I were locked in the room, and he was having sexual intercourse.
> TAYLOR: What point had been reached when the police came?
> SCOTT: Well, when the police tried the door my fly buttons were undone and Jeremy was fondling me ... we stopped. Jeremy put his hand to his mouth and motioned me to sit down. He went to the door and unlocked it ...

In the course of 1962 the affair continued, said Scott, mostly at Thorpe's flat in Marsham Street where, after making love, Scott would have to sleep on a small camp bed.

As the affair deteriorated, however, he grew desperate until, in December 1962, he threatened to kill Thorpe, and was interviewed by police to whom he gave a statement detailing the extent of the relationship. His insurance cards, said Scott, were already a bone of contention since Thorpe had taken them and stamped them for a while, but had never given them back. By 1963 Scott had begun working in Ireland. 'Every time I came over', he said, 'it was for only one reason. It was not to pick up the insurance cards. It was for him, so he could screw me.'

Then came the abortive trip to Switzerland and the matter of the missing luggage. Scott told Thorpe that one of his cases contained certain letters, and Thorpe was 'very angry'. For a long time after Scott had returned to Ireland he continued to phone Thorpe asking for help in getting back his luggage, and finally he decided to write to Thorpe's mother. The letter was read out in court:

'For the last five years,' it began, 'as you probably know, Jeremy and I have had a "homosexual relationship". To go into it too deeply will not help either of us. When I came down to "Stonewalls" that was when I first met him. Though he told you something about the TV programme and Malta. This was all not so true. What remains is the fact that through my meeting with Jeremy that day, I gave birth to this vice that lies latent in every man.'

The letter went on to describe another meeting with Mrs Thorpe's son, and added: 'I think that was the day I realised that Jeremy did not care for me as a friend but only as a — — Oh! I hate to write that!! It upset me terribly and I was rather sick because, you see, I was looking for a friend in the real sense of the word.'

After relating some of his experiences in Ireland, Scott wrote: 'I was to go to England – to Jeremy – to corruption. Your son offered me two pounds after he had satisfied himself ... I came to London with the determination that I would never see Jeremy again. Got very depressed, took all my sleeping tablets and woke up in St Georges Hospital. I was able to discharge myself pretty simply, but they asked me why I had done the whole thing. Could I tell them? – No, I am too loyal – a quality your son fails at so miserably.'

He complained that Thorpe had only spent £30 on

309

attempts to get his luggage back from Switzerland. 'This was the last straw. Was our "love" to be measured in monetary value? – £30 is so little. I was so hurt.'

This 'very hurtful' letter, according to Taylor, was to reveal how much Thorpe feared the threat of exposure. When, in early 1965, he and Peter Bessell had met in the House of Commons and discussed their sexual lives, Thorpe had told him that if the truth about his homosexuality were ever to be made public, he would take his own life rather than face the shame it would bring on him and the Liberal Party.

That meeting was described in court by Bessell himself – the first prosecution witness to be called – on Day Four of the trial. 'He disclosed to me that he was a homosexual,' said Bessell.

'I was concerned', he went on, 'because a number of people had raised the question with me whether he might be homosexual. There was the question of the future leadership of the Liberal Party ... I wanted to determine whether this represented any risk to the party.'

A few weeks later, Thorpe asked Bessell to have lunch with him at the Ritz Hotel and showed him the letter from Scott to Mrs Thorpe. 'He was unusually tense – I would say on edge,' said Bessell. He read the letter, then asked Thorpe if the contents were basically correct. Thorpe said that they were.

From this discussion arose Bessell's long involvement in the affair; he travelled to Dublin to see Scott; corresponded with him; then helped him with small retainer payments during his early months back in London.

Bessell told the court what he claimed had happened when Scott's luggage was finally returned from Switzerland. It was, he said, collected from the railway station and taken to Thorpe's flat in Marsham Street, where Thorpe had opened it and removed two bundles of letters before returning the luggage to Scott in Dublin.

Some time later Thorpe became worried by the possibility

that Scott still had documentary evidence of a relationship, and early in 1968 a plan was hatched by which David Holmes, posing as a reporter from the German magazine *Der Spiegel*, would offer to buy Scott's story and thus acquire any letters he might have. Holmes, who did not know what Scott looked like, was to stand outside Bessell's office on a day when Scott had an appointment there, and would then follow and accost him after he had been pointed out. This elaborate plan was dropped at the last minute because Scott informed Bessell – untruthfully – that he had destroyed any remaining letters from Thorpe.

It was later that year – in November or December 1968 according to the prosecution – that the idea of getting rid of Scott first began to take shape in the mind of Jeremy Thorpe. He and Bessell were discussing the Scott problem in Thorpe's office at the House of Commons. Thorpe said it loomed 'like a black cloud' over him – a threat which might ruin his career. Bessell dismissed such foreboding. Scott, he thought, 'could be handled', and he did not think there was any great cause for anxiety.

At this point the division bell rang in the House and the two MPs went off to vote before resuming their discussion. Thorpe asked Bessell if it was really impossible to find Scott a job in America, and when Bessell said he thought it was, Thorpe announced: 'In that case we have got to get rid of him.'

'Are you suggesting killing him off?' asked Bessell, trying to treat the matter lightly.

The reply was solemn and serious. Thorpe stood up, looked at Bessell, and answered: 'Yes.'

He then went on, Taylor said, to suggest various methods of disposing of Scott's body. It could be buried; dropped in a river; buried under the rubble of a new motorway. All of these, Bessell thought, presented difficulties. It was not until he mentioned the disused tin mines in his Cornish constituency that Thorpe leapt up, shook him by the shoulders and exclaimed: 'A tin mine! That's it!' The body could be dropped down an empty mineshaft.

Bessell said he objected to the whole tone of the discussion. The suggestion was immoral, and one which two grown MPs had no right to be discussing.

Thorpe's reply was: 'It's no worse than shooting a sick dog.'

Bessell told the court that at this point he had left the room and driven away from the House of Commons, only to return some time later that night to find Thorpe still sitting in his office. 'He was sitting there at his desk, head down, and when I came in he behaved as though I had never left the room.' The following conversation, according to Bessell, then took place:

Thorpe: 'I have thought of the person who could kill Scott – David Holmes.'

Bessell: 'Rubbish. David's far too wet.'

Thorpe: 'Well, certainly you and I can't do it.'

Bessell: 'No, we can't.'

Thorpe: 'David is completely loyal, and if he were properly instructed he would be able to carry it out.'

The prosecution said that a few months later another meeting took place, also in the House of Commons, and this time Holmes attended. Thorpe proposed that Holmes should again pose as a reporter and invite Scott to drive with him to Plymouth where, he could say, the editor of his magazine was staying. On the way Holmes could take Scott to a pub where he could get him drunk. They could then drive over to Cornwall, and Scott's drunken state would make it easy to persuade him to get out of the car in some lonely spot and there Holmes could kill him.

'Holmes looked petrified,' Bessell told the court. 'Eventually he managed to catch my eye. I winked and he relaxed.' Thorpe continued to elaborate on his plan, but Bessell interrupted to say that shooting Scott would be noisy and messy. 'In that case', said Thorpe, 'it will have to be poison. You can slip it into his drink, David, in the pub.'

Holmes, according to Bessell, had an excellent sense of humour, and replied: 'It would be a bit awkward if he dropped dead and fell off the bar-stool.' Bessell responded to

312

he joke and remarked: 'That's all right. You can apologise
to the landlord and ask for directions to a convenient
mineshaft.'

Only Thorpe failed to appreciate the joke, commented
Bessell; he turned to him and said: 'This is a serious matter.'

It was left that Holmes would research slow-acting poisons
and report back. After leaving Thorpe, Bessell and Holmes
walked to the Strangers' cafeteria.

'Holmes's reaction and mine were the same,' Bessell told
the court. 'We were astonished at the nature of the plan
which was being put forward. Mr Holmes was not entirely
surprised at Thorpe's obsession about Mr Scott. What surprised us both was the ludicrous plan that had been put
forward, and Holmes was astonished at being cast in the
role of the principal actor.'

In his opening address, Taylor pointed out to the jury
that there was no suggestion of a conspiracy at this stage,
but he submitted that Thorpe was endeavouring seriously
to persuade Holmes to murder Norman Scott. That, he said,
was the evidence for the separate charge of incitement made
against Thorpe alone.

According to the prosecution, the murder plan – what
Thorpe referred to as 'the ultimate solution' – was shelved
when news came that Scott had got married in May 1969.
But Thorpe continued to believe, said Bessell, that it would
be necessary to carry it out, and the three men discussed
the possibility of luring Scott to America where he could be
eliminated, perhaps in one of the thinly populated western
states. Bessell said he was going to Florida anyway, and
perhaps that would do. Thorpe agreed.

Bessell said he and Holmes decided they ought to do
something to persuade Thorpe that the idea was unworkable.
They met up in New York in January 1971 and, over lunch
at the Algonquin Hotel, discussed a 'charade' that would
convince Thorpe that they had seriously tried to carry out
his plan to do away with Scott. They agreed to meet up in
Florida, and Holmes went so far as to buy a toy pistol which
fired plastic pellets a distance of a few feet so that he could

genuinely report that he had acquired 'a murder weapon
According to Bessell, both men enjoyed the joke, and afte
they had got back to New York Holmes telephoned Thorp
to inform him that the plan had unfortunately failed becaus
Scott had not turned up.

'Mr Holmes said he thought Mr Thorpe had conclude
we were two incompetent idiots,' Bessell told the court. 'Bu
since there was no one else he trusted to discuss the plan
Holmes thought that it would be the end of the matter. W
felt our charade had worked.'

Mr Justice Cantley raised an eyebrow. 'It sounds crazy
he commented drily.

'I agree, sir,' said Bessell. Even Thorpe permitted himsel
a smile.

The court heard from Norman Scott how, in 1971, he ha
taken his complaints to the Liberal Party and had bee
examined by a Liberal inquiry team. Later he had moved t
live in Thorpe's constituency. It was after this that Bessel
began to drop out of the picture as he shifted his busines
operations to America. Taylor had summarised the positio
to the jury by taking stock. 'Thorpe had talked of th
ultimate solution, but somehow, on each occasion the crisi
or any major disaster had been averted. In 1974 Mr Bessel
was no longer present to side with Holmes and support hin
in exercising a restraining effect. Scott had moved int
Thorpe territory in North Devon and was talking
indiscreetly.

'There were two elections in 1974, at each of which ther
was this nightmare possibility that the Scott affair migh
become public. Whether for these reasons or for othe
reasons, we submit that sometime, probably in 1974, Holme
became converted to the view that Thorpe was right an
that Scott would have to be killed. When that conversion
occurred, the conspiracy to murder was born.'

Once the plot had taken shape, Taylor contended, th
search was on for a 'hit-man'. David Holmes, in the compan
of a carpet-dealer, John Le Mesurier, with whom he was i

314

usiness, visited Cardiff where Holmes was giving financial
advice to a friend of Le Mesurier's, George Deakin. In the
course of one of their meetings Le Mesurier told Deakin
that a friend of Holmes had a problem with a blackmailer
'a woman had committed suicide,' he said, 'and a three-
year-old child's life was being threatened.' Le Mesurier
asked Deakin if he could find 'somebody who could frighten
the fellow off.'

Deakin, said Taylor, had agreed to help and had mentioned it to a friend called David Miller in about October
1974. Miller said that he did in fact know someone who
would do anything 'for a laugh and a giggle'. On 26 February
1975 at a charity Showmen's Dinner Deakin and Miller
were together. Miller introduced Deakin to an airline pilot
called Andrew Gino Newton whom he had brought along.
In the course of the evening Newton took Deakin aside and
said: 'I understand you want someone bumped off. If you
haven't got anybody, I'm your man.'

'Deakin's reaction', Newton told the court when he took
the stand on the twelfth day of the trial, 'was one of interest,
but we didn't have a dialogue.' That night Newton got
extremely drunk and did not remember being taken back
to his home in Blackpool.

Some weeks later, however, Newton again saw Deakin at
Miller's business premises in Cardiff, and Deakin asked him
if he was still interested. He said he was, and Deakin gave
him a telephone number to call. Newton told the court that
there was talk of the contract being worth £15,000.

About two or three weeks later, Newton claimed, he
telephoned Deakin from Blackpool and they arranged to
meet at the Aust service station on the M4 motorway on
the English side of the Severn Bridge. Deakin arrived in a
BMW car and Newton got into the passenger seat beside
him. Deakin showed him a folder of photographs with what
Newton presumed was Scott's address written on it. Deakin
pointed to the photos without touching them, and said:
'That is him.'

The town of Dunstable was mentioned as the place where Scott was staying, and during a short conversation 'we established the figure was not £15,000, but £10,000.' Payment would be in cash.

TAYLOR: Did you have any questions?
NEWTON: Yes. Only the sort of questions one would expect a hit-man to ask.

The court dissolved in laughter. Only the judge failed to see the funny side and called for order.

NEWTON: I also wanted to know who wanted him killed and why, but I was told I was expected to go through with it and that I already had too much information from the people concerned.

Newton told the court that he took the photographs and left, agreeing that he would telephone Deakin if he had anything to report. He spent a fruitless day in Dunstable, then called Deakin who gave him a number where he could contact David Holmes direct. It was only after he had spoken to Holmes that Newton learned he should have been in Barnstaple not Dunstable. He and Holmes met to talk the whole thing over at the Royal Court Hotel in Sloane Square, London. During the talk Holmes told him that he and Deakin had once met Scott, posing as reporters, at the Imperial Hotel in Barnstaple, and had tried to steal his briefcase. Holmes confirmed that the fee for the job would be £10,000. 'He said he would be far happier if Scott just vanished from the face of the earth rather than having a body,' said Newton. How would he know the job had been done in that case? 'I would know,' replied Holmes.

Newton then described to the court his attempts to make contact with Scott. His first idea, he said, had been to lure Scott to London on the pretence of offering him a modelling job. He had suggested a rendezvous at the Royal Garden Hotel in Kensington, and had gone along with a chisel concealed in a bunch of flowers. But Scott had failed to turn up.

NEWTON: I was going to hit him on the head with the chisel in the hotel room to kill him. I bought the flowers to conceal the chisel, but Mr Scott did not turn up, and I heaved a sigh of relief.

His next move was to talk to Holmes again. He also burnt the photographs of Scott. Holmes arranged an appointment with Scott, but by this time Newton's nerve was beginning to fail.

NEWTON: It was something I did not want to do. It was something I knew from that day on I could not carry out. It was something I had found out about myself as a person.

Nevertheless he kept up the pretence, partly for the money, partly, he says, because he was frightened. 'One hears of kneecaps being blown off,' he said. He approached Scott directly in the Pannier Market, posing as a man called Peter Keene, and pretended that he was there to protect Scott from 'a man in Canada who was being paid a four-figure sum to kill him.' This, Newton admitted, was pure invention on his part.

Finally he persuaded Scott, together with his Great Dane which was an unexpected addition, to drive with him from Combe Martin in Devon to Porlock. He had acquired a Mauser pistol from a friend and he intended to pretend that the murder had been bungled. But the dog presented a problem.

NEWTON: If it had been a Yorkshire terrier or something not very big, that would have been all right, but I thought if I had to frighten Norman Scott I was not sure whether the dog would attack me or run away.

They set off towards Combe Martin, with Newton pretending to be exhausted. Eventually Scott offered to drive and Newton pulled the car off the road.

NEWTON: Norman Scott got out of the car, the dog leapt over the passenger front seat and followed him. My

317

loaded firearm was in my right-hand pocket. I probably had about six rounds in it. As Norman Scott went round the front of the car I got out and started to walk behind the car. Then I pulled the firearm from my pocket, went back to the driver's side and shot the dog.

He then levelled the gun at Scott and told him: 'Right, it's your turn now.' Then he said: 'Oh, it's jammed.' He made a great pretence of trying to unjam the gun in the headlights of the car although he knew it was working perfectly well. He again approached Scott who was beside his dog, and levelled the gun at him. Once again he said it was jammed, cursing as he did so.

NEWTON: Scott still stood there. He made no move to go, so I got back into the car and said, 'I will see you another time' . . . it's as stupid and as simple as that.

Scott had earlier given the court his own account of the shot that had killed Rinka. 'I did not hear anything,' he said. 'The dog just sort of fell against me and sank down. Newton had shot the dog. I couldn't really understand what he had done at that moment.'

After the shooting Newton drove to Miller's house where he stripped down the gun and then test-fired it, later hiding it on the premises. Again, he claimed, he was only play-acting – the sham was to convince Miller that the gun had jammed.

Newton told the court that while he was on bail awaiting trial he had a number of meetings with Holmes who gave him £400 on account and discussed his court appearance. Holmes said he was going to America to help Newton's defence and that 'a letter would arrive to a friend of the court'.

TAYLOR: Is that the phrase – a friend of the court?
NEWTON: That's word perfect. I asked what he meant and he said he could not say.

Holmes's trip to America, according to Bessell, was to see him in order to persuade him to write a 'blackmail' letter

318

about Scott to Thorpe's solicitor. Bessell told the court of a conversation with Holmes after he had finally agreed. He had asked if there was anything else Holmes had not told him about the dog-shooting incident.

After some hesitation, Holmes eventually said: 'All right, Newton was hired to kill Scott.'

BESSELL: I said something like: 'Oh Christ, David, I thought all that kind of thing had been abandoned long ago . . . I thought we had always agreed we would never have anything to do with anything of that sort.'

Holmes explained, said Bessell, that Scott's move to North Devon had changed everything. The threat had become a real one again, and eliminating him had seemed the only solution. Bessell asked him who had hired the pilot, and Holmes said he had. He had met him in a pub in Chelsea. 'Are you really suggesting that you casually ran into a man who made a habit of killing people for money?' Bessell asked him. 'Well,' said Holmes, 'It was more or less like that.'

Bessell described later speaking to Thorpe on the telephone and asking him whether it was true that Holmes had paid £10,000 for Scott's letters, as he had claimed.

'Not to my knowledge,' said Thorpe sharply. But when Bessell pressed him he had answered: 'Wait, let me give you an Isaac Foot answer. If Mr Holmes had taken the ferry, it was essential that these letters should not be found by the police afterwards. We had to get them first.'

According to Bessell, an 'Isaac Foot answer' was one which seemed to say one thing and meant another. 'Taking the ferry' meant crossing from Plymouth over to Cornwall and was a reference to the original plan to silence Scott. The following exchange, said Bessell, then took place:

Bessell: 'So the plan David told me about was real?'
Thorpe: 'Yes.'
Bessell: 'Well, thank God it failed . . . and that it can never be tried again.'
Thorpe: 'Yes . . . yes, that's right.'

As events leading up to Newton's trial in March 1976

and Thorpe's resignation in May began to gather pace, Bessell recorded two telephone conversations with David Holmes. These were played in court, using the Old Bailey's brand new system with transmission to earphones relayed by infra-red signals rather than radio frequencies. Judge, jury, counsel and defendants donned earphones, and heard the following exchanges from a conversation which took place on 7 March – two days after David Holmes had admitted to paying £2500 for Scott's letters:

Bessell: 'Tell me this, how is Jeremy?'

Holmes: 'Well, he's coming back fighting . . .'

Bessell: 'I take it he's in reasonably good spirits.'

Holmes: 'Reasonably good spirits . . . after all, we all knew it was coming.'

Bessell: 'And Goodman is still holding his hand?'

Holmes: 'Absolutely.'

Bessell: 'Good, and Harold is being helpful?'

*

Holmes: 'Well, I have deliberately emerged in the last two days as being a total fool.'

Bessell: 'Yeah, yeah, which is very wise, I think you're right.'

Holmes: 'Yes, absolutely, I mean, we decided, that is how I'd play it.'

Bessell: 'Right, exactly, exactly.'

Holmes: 'Now I may say, of course, nature's on my side as well, but I have come over – I looked at the interview – anyone would think I was ga-ga.'

Bessell: (Laugh) 'No, I don't think that I . . . I'm sure they wouldn't think that, David.'

Holmes: 'You needn't be polite. It was, it was quite deliberate on my part.'

*

The second conversation, on the eve of Thorpe's resignation, included these comments on some of the people involved in the unfolding drama:

Holmes: 'Wainwright is being particularly poisonous . . . going round asking sort of difficult questions and spreading

320

rumour and discontent ... I think Emlyn [Hooson] has been firmly, firmly sat on.'

Bessell: 'Oh, well, Emlyn, yes, I wouldn't take too much notice of Emlyn, because I would say Emlyn has done himself as much damage as he's done anybody.'

*

Holmes: 'Another small point is that Hayward, Jack Hayward, has been asking Jeremy for your address.'

Bessell: 'He's got it.'

Holmes: 'I beg pardon?'

Bessell: 'He's got it, Hayward's got my address.'

Holmes: 'Oh, has he?'

Bessell: 'Yes.'

Holmes: 'What we have been saying is that, that we didn't, um, we are actively defusing him.'

Bessell: 'Yeah. Well, I don't imagine he's going to get himself too publicly mixed up in this mess.'

Holmes: 'No, I think, in fact, his immediate reaction, putting it bluntly, was to say if he [Bessell] has re-appeared again, he owes me some money and I shall ask him for it.'

Bessell: 'Yeah. Well, that's all right.'

Holmes: 'Jeremy rang me up about this and I suggested to him that he should say to Jack, as a majority favour to all of us, would he kindly not make that kind of remark, would he kindly not do anything about it if he cared at all.'

Bessell: 'Right, right.'

*

Bessell: 'Tell me this, how is David Steel doing in all this?'

Holmes: 'He's behaved with dignity and sense and he's one of the few that has ... in that he has always said he would like to be, like to succeed, but he would never fight ... and that he wouldn't even put his name forward until the other one had irrevocably gone ... that, I think, is a very dignified posture.'

The conversation ended with a heart-warming testimonial:

Bessell: 'Take good care of yourself, and I'm very glad indeed to get such good news and particularly glad that things are looking all right for you, David, because you have been, to use a sentimental term, you have been a good and faithful servant to our friend, and I don't mean that in a belittling way, but I mean it in the sense that you have been a most honourable friend, and you don't deserve to suffer ... you are, after all, a private citizen and your privacy and your life has been invaded in the most hideous way.'

There were other people, the court heard, who were just as keen to protect their interests. As Newton's release from prison approached, Le Mesurier had a conversation with Miller which Miller taped:

Le Mesurier: 'All the arrangements that we made with Andrew [Newton] stand. We want Andrew to know that, 'cause if the press get hold of him, he starts blabbering ... the geezer involved in this lot is fucking Lord Goodman ... defending solicitor. These writers already have letters from Lord Goodman threatening them if they mention Holmes's name, they'll be sued for libel, criminal libel fucking slander. Not from some little solicitor tucked away ... this'll be Lord Goodman's office ... so they ain't playing with the boys, you know they've got the money, the real money to go up.'

Le Mesurier was particularly keen that Newton should be reassured that all was well:'... if Andrew comes out and ... he wants to get away somewhere, it's all set up for him, everything is arranged, so we don't want these blokes from the bloody press or from, you know, going round offering him or anybody else all kinds of money to come up with the stuff, because, you know, it'll all start again. No one'll win. It won't do anybody any good.'

Later Miller said: 'You told him he was in for ten grand.'

Le Mesurier: 'That's right, it's all ready for him, and if he came tomorrow and said, "I want ten G's" ... it's all put to one side, it's all ready.'

Then he added: 'You're not talking about people with a few bob, you know. I mean, these people have got a good

322

lot of money. I mean, ten grand was up like that.' A later conversation between the two men, a short time after Newton's release from prison, revealed that the fee had dropped to 'five'. Was that the arrangement? asked Miller.

Le Mesurier: 'Oh, yes, I've spoken to my friends and they, I said, well, you know, I thought it was more actually.' He added that he did think it was twice as much, but 'I was corrected very quickly when I mentioned that amount and they said, "Oh no, it ain't, it's five, you know, that was all arranged so there's no problems with him about that," they said, "because he knows how much it is ..." I said OK, as long as I know, all they're concerned about is getting him paid.'

On 18 April 1977, the court heard, Newton was paid his £5000 fee on St Brides Common, near Bridgend, photographed by a detective agency hired by Miller, apparently for his own 'protection', though he admitted that the *People* newspaper had later paid £8000 for what he called 'this volatile package' of tapes and photographs. Le Mesurier's reaction to the appearance of the detective agency's photographer, hanging out of the car as it passed the pay-off point, had been, according to Miller, complete panic: 'He got very worried and said he wanted to get out of the place. He said, "They have got a picture that will link me with Holmes ..."'

Miller told the court that he had not been granted any immunity in the case, and was advised by the judge that he was entitled to refuse to answer any question which he felt might incriminate him.

The prosecution revealed some of the tapes which Newton himself had made in order to improve the saleability of his own story. He had recorded telephone calls between himself and a reluctant David Holmes.

Newton: '...um, look, I have to get a couple of things straight, right? ... The press, right? ... Now, they have been on to me ... Now, then, something, somewhere along the line somebody must have said something ... what about the Sloane Square? Have you, did you tell anybody?'

Holmes: 'No.'

Newton: 'Well, what about Dave Miller?'

Holmes: 'I don't know him.'

Newton: 'Yeah, well obviously John does, right?'

Holmes: '... let's stick to "my South Wales" and "your South Wales". My South Wales wouldn't know about that anyway ...'

Newton: '... I've been told from er John that you in fact have had a telephone call ... it took the form of a threat ...'

Holmes: '...um, I know who I was told it was from.'

Newton: 'What, MI5?'

Holmes: 'Hmmm ... I think they are concerned that, if the whole subject came up again for some, er, weakness on my part, things that happened that I know nothing about and have nothing to do with, any of us could very well appear as well, is my interpretation.'

Newton: '... there's one person knows the full story, um, you know, at my end ... when I was in the States I got hit by a lorry ... It took three blinking attempts to run me over, you know, and I take great exception to this, you know ...'

Holmes was still struggling to express himself: 'You, you know that in this one, um, one comes up against something called conspiracy which is extremely important to know – a lot of other things and that therefore I would be in exactly the same position and it wouldn't be comfortable ... I mean I think it's uncomfortable for all of us and it simply is a question of sitting it out.'

But Newton was inexorable: 'You know Deakin, Dave Miller.'

Holmes: 'Don't produce any names because I never know about my telephone ... I have every reason to be totally silent.'

Holmes was keen that Newton should go to Rhodesia and look up General Peter Walls who would find him a job there.

Newton: 'In view of the attempt at me, having a go at me, now, you know, I have got an unnatural and not natural desire to try and stay around a bit longer.'

Holmes: 'Well, absolute hand on heart, I do assure you that had nothing to do with anyone that I know ...'

Newton: 'I don't know how long it is going to take to get to Rhodesia but when I go there, I'll certainly make a note of telling somebody ... I don't want anything sort of going wrong, you know, you see.'

Holmes: 'It is the last place in the world that there is any English influence.'

Newton: '... what the press are trying to do ... they want to tie up with this BOSS angle ... the South African involvement.'

Holmes: 'Oh, I see.'

Newton: 'Because it ties up with Salinger [Thorpe's financial adviser]. The last thing I had, some female reporter come and a pair of them came up. Because my name was Niewedonski at one time.'

Holmes: 'Hum.'

Newton: 'They thought I was involved with the KGB.'

Holmes: 'Come back to the one point, to the central factor in, to you, in fact, you have made to me, um, that – if you say nothing, I say nothing.'

Newton: 'All right.'

Holmes: 'And they aren't able to prove anything.'

Later still, Newton pressed Holmes still further.

Newton: 'But what I am trying to get at is that John the Carpet –'

Holmes: 'Hm, yes, but ...'

Newton: '– had suggested that if I go to um Rhodesia ...'

Holmes: 'Stop producing names every conversation, because I mean the whole thing terrifies me. I know who you are talking about, get on ...'

Newton: '...er, Miller, right, I suggest we don't touch him at all.'

Holmes: 'Yeah, OK.'

Newton: 'OK, um, because I think you know his eyes

seem to go round like blinking cash registers or fruit machines himself . . .'

Holmes: 'I'll make sure that nothing else is ever said . . . and just one thing. If it becomes necessary for us to have any more words, talk via my friend in South Wales, don't please arrive in Manchester because there is no way I could provide explanations for that, if it isn't me who answers the door.'

Newton: 'Right well I think that's it then right um yeah I mean don't forget you know that there's a charge you know that they can put on you is – us – a conspiracy to bloody –'

Holmes (interrupting): 'I am remembering that very carefully.'

Newton: '– to murder so now let's keep it quiet OK.'

Holmes: 'Just fine, and you may rely on that.'

Holmes's warning to Newton to stay away from his home had just the opposite effect, and Newton was to make more than one unsuccessful attempt to see him in person before he left for South Africa, on a ticket paid for by Le Mesurier, according to the prosecution. He flew out leaving behind him the headlines he had made with his disclosures about a conspiracy. Miller had phoned Deakin about it.

Miller: 'Hello.'

Deakin: 'Dave?'

Miller: 'Yes, George.'

Deakin: 'Heard anything?'

Miller: 'Yeah, bad news really . . . big article on me . . .'

Deakin: 'Anything on me?'

Miller: 'Nothing, but it's, er, Newton's made a statement with his solicitor to the papers.'

Deakin: 'Yes.'

Miller: 'He is going to name everybody, you know why he has done it, it is obviously money.'

Deakin: 'Yes, well, I'm denying, what are you going to do?'

Miller: 'Well, you know, um, um, I'm just going to look

after myself if it comes down to it ... why has he fucking done it?'

Deakin: 'I don't know.'

Miller: 'You know, didn't somebody come up with the goodies, or what?'

Deakin: 'Yes, yes, they came up with that.'

Miller: '... You seen a solicitor?'

Deakin: 'Well, I have seen mine.'

Miller: 'Yeah.'

Deakin: 'And as I said to him, that as far as I am concerned, they just wanted somebody to frighten somebody.' He added: 'I said it quite jokingly in a place at Blackpool ... what went on afterwards I don't know because that's all I ever did and that was the end of it ...'

Miller: '... the last time I heard was that they are being made to look fools, aren't they, the police? If it all comes out they are really going to go into it.'

Deakin: 'Yes, but there is such a lot of high powers at the moment trying to hush it up still.'

Miller: 'Yeah, well, hopefully, yeah.'

On the seventeenth day of the case, Peter Taylor called a witness called Colin Lambert who had worked in the carpet business of which Le Mesurier was managing director and David Holmes a consultant.

In 1977, after press publicity over the Newton affair, Lambert had asked Le Mesurier whether he had paid £5000 to Newton and Le Mesurier replied: 'Yes, I did.'

Asked by John Bull, junior prosecuting counsel, if he had said anything else, Lambert added: 'Yes, he also remarked that "David says we are going to prison."' He understood that to mean David Holmes.

On another occasion, Le Mesurier had remarked to him: 'We should have hired someone like you because the chap who went to do the shooting was an idiot.'

On the following day two witnesses, Nadir Dinshaw and Jack Hayward, gave evidence about two sums of £10,000 which had been passed from Hayward via Dinshaw to David

Holmes, at Thorpe's request. Dinshaw explained that he had agreed to pass the money to Holmes, provided there was no publicity, and that he had given Holmes the second £10,000 in small amounts of cash.

Hayward testified that he had passed the £20,000 to Dinshaw and was 'merely following instructions' in doing so.

The prosecution now moved to more recent events. Taylor said that as the police net closed around Thorpe he made 'undignified and wholly improper' attempts to tamper with witnesses to his part in financing the plot to kill Norman Scott. These included approaches to both Dinshaw and Hayward and his attempts to persuade them to give innocent explanations of the £20,000 which was, the Crown submitted, used to pay for the conspiracy.

He had even asked his friend, Michael Ogle, to act as an intermediary between himself and David Holmes whom his lawyers would not allow him to contact direct, in order to ascertain whether Holmes might agree that the money was a loan to him.

Ogle's statement was read out unchallenged. In it he said that Thorpe had told him that Holmes had lent money to him in the past. When Holmes had got into difficulties himself, said Thorpe, he had returned the favour using Hayward's £20,000 donation. Both Thorpe and Holmes had recognised that the money had been given for political purposes and Thorpe was also worried because the method of payment might have made it look as though there had been exchange control or income tax irregularities. Thorpe had told Ogle that he could not remember his precise instructions to Dinshaw about the money and now realised that this could lead to a 'disastrous ambiguity'.

According to Ogle, he had met Holmes on several occasions and reported to Thorpe after each conversation. Holmes had agreed that the first £10,000 cheque had gone straight into his bank to reduce his overdraft, but he would not be specific on the second £10,000 which was paid in cash. The two men met for the last time in August 1978. Holmes was worried because conspiracy charges seemed inevitable, and he had wanted Ogle to arrange a meeting with Thorpe so that both men could sort out what happened to the money. Thorpe's lawyers had refused. Holmes had appeared relieved that Thorpe had made arrangements to repay Hayward in full.

Finally, after taking Detective Chief Superintendent Michael Challes through his evidence of interviews and arrests, Taylor turned to the judge and said simply: 'My lord, that is the case for the Crown.'

21. The Trial: Defence

The defence had concentrated from the very first day of the trial on what counsel considered to be the weakness of the prosecution case – the unreliability of the main witnesses.

Thorpe's counsel was George Carman QC, at forty nine a contemporary – they had been at Oxford together. A small, bespectacled man with a precise and academic delivery, Carman represented a complete contrast in size and manner to the genial Peter Taylor beside him. Although he had practised on the northern circuit, where Mr Justice Cantley had been a presiding judge, Carman seemed not to find favour with him as he ploughed remorselessly through the legal submissions of the first two days. His aim was to persuade the judge that some of the prosecution witnesses were so prejudiced by reason of the sums of money they stood likely to gain from a conviction, and the various forms of immunity they had been granted, that even allowing them to give their evidence would amount to a contempt of court.

The judge listened to the arguments with increasing impatience, frequently interrupting to complete a point, or to contradict legal assertions. Halfway through the second day he rejected the pleas and announced that these were matters for a judge and a jury to decide on in the course of the trial.

It was John Mathew QC, an experienced prosecuting counsel, in this case defending Holmes, who began the first cross-examination, on Day Six, of Peter Bessell. His opening words set the tone: 'There are a number of compelling reasons, aren't there,' he said, 'why your evidence should not necessarily be believed?'

Bessell, giving evidence in his deep politician's voice, courteously accepted that the court only had his word to go on that he was now telling the truth. But he pointed out that most of the lies he had told in the past had been in defence of Jeremy Thorpe.

'Not only do you have a credibility problem,' continued Mathew, 'but you have every motive, do you not, to exaggerate and sensationalise about this case?' He understood that by selling his story, Bessell was expecting to make 'many thousands of pounds'.

BESSELL: I expect to make a few thousand pounds which, when various expenses have been deducted including legal fees, will not amount to a very large sum.

At the same time, said Mathew, he stood to make more money if one or all of the defendants were convicted?

BESSELL: I accept I would make more money, sir, yes.

Bessell accepted in cross-examination that his contract with the *Sunday Telegraph*, was geared to the outcome of the trial. The total he might earn for serialisation of his book was £50,000. There had been a £17,000 advance already. If there was an acquittal he would receive an additional £8000. If there was a conviction he would get the full balance of the £50,000.

Mathew then turned to the form of immunity which Bessell had been granted. This included no criminal proceedings by the police in respect of anything arising out of the case, or anything referred to in court. He was also immune from private proceedings. These were surely, said Mathew, the widest terms of immunity that any prosecution witness had ever been given in Britain.

Bessell said that might be so, but they still did not render him immune from charges of perjury if he lied in court.

Mathew then asked him about his 'disappearance' in January 1974. Was this 'the lamentable last act of a discredited figure'?

BESSELL: Regretfully I do admit that, sir.

MATHEW: Do you also agree . . . a discredited politician?
BESSELL: No, sir.
MATHEW: A disastrous businessman?
BESSELL: Yes.

Mathew proceeded to question Bessell about the evidence he had given which related to his client, David Holmes. He suggested that Bessell had lied by saying Thorpe wanted Scott killed in 1969 and 1970 and had further lied by saying an attempt had been made to carry out the job. Bessell denied it. Mathew suggested that the conversation they had had about an 'ultimate solution' in the early part of 1969 had been 'light-hearted banter'.

BESSELL: I cannot accept that. It was a serious proposition.

Mathew quoted Bessell himself as saying, 'It sounds like a fairy tale' – and a fairy tale it was, wasn't it?

BESSELL: No, sir, it is not.

On the afternoon of the sixth day George Carman got to his feet and began a cross-examination which was destined to be the dominating feature of the trial, and quite possibly its turning point. He began gently, by proposing four reasons which, in his view, might have persuaded Bessell to return to England to give evidence; a sense of justice; loyalty to the Liberal Party; revenge; money. Bessell accepted the first two, and firmly rejected the others.

Carman then asked Bessell why, as a lay preacher, he had not felt it incumbent on him to tell the party that his leader was 'a man intent on murder'.

BESSELL: My first loyalty was to Mr Thorpe. I believed this could be prevented. I saw no purpose in seeking to damage his career in that way.

Carman said he found that attitude 'incredible'.

CARMAN: Something more totally incredible – before Mr Thorpe, on your account of the matter, in his mind was sending Mr Scott to his death in 1971 in the United

States, you have asserted he proposed the murder of *another* person to you, in 1970.

BESSELL: Yes, sir.

CARMAN: A man called Hetherington – a man Thorpe had never met?

Bessell, showing no surprise, answered calmly: 'Yes, sir.'

CARMAN: If your evidence has any vestige of truth, by the time you went to the United States and met Holmes, the leader of the Liberal Party had proposed not only the death of Norman Scott, but that of another human being ... but this time you, not the unfortunate Holmes, was the deputed assassin. Mr Thorpe was perfectly serious?

BESSELL: Yes, sir.

The 'Hetherington incident' was to be examined off and on over the next two days, and was to lead to one of the more dramatic moments in court. Bessell's contention, as described in his *aide-memoire* drawn up in 1976, was that at the time of the General Election of 1970, a man called Hetherington, claiming to be a relation of Norman Scott, or his wife, had approached Bessell, and had threatened to expose the alleged homosexual relationship between Thorpe and Scott.

Bessell had consulted Thorpe who had been very anxious about it, and had suggested that unless Hetherington was 'disposed of', he might be a continuing source of trouble. Bessell told him: 'Leave it to me. Go away and fight the election, and I will deal with it somehow.'

The weekend before the election, he had met Hetherington at 2 am outside Plymouth station. Hetherington had handed over documents which Bessell concluded were forgeries. He had promised the man £2000, but had only given him £170.

CARMAN: When you went off to deal with Hetherington, you say Thorpe did not know whether you were going to kill him?

BESSELL: No, I am sure Thorpe knew I had no such intention. I left him confident that I would deal with it somehow.

After the election, Bessell says he told Thorpe: 'It is resolved, don't worry about it.'

CARMAN: Are we in the world of reality or fantasy?
BESSELL: We are in the world of reality.

The word 'resolved' did not mean that he had murdered Hetherington.

MR JUSTICE CANTLEY (intervening): Did you murder him?
BESSELL: No.

Carman now revealed that in December 1977, at Thorpe's suggestion, Lord Goodman had written to the Director of Public Prosecutions, outlining Thorpe's version of this extraordinary episode. Carman did not submit the text of this statement to the court, but put Thorpe's side of the story. According to him the whole thing had been an episode of pure comedy. One day Bessell had taken Thorpe on one side and told him that the Hetherington matter had been resolved.

'Hetherington has been eliminated,' Bessell had whispered. 'I've bumped him off!' He announced that he had poisoned Hetherington using a clear liquid common in the dry-cleaning business – with which he was familiar. He had then thrown the body down a mineshaft.

Thorpe had roared with laughter, said Carman. 'Peter,' he had said, 'if you spent less time murdering people, and more time canvassing, your successor might not have lost his seat!'

The implication of Carman's account was clear: the whole saga of poisoning and mineshafts was a product of Bessell's fertile imagination. But Bessell was unshaken: 'There is not a word of truth in [your account],' he said.

CARMAN: ... you must have thought you had a ghastly maniac leading the Liberal Party?

BESSELL: Yes, at one stage I thought Mr Thorpe had a crazy, sick obsession about murder . . .

CARMAN: You haven't left out any other murder proposals have you?

BESSELL: No, it was the first time – there were no others.

CARMAN: You are not going to tell us of a third or fourth murder proposal tomorrow, are you?

BESSELL: No, sir.

The dramatic conclusion to this exchange came on the following morning of the hearing; Bessell had claimed that the meeting with Hetherington had taken place on Sunday 14 June – the weekend before the General Election – and he had telephoned Thorpe about it on the Monday following.

Carman now produced a cutting from the *Western Morning News*, dated 16 June 1970, and asked Bessell to read it out. Stumbling slightly, Bessell read the headline and the story, and described the photograph. All showed that on the day when he had supposedly been telephoning Thorpe to tell him about the Hetherington meeting, he had actually been sharing a political platform with him, in full view of the crowds at Newquay in Cornwall.

BESSELL: There is no question. I have got it wrong. This proves it beyond doubt . . . somehow, somewhere I have made a mistake over dates.

CARMAN: It takes a long time to nail down some of your lies. That is one we have nailed.

Although Bessell continued to maintain the basic truth of the story, it was a bad reversal.

Carman went on to suggest that Bessell's evidence on vital matters was often a 'tissue of lies'. He made it clear that he was gravely suspicious of the way Bessell had co-operated with the journalists Penrose and Courtiour, and suggested that the famous *aide-memoire*, which was an important part of the police case, had been 'orchestrated' by the three of them. Bessell rejected this robustly, and pointed out again that most of the lies he had told had been on Thorpe's behalf.

CARMAN: Have you told any whoppers since 1976?
BESSELL: Not to my knowledge.
CARMAN: You have told quite a few in this case, haven't you?
BESSELL: No, sir.

As Carman turned to the judge and asked whether they might now adjourn at the end of the sixth day, Mr Justice Cantley remarked: 'Oh, I think we have got time for one whopper if you like.'

Jeremy Thorpe was noticeably more cheerful as he arrived at the court next day, doffing his hat to the crowd before walking through the revolving door with his wife Marion. His mother Ursula, who had been in court for the first day, had left matters in her daughter-in-law's hands for the time being. Bessell, in spite of his savaging, looked quite unperturbed and continued to give his evidence in a clear unwavering voice. The judge had allowed him to take the stand in one-and-a-half-hour stints because of his health (he suffered from emphysema), but he did not appear to be faltering. His third day of cross-examination, however, was to be his worst yet.

Carman moved on to the attempted fraud against Jack Hayward and described the proposed £240,000 commission he expected on the Mobil deal as 'a bribe'.

CARMAN: On any view of it, you were not entitled to one penny of it?
BESSELL: That is correct.

Bessell insisted that the original idea to defraud Hayward had been Thorpe's, and that Thorpe was heavily involved in carrying it out. Not for selfish reasons, however, but only to help Bessell pay off his debts.

CARMAN: It was an attempted fraud by you?
BESSELL: Yes, but I had to do this and do it reluctantly,

because your client was concerned to help me and not himself. But he too was involved, in this, and knew of the nature of what was proposed to perpetrate upon Mr Hayward.

CARMAN: That, I suggest, is another very wicked invention by you. Mr Thorpe was totally deceived by you at that time as well as Mr Hayward.

BESSELL: No, he was not. He was fully aware of it, and regretfully I have to add it was he who suggested it to me.

CARMAN: Are you saying that Mr Thorpe suggested a fraud on the principal benefactor of the Liberal Party to line your pocket with a quarter of a million pounds?

BESSELL: That is precisely what I am saying.

Carman then produced two letters Bessell had written and sent to Thorpe in early 1974. One was a draft letter to Hayward, clearing Thorpe of any involvement in the fraud and apologising to Hayward. The other was a covering letter to Thorpe. Both contained deceptions, but Bessell claimed that they were meant to be read between the lines by Thorpe. However, he conceded that some parts were more lying than others. Carman, in a devastating piece of legal knifework, proceeded to take Bessell through the letters line by line, pressing him to say which were true, which were false. Finally even Bessell had to confess that there was not always a straight answer.

CARMAN: Very well, Mr Bessell, I am perfectly ready to accept the answer 'partly true, partly false'.

The jury was then treated to the spectacle of Bessell replying 'true', 'false', 'partly true and partly false' or 'unable to say which' as Carman read inexorably through his letters. At the end of it all he turned to Bessell and shook his head sadly: 'Oh, Mr Bessell. It is a tangled web of lies that you tell.'

Bessell agreed that the fraud was a serious one. 'I should not have allowed Mr Thorpe or myself to have any part in this disgraceful, inexcusable, totally damnable episode.'

CARMAN: I don't want you to use the witness-box as a confessional, Mr Bessell.

BESSELL: I was merely expressing my emotion of the moment.

As if this was not enough for one day, Carman now revealed that for a long period of time, between 1967/8 and 1974, Bessell had been addicted to the sleeping drug Mandrax. In a letter to Thorpe written in October 1975 he ascribed some of what he called 'the madness of Christmas 1973' to his dependence on the drug.

Some time in 1967, he said, a doctor had prescribed Mandrax. 'At first I took it when I needed it. Then it became habitual and gradually I doubled and even trebled the prescribed dosage.' At one stage he was getting simultaneous prescriptions from two or three doctors.

In the course of the letter he told Thorpe that he did not know if the cumulative effect of the drug, combined with other pressures, had been the cause of what he did. 'I was like a desperate animal, cornered, at the end of my tether.'

Relatively little time was spent on examining Bessell's description of the conversations which concerned the 'ultimate solution'. Carman, however, pointed out that when Bessell had first described these discussions to Penrose and Courtiour in 1976, he had recounted circumstances which differed substantially from his present version; yet Bessell had said it was imprinted on his memory. How, Carman asked, could he get so important an exchange so badly out of context?

Bessell accepted that the detail had changed, but the main burden of the conversations, he insisted, was real enough.

Finally, Carman wound up, saying that Bessell was now a man 'incapable of belief'.

BESSELL: If I believed I was no longer capable of being believed, I would not be here at the Old Bailey. I would be at Oceanside, California.

Peter Taylor, re-examining Bessell, now produced a letter

which, he said, was a 'covering' letter sent by Bessell to Thorpe together with the 'Mandrax' letter. It was a light-hearted one, written to 'Lord Thorpe of Barnstaple' by 'Count Besili of Bodmin', and it read in part:

> Further to my letter of last week, subject to your advice on Hayward, it appears that quiet guns will be fired shortly, and from one corner of the empire to the other, there will be fasting, feasting and rejoicing at the news that Count Besili is alive and skulking in California.
>
> In anticipation of this nerve-shattering event, I have drafted a letter for Jack Hayward. If when you have read it you consider it to be alright, all you have to do is ask one of your minions to call Fancy-Knickers [his solicitor Charles Negus-Fancy] and say 'Tell his Grace the Hayward letter is OK.' On the other hand, if you have serious objections, I shall have to ask you to pick up the telephone....
>
> I am also enclosing a letter to you. The Mandrax story is true and can be checked. I think it is important that I use it in writing to you. Hayward is not a fool and is unlikely to believe that I would not make an explanation to you. An abject, contrite apology without a logical reason, would not impress me and I doubt it would cut ice with him.
>
> To some extent it also protects you, since he must wonder why you trusted me and how you could possibly have been duped by me, when we had been such close colleagues. If you want the letter changing, let me know.
>
> And so, the crimson sun sets over the azure blue Pacific while the black widow spiders creep from their holes into my bed and buzzards hover over Richard Nixon 17 miles away, at San Clemente.
>
> I beg to remain, my lord, your faithful servant,
> Besili

Mr Bessell told the court. 'It was a normal sort of letter that Thorpe or I would have written.'

The cross-examination of Norman Scott began on Day Eleven. He was examined briefly by Mathew who was anxious to learn why Scott had not reported the theft of his documents from the Imperial Hotel, Barnstaple, to the police. 'Because the local police would not have helped me,' replied Scott, ' . . . . because I knew it was involved in this business.' Gareth Williams QC, for Deakin, established that neither of the two men who had interviewed Scott at the Imperial Hotel had resembled Deakin. Carman's cross-examination was a brief affair compared with the Bessell marathon, but it was no less dramatic. This time things did not go all the defence's way.

Carman began by asking Scott about the early psychiatric treatment he had had, and the doubts he had experienced over his own sexuality. Scott's answers were given in a low, hesitant voice and several times he was asked to speak up. He apologised – he had a sore throat, he said. Soon, however, he was talking readily.

Carman asked him if he remembered a time before he had been to see Thorpe at the House of Commons, when he was living with two friends in a small Oxfordshire village. Scott replied that he had been heavily drugged at the time, and could not remember much about it.

CARMAN: You can't remember telling them that you knew Jeremy Thorpe?

SCOTT: I still had a bundle of love letters of Jeremy Thorpe that he had written to Van de Vater.

CARMAN: Never mind what you say are love letters between Mr Thorpe and Van de Vater. Answer the question.

MR JUSTICE CANTLEY (intervening): That was just a bit of dirt thrown in. Listen to the question, and answer, and behave yourself.

CARMAN: You had met Mr Thorpe and talked to him for five minutes or less. He hadn't written you a single letter before you went to the House of Commons, neither had you written a single letter to Mr Thorpe before that. Why did you say that Mr Thorpe was a friend of yours?

SCOTT: Because when I had had the therapy at the hospital I was going through a delusion, and I had these letters. I was using these letters to say that I had had a relationship with him already ...

CARMAN: You were saying you had a sexual relationship with Mr Thorpe *before* you went to the House of Commons?

SCOTT: Yes.

CARMAN: Quite obviously that was not true.

SCOTT: No, it wasn't.

CARMAN: In fairness to you, were you saying it because you were suffering from a delusion?

SCOTT: Yes.

CARMAN: And you had suffered from other delusions had you not?

SCOTT: Yes, sir.

The exchange, with its implication that Scott might have invented the sexual side of the relationship altogether, was a blow to Scott's credibility. It underlined the general burden of Carman's suggestions that the sexual episodes had never taken place; but Carman had his own admission to make, which would capture the headlines next day. He said that he wanted to get one thing clear: 'You knew when you went to the House of Commons that Mr Thorpe had homosexual tendencies.' He said, 'You had good reason to believe it.'

SCOTT: I had seen letters.

CARMAN: There is no mystery about it. You knew this to be the position so that is why you went there.

SCOTT: No.

It was the first public admission made on Thorpe's behalf about the nature of his sexuality at the time, and it was repeated by Carman later in his cross-examination. The admission was made as a result of an agreement between prosecution and defence teams, and its effect was to remove a major issue of contention between the two sides. But Scott would not accept the inference that it was Thorpe who had rejected Scott's sexual advances. 'That is ridiculous,' he said.

During the day, Scott made a number of outbursts as he was pressed again and again on the question of his allegations against Thorpe. Twice he was rebuked by the judge. During a series of questions about the truth of his police statement in 1962, Carman asked him if he felt vindictive towards Thorpe.

SCOTT: No, just great pity because he will be a much sadder man in the end when he goes to see his God. Now he is endeavouring to destroy me totally, but he won't.

Pressed again, Scott shouted: 'Do you think I enjoy saying these terrible things. It is a most horrendous thing.'

CANTLEY: If only you had spoken as loudly as this at the beginning of your evidence we would have heard every word you said. You can speak up.
SCOTT: Yes, I can.
CANTLEY: I will remember that.
SCOTT (shouting): I am in contempt of court. I have gone on long enough. I will not have myself destroyed in this way.
CARMAN: Are you going to answer any further questions from me?
SCOTT: Not if I am going to be treated like a criminal.

Scott's second outburst occurred when he was being questioned about the incident in Thorpe's office when, he said, a policeman called just as Thorpe was making love to him.

CARMAN: Thorpe had arranged for the police to come by appointment and yet that is your allegation?
SCOTT (shouting): Jeremy Thorpe lives on a knife-edge of danger.
CARMAN: What about you?

SCOTT: I have lived in danger of my life for many years because of your client and my relationship with him.

Carman clearly felt that there was not much more to be got out of these exchanges, and wound up his cross-examination with unexpected speed. Scott left, and the tension dropped abruptly.

Andrew Newton came badly out of his cross-examination. He had grown a beard and seemed to have fleshed out since Minehead. There was less jauntiness too. Once again the jury found themselves listening to a self-confessed liar. Replying to John Mathew, he agreed that he had lied on oath during his trial at Exeter after the shooting of Scott's dog, 'to save my own skin'.

NEWTON: What I am saying is that I lied – of course I lied – as your clients are going to.

Summing up Newton's evidence, Mathew said: 'Trickery and deceit have been your trademarks in this matter?'

NEWTON: Yes.

His most obvious – and freely conceded – weakness as a witness, was the amount of money he stood to make from the case. He agreed that he intended to 'milk' it for as much as possible. He had already obtained £10,950 from newspapers and television, and he claimed to have had an extraordinary discussion with the London *Evening News* when prices were placed on the 'heads' of politicians who might be implicated in the story. There was £150,000 for Harold Wilson, £100,000 for Jeremy Thorpe, and about £60,000 for David Holmes.

MATHEW: These were prices offered if you could prove that they were involved in a conspiracy to murder?

NEWTON: Yes.

The key exchange took place early on in the day, when Mathew suggested to Newton that he had gone to Exmoor with Scott in order to frighten him – no more.

343

Newton agreed that that was his intention and that was what he had succeeded in doing. But he denied that that was what he had been *hired* to do.

Mathew told Newton he would be suggesting to him that as far as Holmes was concerned Newton was never asked to do anything other than 'put the fear of God into Scott to shut him up'. The first job he had been asked to do was simply get back the documents Scott had, then get him to sign a statement saying that everything he had alleged was a pack of lies.

NEWTON: That is a good story. That is not true.

Mathew put the suggestion to him again.

NEWTON: I dare say that if you repeat it often enough someone will believe you, but it is a pack of lies.

Newton agreed that he had been given immunity by the Director of Public Prosecutions, but he did not accept Mathew's suggestion that he could now say anything without fear of prosecution. 'If I commit perjury here I can be prosecuted,' he said.

But his confidence was badly dented when Mathew questioned him about the incident in America when, he claimed, a lorry-driver had tried to kill him by running over him three times.

Mathew produced the FBI report on the incident which showed it had been a minor and unintentional accident. Newton was outraged. 'I don't know who has invented this,' he fumed. 'Perhaps you better ask the politicians or something ... the FBI – oh, how convenient. You see what they're doing. In Cuba, in Chile. We have a piece of paper by the FBI. How ridiculous. Oh, take it away.'

CANTLEY: No, we won't take it away. We want to give it an exhibit number.

Newton wound up the fourteenth day of the trial with an uncharacteristically gloomy reflection: 'One day someone will write his memoirs about this and you'll look back and think: "Oh, perhaps Newton was telling the truth." I suppose we've got to wait twenty five years for that'.

Gareth Williams, next day, took Newton at a rattling Welsh pace through the Showmen's Dinner in Blackpool with its topless dancers, drunkenness and fighting. He wondered if Newton could really remember the precise details of what was said if he had been so paralytically drunk. Surely it was the case, he suggested, that Deakin's only involvement was to put Newton in touch with Holmes on an agreement to frighten. Other than that, Deakin had no part in the matter at all. Newton disagreed. He remembered the salient details well enough.

To Denis Cowley QC, representing Le Mesurier, however, he conceded that, as far as he was concerned, there was no mention of Le Mesurier's name until about fourteen months after the killing of Scott's dog, when a £5000 pay-off was made.

On the nineteenth day of the trial the defence suffered a setback at the hand of the main police witness, Detective Chief Superintendent Challes, when he came back to the court with the answers to some questions put to him earlier by Carman, on Thorpe's behalf. Carman had submitted that in 1971 Thorpe had asked the Home Secretary, Reginald Maudling, and the Commissioner at Scotland Yard, Sir John Waldron, to investigate Scott's allegations.

Challes, however, said there was no such evidence in the files. Thorpe had indeed approached both men, but not to ask for an investigation. Next day, in an agreed statement, Thorpe admitted, through his counsel George Carman, that he had not made the request.

Friday 8 June – Day Twenty-one of the trial – was to witness a series of shocks. The first came when David Holmes, due to go into the witness-box, announced through his counsel that he would not be giving evidence on his own behalf.

Immediately after this, George Deakin, pale but self-possessed, took the stand and announced: 'I am here because

I have nothing to hide.' Answering a question from his counsel, Gareth Williams, he explained that all he had been asked to do was to help find someone to 'frighten' an unnamed blackmailer. He knew nothing about Jeremy Thorpe and had no experience of political life. And he had not taken to Andrew Newton, particularly when he learned that he had been chatting up his wife.

Le Mesurier was a fellow-member of the Carlton Club in Port Talbot, and it was through him that he had been introduced to David Holmes. When Le Mesurier had announced that a friend of Holmes was looking for someone who would frighten off a blackmailer, he had offered to do what he could to help.

It was Deakin's apparent lack of curiosity about this proposition that exercised Peter Taylor when he began cross-examining him. Was it really possible, he asked, to want to know so little about the background – who was involved, how much money was being offered, what the frightening job was really for? Doggedly, Deakin contended that it had simply not bothered him.

When Miller had told him in Blackpool that Newton was 'the boy for your problem', he had snapped back: 'It's not my bloody problem.'

He had only met Newton once after the Blackpool meeting, and that was at Miller's premises when he had given him Holmes's telephone number. There had been no meeting at the Aust service station, and he did not own a BMW car. He had never been to Barnstaple, let alone the Imperial Hotel to steal Scott's briefcase. Nothing he had said on tape was other than innocent. Even the curious phrase, 'I'm denying', made to Miller, was a reference to holding off the press rather than refusing to talk to the police.

Mr Justice Cantley found little reason to intervene during most of Deakin's evidence, but he moved in abruptly when Deakin's counsel asked him who he had been told was previously active in 'hushing up' the affair. Deakin responded with: 'Harold Wilson, the Prime Minister, Lord Goodman', but was promptly interrupted by the judge with,

346

'Thomas Cobbleigh?' The judge went on: 'We keep getting these names and everybody gets wildly excited although it's hearsay upon hearsay. . . .'

As Deakin stood down, the next two shocks of the day came in quick succession. First, Denis Cowley, for le Mesurier, announced that he, like Holmes, would be calling no evidence. Then, just as everyone was expecting the court to be adjourned at the end of the day, George Carman rose and announced: 'My lord, on behalf of Jeremy Thorpe, I call no evidence.'

There had always been speculation that Thorpe, and some at least of his co-defendants would exercise their right not to give evidence and face cross-examination, but the brief and stark announcements when they came took almost everyone by surprise.

Peter Taylor was unperturbed, however, as he remarked to the judge that perhaps they might leave final summing-ups until the Monday of the following week since 'the case can now be said to be well in advance of schedule.'

Over the next five days, prosecution and defence both summed up their final positions, more than once with a dash of eloquence. Taylor set the pace by describing Thorpe's story as 'a tragedy of truly Greek or Shakespearian proportions'.

It led to the 'slow but inevitable destruction of a man by the stamp of one defect'. The combination of Thorpe's homosexual tendencies and his determined ambition was 'the key and the only key' to the conflict which followed.

Taylor then advised the jury on five matters: the press, the substance of the evidence, the witnesses, the possibilities of fabrication and collusion, and the undisputed facts of the case. He was actually able to list sixty-six of the latter, all uncontested by the defence which, he claimed, were the bedrock of the prosecution case. He stressed that in spite of the defence attacks on the witnesses, and their suggestion of collusion and fabrication, all the jury had to do was look at the evidence itself and decide whether that was true.

347

'The mere fact that a man has sold his story to the press does not mean that story is false.' A man could tell many lies, but still be believed.

When he turned to Thorpe, and his role in the laundering of the Hayward money, Taylor was blistering. Thorpe, he said, had 'lied, lied and lied again' about the money.

Thorpe had given no fewer than seven conflicting accounts of the money 'which we say was obtained and used to finance this conspiracy.'

He traced the money from Hayward to Dinshaw, to Holmes. The first payment of £10,000 had gone to pay off Holmes's overdraft. Holmes had paid £2500 for letters in 1974, and a further £5000 to pay off Newton in 1977.

'You may think the money is crucial in this case because the money links all of these men together; the money from Mr Jack Hayward, procured by Mr Thorpe, passed clandestinely to Mr Holmes and then used to pay off Mr Newton via Mr le Mesurier.'

John Mathew for David Holmes, however, offered a very different explanation for the money. The clandestine route and the secrecy surrounding the payments all suggested illicit election expenses, he said, rather than money for a killer. Would Holmes or Thorpe have entered into a contract if the only way they could pay for it was by getting cash in a way which could later be traced back?

Mathew conceded that there was strong evidence of a conspiracy to frighten, to which David Holmes was party. But there was no plot to kill. The only two witnesses to have given relevant evidence against Holmes on the conspiracy to murder were Bessell and Newton, and their evidence is 'so tainted with doubt and so comprehensively incredible that you cannot possibly rely upon it in any way.'

He ended by making this plea to the jury: 'This case can never have a happy ending, whatever your verdict may be, because the scars are too deep and will remain. But there can be a just and fair ending to the agonies which, albeit brought on by himself, must have been suffered by Mr Holmes in recent times.'

348

George Carman referred to the trial as 'the watershed of Jeremy Thorpe's life'. In his closing speech he said: 'Privately he is a man with a life that has had more than its fair share of its grief and agony. Nature so fashioned him that we know that at the time he had the misfortune to ever meet Norman Scott, he was a man with homosexual tendencies.'

Thorpe's political life and future were now irrevocably and irreversibly denied to him, said Carman. His frailties and weaknesses had been exposed remorselessly to public gaze. But he was innocent of the charges laid against him.

Carman spoke scathingly of the 'unholy trio' of witnesses who had testified against him. Peter Bessell, he said, 'may go down at the end of this case as the Judas Iscariot of British politics of the twentieth century ... a man so devious, so unprincipled, so cunning, and so sophisticated a liar that you could not in all conscience safely act on his evidence.' The second witness, Norman Scott, was a liar and a scrounger, and with the third, Andrew Newton, you had to guess when he was telling the truth.

Explaining why Thorpe had not gone into the witness-box, Carman said: 'It does not prove his guilt. On the contrary, it is a right invested by law that a defendant can remain silent. We are not here to entertain the public or provide journalists with further copy.'

Thorpe's wife Marion and his mother Ursula were in court as Carman spoke of the 'untimely death' of Caroline Thorpe, and then paid tribute to his present wife 'whose constant presence in this court speaks eloquently for itself.'

After going in detail into Scott's claims of a homosexual relationship with Thorpe, Carman questioned the prosecution interpretation of the money from Hayward. 'I'm not going to solve for you the mystery of this money. You can spend a long time trying to work it out ... and come up with six different answers.' But, he said, the Crown had to prove it was referable to guilt. This was only one possibility – there were others they had not explored.

Carman also questioned whether Thorpe's approaches to Maudling and Waldron in 1971 were evidence of 'fixing the record' as the prosecution had contended. 'The Maudling correspondence is a fine example of something which, in analysis, favours Mr Thorpe rather than points to his guilt,' he maintained. 'It points to exposure rather than cover-up. It points to accuracy rather than inaccuracy. It points to legitimate channels of investigation and not murder.'

Gareth Williams paid an unexpected compliment to the Director of Public Prosecutions when he spoke for Deakin. The decision to prosecute, he said, was 'an act of courage'; it upheld the rule of law 'so that even the mighty in this land are in the end subject to the same ventilation as the most obscure.'

And obscure, said Williams, was what George Deakin was – 'just someone of no consequence who could be used and not told the whole story . . . someone of no account – a tool.' Deakin alone had treated the jury with respect and had given his explanation, though he had known he would be cross-examined. 'He does not have any powerful friends,' said Williams. 'He does not write letters to the Home Secretary . . . "Dear Reggie . . ." He does not seem to be on close and affectionate terms with the Commissioner of Metropolitan Police.'

Williams reserved his greatest scorn for Newton, whom he described as a sort of 'moral amputee'. He was not just a man from whom you would hesitate to buy a second-hand car, you would not even sell him one. 'If you sold him a car with a wheel wobbling, he was likely to say it was a conspiracy to murder him . . . if the paint rusted he would say it was death rays from the KGB.'

Denis Cowley, for Le Mesurier, said his client had an impeccable character. 'Is he the sort of man that you think was going to be engaged in a scheme to kill someone whom he does not know, and has never met and has nothing to do with?' The evidence against him was sketchy, and his only involvement with Newton was in the pay-off.

At the end of the twenty-sixth day, the court retired for the weekend, to prepare for the judge's final words to the jury on Monday 18 June.

350

22. The Trial: Judgment

The summing-up of Mr Justice Cantley was to become a matter of heated debate in the days following the trial. Seldom has a high court judge been more outspoken in his condemnation of witnesses in court, or used such terms of open abuse to describe their conduct. Critics were quick to point out that Cantley's colourful language was reserved for prosecution witnesses alone, while defendants were dealt with in milder language.

Inevitably it was the judicial expletives which caught the headlines, but the speech itself, taken over its two-day course, was more even-handed than these suggest. Since, as we shall see, parts of the summing-up were to have a strong influence on the jury when they came to decide their verdict, it is worth setting out what Mr Justice Cantley actually said.

He began by warning the jury not to be overwhelmed by the complexities of this 'rather bizarre and surprising' case, and by telling them bluntly that he expected not only a 'true verdict according to the evidence', but a unanimous one as well. If they were not sure about the guilt of any of the defendants, then they must acquit.

'It is right for you to pause and consider', he said, 'whether it is likely that such persons would do the things these persons are said to have done. But if, however unlikely you would otherwise have thought, you are ultimately convinced by the evidence, that they did, then, however sadly, you will have to convict.'

The judge then dealt with the decision by Thorpe, Holmes and Le Mesurier not to go into the witness-box. It was, he said, a course of action which added nothing at all to the prosecution case, and from which no inference of guilt should be drawn. There were various reasons why they should have decided not to give evidence other than guilt, and the jury would be wrong to speculate. On the other hand, it did not add to the defence case either – it was a 'neutral action'.

If the jury had a reasonable doubt, he stressed, the prosecution had failed to prove its case, and they should acquit.

The four accused, he said, were men of hitherto unblemished character. Thorpe, for instance, was a Privy Councillor, a former party leader, and a national figure. 'What is the effect of the defendants' good character in a criminal trial?' he asked. 'Normally it has its most important effect when the defendant goes into the witness-box and gives evidence, because the jury is then reminded that they have been listening to the evidence of a man with good character, and give it the attention which a man of good character deserves.'

In this case three of the accused had not gone into the witness-box but that did not mean that their good character should be ignored.

Turning to the charges themselves, the judge said that the charge of incitement, against Thorpe, related to the evidence of Bessell alone. The jury would have to decide whether Thorpe genuinely tried to persuade Holmes to kill Scott, even though he failed.

The other charge, conspiracy, was, he said, an agreement by two or more persons to murder, provided that they intended at the time to carry it out. The fact that the deed was not carried out was irrelevant.

'The most famous conspiracy of all is the gunpowder plot to blow up the Houses of Parliament,' said the judge. 'Of course they did not blow it up, and when Guy Fawkes was caught, he hadn't even tried to blow it up. But he and others had conspired to blow it up, and the allegation in this case is that these defendants agreed to join in a course of conduct which, if carried out successfully to completion, would have

352

3

resulted in the murder of Scott by one of the conspirators, namely Newton.'

The relation between conspirators may be slight – they need not meet, plan together, or even know each other. But no one could join a conspiracy to murder *after* the murder had taken place. In this case it was too late to join the alleged conspiracy after the shooting incident in October 1975. This was relevant when the case of Le Mesurier was considered because his counsel maintained he was not really in it until after the shooting.

'If, for example, Le Mesurier joined what he thought was a conspiracy to frighten somebody, and then found out in October 1975 that the real object was murder, the mere fact that he helped after that to hush it up would not make him a member of the conspiracy to murder.'

A conspiracy to frighten someone was a criminal conspiracy, but the defendants were not charged with that. The jury had to decide whether they conspired to *murder* someone. If the jury decided, first, that there was a conspiracy, and secondly that it was to murder, they should then go on to consider the case of each accused separately.

The judge then discussed 'the tainting of the evidence', about which so much had been said. 'I think more time has been taken in this case in evidence to establish a homosexual relationship between Mr Thorpe and Mr Scott and the activities of what we can collectively call "the media" than has been spent on the real nub of the case.'

Mr Justice Cantley then proceeded to devote some time to the subject himself, observing that journalism was an honourable profession, and that many journalists must be feeling uncomfortable at some of the things they had heard during the case. A vigilant and inquiring press, he said, was of great service – 'and so we must respect and support the freedom of the press, not only to report but to inquire.'

'However, when a state of affairs is created of offers to witnesses who have low moral standards, of big money or the prospects of big money for a sensational story, then the rights of the individual to justice become endangered.'

By offering money to witnesses, he said, newspapers were indulging in 'a double vice'. The payment might either induce a witness to tell lies in which case an innocent man might be convicted. Or the witness might be telling the truth, but because the jury knew that he had a financial interest they might not accept his evidence and a guilty man would be acquitted. 'The pursuit, not of justice, but of profit, has tampered with the quality of important evidence,' he concluded.

This discussion about tainted evidence led the judge on to tainted witnesses. He reminded the jury that the defence had said that the court was not 'a court of morals', and pointed out: 'I am not quite sure what a court of morals is, but this is not one of those.' The jury should consider only the charges and not make judgments because a man might in their view have behaved badly.

The first witness to come in for one of the judge's sharp comments was Peter Bessell. He was, said Mr Justice Cantley, a very intelligent and articulate man. 'He must have impressed the electors of Cornwall very much.' He was a lay preacher, and at the same time, as Bessell himself had put it, sexually promiscuous – 'and therefore', added the judge, 'a humbug'.

Much of his evidence, up to the alleged incitement to murder, was corroborated by letters or documents, though what really happened to Scott's luggage before it reached Dublin, and whether letters were actually removed by Thorpe 'we shall never know'.

On the incitement charge itself the only evidence was Bessell's. According to him, Thorpe's suggestion that they would have to get rid of Scott, and the discussion about various methods of disposing of the body, took place in Thorpe's room at the House of Commons.

But he had given another version to the journalists Penrose and Courtiour, to whom he had said that the conversation took place in a different place and at a different time. In the end, said the judge, 'If you accept that evidence and come to the conclusion that Thorpe was seriously trying to persuade Holmes to murder Scott, whether by shooting, poisoning or some other means, that would be incitement to murder.'

In 1969, said the judge, Scott had apparently been hysterical because he could not get maternity benefits for his wife. According to Bessell, he had said he would make trouble for Thorpe and the Liberal Party if he was unable to get the benefits, and would sell his story to a newspaper.

The judge remarked: 'That is blackmail. Is it true? If it is true, then as early as 1969 Scott was alive to the possibility of selling his story.' There was corroboration that Bessell had told him he would help him get his cards, and corroboration that following the divorce proceedings Thorpe had paid the fees incurred by Leonard Ross.

On the question of the 'U.S. charade' – when Bessell and David Holmes had supposedly pretended that they were trying to dispose of Scott – the judge pointed out that once again Bessell had given a different version to the Pencourt team when he had first described the incident to them. There was, however, corroboration that the actual meeting in New York had taken place.

In 1976, Holmes, according to Bessell, admitted that he had hired the pilot (Newton) to kill Scott, said the judge. He said he had been persuaded that it was the only solution. Yet, in two taped telephone conversations between Holmes and Bessell some time later the tone of the exchanges between them was 'very cordial'. They were 'not the conversation of a man who feels he had been deceived by Mr Holmes,' observed the judge. There was, for instance, a curious passage in the transcript of the conversations where Bessell tells Holmes that he is 'a good and faithful servant to our friend' and 'a respectable private citizen'.

Mr Justice Cantley commented: 'I say that was a curious comment – to say of the man who has told you he is trying to murder someone – "you are, after all, a respectable private citizen."' Either it helped to establish Bessell's credibility, or it showed he was 'broadminded to an unusual extent'.

Later in his summing-up the judge turned to consider to

what extent Bessell's evidence might have been affected by his dealings with Penrose and Courtiour, and here he was less inclined than the defence to ascribe to them any sinister motive.

'They are mystery men as far as we're concerned,' he said. 'Every time Mr Carman has mentioned them you could detect the faint smell of brimstone,' and Mr Mathew had referred 'in a rather menacing way' to the fact that neither had appeared in the witness-box. 'It is not their fault,' he pointed out. 'We don't know what they could have said about themselves if somebody had given them the opportunity.' And he added: 'We don't to this day know how to pronounce the name of the junior partner, Mr Courtiour.'

The judge then raised the question of whether Bessell's contract with the *Sunday Telegraph* could be held to have affected the weight or credibility of his evidence. It was a matter, he said, of determining the period when Bessell's evidence had *crystallised*.

'Before he had crystallised the *aide-memoire* [in September-November 1976] he had made contact with Messers Penrose and Courtiour. So, although his evidence may have crystallised by the time of his *aide-memoire*, in that it hasn't varied much since then, it is said, there is some evidence that he may have had publication of an adequately sensational book in mind before the *aide-memoire* came.'

In the light of that, said the judge, Bessell's 'deplorable contract' with the *Sunday Telegraph*' ceased to have the significance it would otherwise have had.

'But I will refer to it,' he announced, 'if only to give it unfavourable publicity.' He then proceeded to analyse the deal – by which Bessell stood to make double the money on a conviction – at some length and in a caustic manner, while concluding that because Bessell had formalised his evidence well before the contract was signed, 'it cannot have produced the mischief it might otherwise have done.'

Equally, the notorious 'Hetherington incident', in which Bessell claimed that Thorpe had asked him to eliminate a man who had incriminating evidence against him, went

356

against Bessell's credibility but did not destroy it. He warned the jury that just because a man told a lie in a case did not mean that he was telling lies all the time. He called it the 'snakes and ladders' of litigation. 'You cannot say a witness is disqualified and down the snake he goes if he is caught out in one lie.'

In the end, the judge said, if the jury viewed Bessell's evidence with suspicion, they should be slow to act upon it, unless it was supported by other evidence.

If Bessell was believed, it proved there was a homosexual relationship between Thorpe and Scott; that Thorpe was anxious over a period of years about the danger of this scandal becoming public; that because of that anxiety he took, mainly through the agency of Bessell, steps to deal with Scott privately. There were matters capable of corroborating the substance of those matters.

It had been admitted that Thorpe had homosexual tendencies. And when it came to the evidence of Scott there were some documents which were capable of corroborating that part of the story. If Bessell were to be believed, he proved that Thorpe had unsuccessfully tried to persuade Holmes to kill Scott. But that charge depended entirely on Bessell's evidence. So too did the talk of an 'ultimate solution', on the further occasions when Bessell said it had cropped up.

His final word on Bessell left the decision in the jury's hands: 'When I say you must look at Bessell's evidence with suspicion, it does not mean you cannot believe it if there is no corroboration.'

When it came to Norman Scott, the judge found it impossible to conceal his distaste for the man. 'I am sure you remember him very well,' he told the jury. 'His hysterically warped personality; an accomplished liar; very skilful at exciting and exploiting sympathy.' Reminding the jury that he had fraudulently pledged other people's credit, including that of Bessell and Thorpe, the judge added: 'He is a crook.'

Scott had claimed that he and Thorpe first met early in

357

1960 when Scott was working for a man calling himself the Hon. Van de Brecht de Vater – a bogus name. 'He had', remarked the judge, smiling at the jury, 'made a name for himself.' After Scott had been to the House of Commons to see Thorpe, he raised with him the problem of the insurance cards. He said they were still with Vater, and Thorpe said he would sort them out.

'If that is true,' said the judge, 'it is the most unfortunate thing Mr Thorpe has ever said to anybody, for if anybody had done Scott wrong – although Scott would never be able to understand it – it must have been Van de Vater.'

The judge then examined the evidence of the 'Bunnies' letter. 'All I can say is that this is capable of corroborating some homosexual relationship between the two, but not necessarily. It is for you the jury to decide whether or not you take a different view.' The jury might remember a reference which George Carman had made to Thorpe's 'flamboyant' style of writing. 'It is capable of corroborating a homosexual relationship. I do not mean that it necessarily corroborates what lawyers call buggery, which is alleged to have happened. A man might write to a girl he liked and say "I miss you", but that would not be capable of suggesting that they had had sexual intercourse. We must not assume that mere affection implies buggery, no more than a letter to a girl you hope to see or perhaps marry, is able to imply sexual intercourse.'

The judge smiled as he added: 'I miss you   . I would not write that to a man, but I may have written something like that to a girl.'

Scott's admission that in 1961, having met Thorpe for only a few minutes at Van de Vater's stables, he was already claiming to have had a homosexual affair with Thorpe, was a severe blow to his credibility, said the judge. If Scott was prepared to say that, when there was no foundation to it, to what extent could the jury rely on the full details of what he was saying?

Another lie Scott had told involved his adoption of the name 'Lianche-Josiffe', and the assumption of the new surname, 'Scott', by which he could pretend to be a relative of Lord Eldon, whose family name was Scott. 'He has told many lies to improve his image,' said the judge.

Between 1971 and 1975 Scott admitted telling other lies. 'He said that he told many amazing lies to be able to eat. It is another way of saying he was living on his wits.'

And there was another aspect of Scott's character which aroused the judge's suspicions – the possibility that he was a blackmailer. He knew when he first went to the House of Commons that Thorpe had homosexual tendencies; Mr Carman had suggested that he was hoping to make something out of these tendencies; he had stolen letters from Van de Vater.

'He said they were from Thorpe. We have not seen them, but let us assume they were. What did he keep them for? Why was he so upset when he lost them?' The judge added: 'Do you agree with Mr Bessell that he is not a blackmailer?' Scott had made money from various newspapers and television companies, and in 1973 he had moved into Thorpe's constituency and was talking openly in pubs of his relationship with Thorpe.

In conclusion, the judge said: 'He is a fraud. He is a sponger. He is a whiner. He is a parasite. But, of course, he could still be telling the truth. It is a question of belief.'

Having delivered this uncompromising assault on Scott's character, the judge warned the jury not to be over-influenced by it. 'Don't think that when I have been giving you these recitals, and failing to conceal my opinions of Scott, that I am suggesting you should not believe him. That is not for me, I am putting both sides . . . I am in the middle. It is a question for you. If you believe the important things he said against Mr Thorpe, that proves a homosexual relationship which ceased in 1964 . . . If you believe him, it proves he successfully exploited that relationship for some time . .'

There was little doubt in the minds of reporters listening to the judge's diatribe that Scott's standing as a witness had been virtually demolished. The next morning's *Daily Mail* simply ran the words 'Parasite, Whiner, Sponger, Crook and Liar' in a 72-point headline straight down their front page. Whether the jury, locked safely away from newspapers and television, felt the same, would emerge later.

The second day of Mr Justice Cantley's summing-up began with an equally blunt assessment of Andrew Newton. Having reviewed his evidence about various clumsy attempts to track down Norman Scott the judge concluded: 'What a chump the man is! To frighten or murder – that is no way to go about it.' But he made this important observation: Newton had offered Scott a large sum for papers and documents, but Scott had refused it. Newton had said that Scott appeared to believe that ruining Thorpe was more attractive than money.

'Pausing there,' said the judge, 'supposing this suggestion was made. You have already seen that Newton as an assassin – or even a frightener – was a highly incompetent performer with all his self-advertisement. But supposing this proposal was made, and supposing Scott had accepted it. What was Newton going to do then? There was no arrangement. There was no money. What a mess there would have been if Scott had said "yes". Newton would have had to go back to the people who are supposed to have sent him to murder Scott, if this was a conspiracy to murder, and ask for money to buy the documents. That would have put the cat among the pigeons, wouldn't it?'

Did Newton pretend to try and shoot Scott or did the gun genuinely jam? Newton himself had changed his story twice. The judge said there were four indicators to guide the jury:

The man who supplied the gun said Newton had complained it jammed.

A firearms expert told the court that he fired twenty seven shots and it had jammed four times.

David Miller said that when Newton stripped the gun down in his house after the shooting there was a bullet jammed under the firing-pin.

Finally, Newton himself at his Exeter trial said that the gun had jammed.

'He has told quite a different story on two occasions, and the expert says that this gun does jam.' In the end, the jury would have to decide for themselves.

After Newton's release from prison in April 1977 Newton was paid £5000 in cash by Le Mesurier, who also obtained his ticket to Rhodesia. This was corroborated by tapes made by Newton, 'in order to protect himself'. But these tapes were also invaluable in gaining him nearly £11,000 in fees from newspapers and television stations. 'I doubt whether he has paid any income tax,' observed the judge.

'One has to look at his evidence with great care, not only because he is an accomplice . . . but also because he has the clearest possible motives for making a sensational story.'

Having dealt with Newton, Mr Justice Cantley made a significant point on the prosecution's behalf. Did the jury think, he asked, that a conspiracy to frighten Scott would have been sufficient to silence him? To illustrate his point, the judge returned to his verbal assaults on the hapless Scott: 'He is a spineless, neurotic character, addicted to hysteria and self-advertisement rushing to others for help whenever he felt it would do any good. Would he be expected to keep quiet if thoroughly frightened? Or would conspirators of ordinary intelligence expect him to be silenced by being thoroughly frightened? The answer might be "yes" or "no", we don't know.'

Nobody had told the court how he was going to be frightened, except Deakin who had assumed it would be by a threat of violence, and Newton who had said it would be done by pretending to shoot Scott. Newton had taken Scott on to the deserted moor with a loaded pistol and live ammunition. Suppose he thoroughly frightened Scott either by pretending the gun was jammed, or shooting at him and deliberately missing him. He would hardly give him a lift back after that. Scott would be left on the moor. What would happen next? Would Scott say he had better not mention names or say anything about it? Would people who knew Scott expect him really to keep quiet?

In the end the jury would have to consider all these points before deciding which kind of conspiracy it was. 'Of course,' said the judge, 'it was all a very futile performance. Whether there was a conspiracy to frighten or a conspiracy to kill, nothing seems to have been properly thought out. The way Newton went about it made his detection and arrest inevitable.'

The judge was now reaching his concluding points, and he began them by summarising the case against each of the accused.

Holmes: It was conceded that he was a party to a conspiracy, but not for anything more than a conspiracy to frighten. He had paid £2500 in February 1974 when he was not flush with money. One inference was that he was anxious to quieten Scott, but not to the extent of killing him.

The evidence that he intended to kill Scott rested on Bessell to whom he had allegedly admitted it. If the jury believed Newton, then he had been instructed by Holmes to kill Scott. Newton was an accomplice and it would be dangerous to accept his evidence as corroboration. So was there any corroborating evidence?

There was the taped telephone call between Newton and Holmes in which Newton had reminded Holmes that there was a charge of 'conspiracy to . . . bloody murder'. Between the words 'bloody' and 'murder' Holmes says he is remembering that very carefully. The jury had to consider whether they were confident that the conversation was a tacit admission that Holmes was in a conspiracy to murder or whether there was some other explanation. There was no other evidence to help them decide on this.

Deakin: The judge observed that he was the type of man whose taste probably ran to 'a cocktail bar in his living room' in tones that suggested there was not a cocktail bar in Mr Justice Cantley's living room. On more material issues there was evidence from Newton that Deakin had been recruited to kill somebody, and then briefed at the Aust service station about Scott. But there was no corroboration. It was contradicted by the evidence of Miller – 'the last of the dubious commercial witnesses' and himself an accomplice – and by Deakin's own evidence.

Le Mesurier: The jury had been invited to consider that he never knew it was a conspiracy to murder until after it had been abandoned. Against him there was the evidence of Colin Lambert, 'a sturdy sort of witness', said the judge, who worked for Le Mesurier. Lambert had said Le Mesurier told him: ' . . . We should have hired someone like you because the chap who went to do this shooting was an idiot.' Why had Le Mesurier used the word 'we' and not 'they'? It might have been that Le Mesurier was trying to make out he had a bigger part in something than he actually had.

'It has been put to you', said the judge, 'that when he said "we should have hired someone like you", he was saying something very dangerous, but very foolish, nothing more.'

Thorpe: The evidence against him was 'almost entirely circumstantial', said the judge. The prosecution had asked the jury to consider his motive and interest in silencing Scott. 'Motive and absence of motive may, in a particular case, be relevant,' conceded the judge. And he went on: 'In this case motive, although it certainly isn't conclusive – far from it – is not irrelevant in the case against Thorpe. It is a matter you can take into account.'

That motive was reinforced by Scott's behaviour in repeating his allegations against Thorpe year after year. 'You had the opportunity of seeing Mr Scott in the witness-box and you see his vindictive attitude,' the judge told the jury. 'Mr Scott said of Thorpe – "I pity him." But he doesn't. He hates him, whether with justification or not is a different matter.'

It would be quite wrong for the jury to suggest that Thorpe's natural reaction would be to kill Scott. 'But it would be in his interest if Mr Scott stopped spreading his scandal, and he would also be greatly benefited if, one way or the other, Mr Scott was silenced.' There was, of course,

Bessell's evidence – 'and I warned you about the danger of Bessell.'

Finally there was the money. The judge had already spelled out the evidence given by Hayward and Dinshaw – 'nice, respectable witnesses' – and had given the jury a detailed timetable from 28 February 1974 when Holmes paid £2500 for Scott's letters, to 18 April 1977 when Newton received £5000. During this time two payments of £10,000 were made by Hayward after requests from Thorpe.

The prosecution, said the judge, had suggested that these sums were raised to finance the conspiracy. No explanation had been given by the defence to the jury about what it was for. Thorpe had told a number of stories about it, which could not all be true.

'If, in the end,' said the judge, 'the only inference you can draw from the evidence about the money is that Thorpe obtained it by telling lies to Mr Hayward, that does not do anything to the prosecution case. The fact that a man obtains money by deceit does not amount to any sort of proof that the man was a member of a conspiracy to murder someone else.'

At this point, Mr Justice Cantley looked up at the clock which showed that the afternoon session was drawing to a close, and announced that he had very little to add. He proposed to send the jury out shortly after the court resumed next day.

On the morning of Wednesday 20 June, after only five minutes' discussion, the judge dispatched the jury to consider their verdict in the spartan jury-room behind the court, with the words, 'Take as long as you like. There is no hurry. We shall wait for you.' With a smile and a wave, he added: 'You may go now.'

There was a moment's silence round the court, then lawyers, journalists, judge and jury rose to their feet and shuffled out. For some time, as if reluctant to leave the court at all, reporters hung round the doorway discussing the course of the case, hazarding uncertain bets about the verdict, canvassing opinion from every passing barrister. Then they began dispersing to pubs, coffee bars, or the Old Bailey canteen itself. It would be a long wait – the jury was to take the judge at his word.

For the defendants this meant two nights in Brixton jail. Following a long-standing tradition, their bail was withdrawn as soon as the jury retired, and they were driven off in a police van. Thorpe, who was handcuffed to George Deakin, lay on the floor of the van and covered his head with a coat in order to avoid the indignity of being photographed in this situation. Their reception at Brixton was a rough one. All were stripped, medically examined, bathed, then consigned to cells which they were to share with other prisoners. Only Thorpe was spared the indignity of the cell. On the first night he was moved to the prison hospital after complaining of a stomach upset.

Each day they were brought back to the Old Bailey to wait on the verdict. They passed the time in a room overlooking Newgate. As the wait lengthened a bizarre intimacy sprang up between them which had been totally absent before. During the trial relations between the individual defendants were highly circumspect. Now the sense of a shared fate brought them together in games of cards and chance. Le Mesurier introduced his co-defendants to 'Lie Dice' which involved a good deal of licensed bluffing and good-natured accusations of 'liar'. Deakin remembers it being played with great exuberance.

The jury were meanwhile coming to grips with the evidence. The first thing they had done on retiring was to take a straw poll which resulted in an even split of six for and six against acquittal. Within an hour, however, they had moved to a majority of ten to two in favour of acquittal. The argument which had swayed them was that the burden was on the prosecution to prove the charges beyond 'reasonable doubt'.

The incitement charge against Thorpe had been thrown out within minutes of the retirement because it was based solely on the word of Bessell, and because Holmes had not gone into the witness-box to offer any confirmation.

The judge had told them to consider first whether there was evidence of a conspiracy to murder, then to go on and consider the parts played in that conspiracy by the four accused. In the event they never got beyond that first question.

By Day Two there were eleven for acquittal, one against. The arguments had ranged from the sophisticated to the emotional – one member of the jury felt that Marion Thorpe had suffered enough. The question of the money exercised them for some time. It was obvious, they felt, that the £20,000 had gone from Hayward to Holmes, via Dinshaw, at the request of Thorpe. But they did not have any bank statements to demonstrate what had then happened to it. They did not have a sufficient link to show where the money that had been paid to Newton had come from. Again, there was a 'reasonable doubt'.

They were unhappy about the witnesses they had seen. Bessell left them confused. If Bessell really had been as appalling as the defence had said, then why had Thorpe been so close to him? On the other hand the sheer weight of the defence assault on his character – in particular Carman's – told in the end. They accepted that some of the witnesses stood to gain financially by a conviction, and thought that Bessell's contract in particular did little to help his evidence. To many on the jury, even the £25,000 he was guaranteed, represented five years' salary. When he heard the evidence on this point, one juror had written in his notes, 'half price acquittal!' In the end they refused to accept his evidence except where it was corroborated.

As to the matter of Scott's evidence about a homosexual relationship with Thorpe, the jury eventually came to the view that it was unnecessary to come to any joint decision – what was material were the allegations and the danger they meant to Thorpe.

Newton, they concluded, was unreliable because he was clearly interested financially in the result. The evidence from New York about the reality of the 'murder bid', which turned out to be a truck accident, impressed them forcibly.

The gun-jamming incident became an important issue in convincing one of the two doubters to join the majority in favour of acquittal, and make it eleven to one. The jury considered that Newton clearly knew how to use a gun, and thought it odd that if it had jammed he could not free it. This led them to the conclusion that Newton was not trying to kill Scott.

Deakin impressed them by giving evidence and sticking to his story, and his counsel, Gareth Williams, made the most favourable impression of all the lawyers. They were disappointed that none of the other accused had given evidence since there were a number of things they would have liked answers about.

One of the strongest prosecution points, they felt, was the argument put forward both by Taylor and by Mr Justice Cantley, that a conspiracy to frighten was a singularly pointless plot. However there was no positive evidence to tilt it further towards a murder conspiracy. Although Taylor had pointed out that the original offer of £10,000 was a very high fee if the conspiracy had only been one to frighten, they felt that this was inconclusive since none of the organisers would have known precisely what the 'going rate' for the job was.

Other matters raised included the 'character' of Thorpe, about which the judge had spoken. The jury was impressed by his standing and public reputation, but puzzled by his close relationship with Bessell.

They were struck by the difference in the accounts Bessell had given of the conversation about Scott he had had with Thorpe. To the court he had mentioned the House of Commons as the place where it had occurred, but to the journalists Penrose and Courtiour he had mentioned Thorpe's flat as the venue.

They took Mr Justice Cantley's warning about returning a unanimous verdict extremely seriously – hence the long delay. In the end, the twin arguments about 'reasonable doubt' and the quality of the prosecution witnesses converted the final doubter on the jury, and at 2.34 on the afternoon of Friday 22 June they filed back into Court Number One. They had been out for 51 hours and 59 minutes. The four defendants had been enjoying a splendid lunch of smoked salmon, beef and French wine, provided by Clement Freud. The main topic of conversation had been the possibility of a 'hung' jury. George Deakin recalls Thorpe saying it would be unlikely that Peter Bessell would attend a re-trial – he understood that the *Sunday Telegraph* had already cancelled Bessell's contract.

Every seat in the court was filled as the four defendants were led back up to the dock where they stood stiffly, staring straight ahead.

The court administrator asked the jury foreman, a grey-haired, middle-aged lady, if they had reached a verdict on which they all agreed. She said they had.

Then each name was read out in succession. First, Holmes: 'Not guilty'. Deakin: 'Not guilty'. Le Mesurier: 'Not guilty'. Thorpe: 'Not guilty'. And Thorpe again, on the charge of incitement: 'Not guilty'.

Thorpe stared straight ahead, rigid and motionless. He scarcely noticed when Le Mesurier grasped his right arm in congratulation. The others relaxed and waved in delight at friends and relatives in the court as reporters raced for the exits, only to be checked by a peremptory order from the judge. Slowly Thorpe came to himself. Turning round stiffly towards his wife, he began to smile. Then, in a gesture that was vintage Jeremy Thorpe, he tossed the three cushions, which had been supporting his back, high over the glass partition, one by one. He leaned over and embraced Marion from the dock.

Outside, the crowds were ten deep, held back by a frail row of police when the Thorpes emerged, hand in hand, into the sunlight. As Thorpe walked out through the open door and saw the waiting people, he raised both arms over his head in the politician's traditional gesture of triumph.

Norman Scott spent the day of the verdict on his tiny farm in Chagford tending his animals, which at that time included three horses, divers chickens, ducks and guinea fowl, and four dogs. A small flock of the world's press was also in attendance. Scott helped the newsmen pass the time with an impromptu game of football on the moor.

When news of the verdict arrived Scott said he was not greatly surprised, but was irritated when a reporter suggested that it implied the jury thought he had been lying. 'Certainly not,' said Scott, 'I did not bring the case. It was brought by the Director of Public Prosecutions.' Scott's most waspish remarks, however, were reserved for the judge's aspersions on his own character – 'Let him say one of those things he said about me outside the court, and I will have him back in court – and he will not be sitting in the judge's chair.'

Scott's own plans for the future were vague. He liked the Dartmoor area where he had found acceptance but he had almost given up hope of being re-united with his girlfriend and daughter. He had a notion that his next important move might be a trip to Tibet. It seemed as if the quest for Shangri-La would continue.

Press comment after the trial tended to focus on the questions that had been left unanswered. While there could be no quarrel with the verdict, many commentators felt the uncontested evidence alone signalled the end of Thorpe's political career. The *Daily Telegraph* editorialised severely: 'Mr Thorpe exercised the undoubted right of every citizen, but his public image might have been better served had he explained the whole course of his behaviour publicly and on oath.' There were also indications of other matters for concern. It emerged, in the columns of the *News of the World*, that John Le Mesurier was preparing a book in which he claimed the role of prime mover in a conspiracy to frighten Norman Scott into silence. Le Mesurier had, through his counsel at the Old Bailey, previously intimated that he had not known of any conspiracy against Scott until after the shooting. Moreover, Newton's evidence at Minehead and the Old Bailey had not included any reference to Le Mesurier as a leading conspirator before the shooting.

There was also an intriguing footnote to Scott's evidence, though it was in no way material to the verdict. We traced the psychiatrist, Dr Anthony Willems, who had first treated Scott at the Ashurst Clinic immediately before Scott came to London to take up Thorpe's offer of help. Scott had told the court that he had in the course of this treatment told stories of a sexual relationship with Thorpe *before* their meeting at the House of Commons. This 'disclosure' had undoubtedly helped to undermine his credibility in the eyes of the court and was commented on in Mr Justice Cantley's summing-up. Dr Willems, however, told us that while he had naturally discussed Scott's sexual fantasies in the course of his treatment the name of Jeremy Thorpe had not been mentioned. He had kept his case notes on the course of Scott's treatment and was positive that this was so. Not for the first time, it seems, Scott had to be counted among his own worst enemies.

Two Sundays after the verdict, a remarkable celebration took place in the tiny eleventh-century church of Bratton Fleming, on the edge of Exmoor. It was billed as a 'Thanksgiving Service for Marion and Jeremy Thorpe', and such was the expectation of a large crowd of thankful worshippers that a public address system was installed, linking the church with the village hall.

The service was conducted by one of Thorpe's most loyal admirers, an ebullient vicar called the Reverend John Hornby, rural dean of Shirwell in North Devon. He had not sought the approval of his superiors, but had chosen as his text: 'With God nothing shall be impossible.'

The church was far from full by the time Jeremy and Marion Thorpe arrived, accompanied by Jeremy's son Rupert, to take their place in the front pew, and the village hall was not in the end needed. The lesson for the day was taken from Ecclesiastes: 'Let us now praise famous men ...'

The Church of England has no form of service in the

370

rayer book for an acquittal. The Reverend Hornby was undaunted. 'We have the opportunity to give thanks to God for the ministry of his servant Jeremy in North Devon,' he proclaimed. 'In the long dark days of Minehead and the Old Bailey, God granted Marion and Jeremy that fantastic residence which has aroused the admiration of the whole world ... the darkness is now passed and the true light shines. This is the day the Lord hath made!'

Some of the listening congregation felt the vicar might be going a little far here, and when he went on to speak of Thorpe's acquittal in the context of the miracle of the Immaculate Conception and the Resurrection, there were those who wondered whether this was quite the point to stress. The Thorpes, however, seemed happy to be back again on their own ground and amongst friends.

Outside, after the service, a BBC reporter approached Thorpe and asked him whether he would be standing again as Liberal candidate for North Devon.

'That', said Thorpe jovially, 'reminds me of the remark once made by Harold Macmillan in Moscow —'

'You mean, the wrong question, in the wrong place, and at the wrong time?' said the BBC man helpfully.

'That's it – hole in one!' beamed Thorpe as he set off to join the crowd in the local pub. Like so many other questions, it was one which, for the time being, he preferred not to answer.

Acknowledgements

For kind permission to reproduce photographs, the author and publishers are grateful to the *Sunday Times* (Jerem Thorpe aged six); the Oxford Union (group photograph 1951); Syndication International Ltd (Thorpe's first marriage John Le Mesurier; Sue Scott; Rinka); Sport and General Pres Agency Ltd (Thorpe with his son); Associated Press Lt (Marion Thorpe at the piano); Camera Press Ltd (Mario Thorpe with Jeremy Thorpe and his son; Lord Goodma – photo by Patrick Lichfield; Richard Wainwright – phot by Jon Blau; Emlyn Hooson – photo by Jon Blau; Reginal Maudling; Lord Beaumont; Lord Byers; Cyril Smith – phot by Jon Blau; Henry Kissinger – photo by Karsh of Ottaw Gerald Caplan; Thorpe campaigning in Barnstaple – phot by Jane Bowen); Barratt's Photo Press Ltd (Thorpe with hi mother); Thomson Newspapers (Thorpe after election a Liberal Party leader); George W.F. Ellis (Peter Bessell wit Thorpe); London Express News Service (Norman Scott George Deakin; Gordon Winter); Keystone Press Agenc Ltd (Thorpe with Harold Wilson and Lady Falkender; Davi Ennals; George Thomas; Sir Frank Soskice; Barbara Castle the Press Association Ltd (Sir David Napley; David Holmes Jack Hayward; Nadir Dinshaw; George de Chabris); John Hillelson Agency Ltd (Andrew Newton); Billett Potte (David Steel).

Index

170–2, 174, 179–81, 336–7;
Hardinge letter 176;
Newton's trial 233, 238,
262–4; Scott's trial 238–40;
1974, offered cabinet post by
Heath 191–4; asks Hayward
for funds 106, 196–9, 200–2,
203–4; documents in
Bessell's office 202–3;
phones Bessell in California
242, 319–20; support from
Wilson 244, 245–6, 252–3,
257–8; Holmes's admission
253–4; Wainwright's
campaign 264–5; *Sunday
Times* publication of letters
267–9; 1976, resigns
leadership 269–70, 320;
Pencourt inquiries 272, 276,
284; de Chabris 277–8.

Gives accounts of role in
Scott affair: to Byers 148–50,
to Proven Sharpe 248, at
National Liberal Club press
conference 284–6, to *Sunday
Times* 259, to police, 1978
290–1; denies Scott's
allegations 63, 133, 134, 158,
185, 240, 270, 290; denies
plot allegations 283, 290–1,
293; pressurises Hayward
and Dinshaw 288–9, 328;
charged with conspiracy
292, and incitement 293; at
Liberal assembly 293; at
Minehead 284ff; fights 1979
General Election 300–2; at
Old Bailey 304ff, mentioned
in trial evidence about
'ultimate solution'
discussions 311–13, 332,
354, 367, offers no evidence
347, summary of evidence
against 363, verdict 368;
thanksgiving service 370–1.
Letters: to Scott, Feb. and
Sept. 1962 42, 44, 45, 67,
130, 132, 136, 139, 141, 147,
151, 265, 267–8, 308, 358;
'missing letters' in Swiss
luggage 64, 69, 309, 310,
354; to Gieves Ltd, 1963 46;
to Marie Quirke, 1965 51–2;
to Maudling, 1971 148, 350;
to Byers, 1971 149–50; to
Hayward, April 1974 197–8;
to Hayward, May 1974 198;
to Hayward, Nov. 1974
200–2; to Hayward, 1975
203–4; to Bessell, 1976
249–51; to Steel, 1976
269–70.

Thorpe, John   11, 13, 14, 16
Thorpe, Lavinia   11
Thorpe, Marion   189, 237,
249, 252, 253, 259, 301, 302,
366; engagement and
marriage to Thorpe 160–2,
174; Scott's visit 205; at
press conference 284–6; at
Old Bailey 336, 349, 368;
thanksgiving service 370–1
Thorpe, Rupert   111, 161,
197, 204, 205, 223, 370
Thorpe, Ursula   11, 33, 78,
133; in Thorpe's early life
11, 12, 14, 17, 23, 29, 31;
Stonewalls 40–1, 133, 306–7;
Scott's letter 52, 63, 64, 65,
83, 202, 309–10; Thorpe's
2nd marriage 160, 161; at
Old Bailey 336, 349
Tracey, Lee   157, 159–60
Travellers Inns Ltd   58
Twentieth Century Securities
59, 177

United Bahamian Party   172,
173
Up Against the Law   212

Van de Vater, Brecht   37, 39,
44, 340, 358, 359
Vassall, John   33, 48, 139, 141